THE GOOD RESEARCH GUIDE

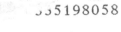

THE GOOD RESEARCH GUIDE
for small-scale social research projects

Martyn Denscombe

Open University Press
Buckingham · Philadelphia

Open University Press
Celtic Court
22 Ballmoor
Buckingham
MK18 1XW

email: enquiries@openup.co.uk
world wide web: http://www.openup.co.uk

and
325 Chestnut Street
Philadelphia, PA 19106, USA

First published 1998
Reprinted 1998, 1999

A catalogue record of this book is available from the British Library

ISBN 0 335 19806 6 (hb)   0 335 19805 8 (pb)

Library of Congress Cataloging-in-Publication Data
Denscombe, Martyn.
  The good research guide: for small-scale social research projects
  Martyn Denscombe.
    p. cm.
  Includes bibliographical references and index.
  ISBN 0-335-19806-6 (hbk) – ISBN 0-335-19805-8 (pbk.)
  1. Social sciences–Methodology–Handbooks, manuals, etc.
  I. Title.
  H61.D35 1998
  300´.7´2–dc21   98-12010
                                                                         CIP

Typeset by Type Study, Scarborough
Printed in Great Britain by Biddles Ltd, Guildford and King's Lynn

▶ ▷ ▷

CONTENTS

List of figures		vi
Acknowledgements		vii
Introduction		1
Part I	**Strategies**	3
1	Surveys	6
2	Case studies	30
3	Experiments	43
4	Action research	57
5	Ethnography	68
Part II	**Methods**	83
6	Questionnaires	87
7	Interviews	109
8	Observation	139
9	Documents	158
Part III	**Analysis**	173
10	Quantitative data	177
11	Qualitative data	207
12	Writing up	224
Frequently asked questions		239
References		242
Index		245

▶ ▷ ▷

LIST OF FIGURES

1	Raw data example	181
2	Array of raw data example	181
3	Tally of frequencies example	182
4	Grouped frequency distribution example	182
5	Table example	185
6	Contingency table example	185
7	Simple bar chart example	186
8	Horizontal bar chart example	186
9	Stacked bar chart example	187
10	Histogram example	188
11	Scatter plot example	188
12	Line graph example	189
13	Pie chart example	190
14	Chi-square and contingency table examples	200
15	Correlations and scatter plots examples	203

▶ ▷ ▷

ACKNOWLEDGEMENTS

There are those close to home who contribute to the completion of a book by putting the author in a position to start, sustain and finish the book. For this reason, and many others, I would like to dedicate this book to my wife Viv, to my sons Ben and George, to my mother Kathleen and to the memory of my father Roy. Thanks especially to Viv – this book is for you.

Friends and colleagues have also played their part, in particular David Field, Derek Layder and Barry Troyna. Barry couldn't stay for the completion of the book – he's sadly missed. Finally, colleagues at De Montfort University deserve my thanks for being good to work with. At the risk of offending the rest, I will name but a few: Brian Allison, Mike Hart, Pete Lowe, Lynton Robins and David Wilson.

Martyn Denscombe
Leicester

▶ ▷ ▷

INTRODUCTION

A book for 'project researchers'

Social research is no longer the concern of the small elite of professionals and full-time researchers. It has become the concern of a far greater number of people who are faced with the prospect of undertaking small-scale research projects as part of an academic course or as part of their professional development. It is these people who provide the main audience for this book.

The aim of the book is to present these *'project researchers'* with practical guidance and a vision of the key issues involved in social research. It attempts to provide project researchers with vital information which is easily accessible and which gets to the heart of the matter quickly and concisely. In doing this, the book is based on three premises:

1 Most of what needs to be known and done in relation to the production of competent social research can be stated in *straightforward language*.

2 The foundations of good social research depend on paying attention to *certain elementary factors*. If such factors are ignored or overlooked, the research will be open to criticism and serious questions may be raised about the quality of the findings. Good research depends on addressing these key points. The answers may vary from topic to topic, researcher to researcher. There may be no one 'right' answer, but the biggest possible guarantee of poor research is to ignore the issues.

3 Project researchers can safeguard against making elementary errors in the design and execution of their research by using a *checklist approach*, in which they assure themselves that they have attended to the 'minimum' requirements and have not overlooked crucial factors associated with the production of good research.

▶ ▷ ▷ **Part 1**

STRATEGIES FOR SOCIAL RESEARCH

The process of putting together a piece of good research is not something that can be done by slavishly following a set of edicts about what is right and wrong. In practice, the *social researcher is faced with a variety of options and alternatives and has to make strategic decisions about which to choose.* Each choice brings with it a set of assumptions about the social world it investigates. Each choice brings with it a set of advantages and disadvantages. Gains in one direction will bring with them losses in another, and the social researcher has to live with this.

There is no 'one right' direction to take. There are, though, some strategies which are better suited than others for tackling specific issues. In practice, good social research is a matter of 'horses for courses', where approaches are selected because they are *appropriate* for specific aspects of investigation and specific kinds of problems. They are chosen as 'fit for purpose'. *The crucial thing for good research is that the choices are reasonable and that they are made explicit as part of any research report.*

Horses for courses

▶ Approaches are selected because they are *appropriate* for specific aspects of investigation and specific kinds of problems.

▶ 'Strategic' decisions aim at putting the social researcher in the best possible position to gain the best outcome from the research.

▶ In good research the choices are (a) reasonable and (b) made explicit as part of any research report.

Key decisions about the strategy and methods to be used are usually taken before the research begins. When you have embarked on a particular approach it is not easy to do a U-turn. Particularly for small-scale research, there tend to be tight constraints on time and money, which mean that the researcher does not have the luxury of thinking, 'Well, I'll try this approach and see how it goes and, if it doesn't work, I'll start again with a different approach . . . put Plan B into operation.' In the real world, research projects are normally one-off investigations where, if you do not get it right first time, the research fails.

To avoid starting on a path that ultimately gets nowhere there are some things which can be taken into consideration right at the outset as the researcher contemplates which approach to choose. In effect, the checklist on the following page can be used by the project researcher to gauge if what he or she has in mind is a 'starter' or a 'non-starter' as a proposition. If the researcher is able to score well in the sense of meeting the points in the check-list – not all, but a good majority – then he or she can feel fairly confident that the research is starting from a solid foundation and that it should not be necessary to back-track and start again once the project has got under way.

Key decisions about social research ✓

Issue	Factors to be considered	
Relevance Does it really matter whether the research takes place?	▶ Is the research significant in relation to *current issues* in society?	☐
	▶ Will the research *build upon existing knowledge* about the topic?	☐
	▶ Are specific *theories to be used*, tested or developed?	☐
Feasibility Can it be done?	▶ Is there sufficient *time* for the design of the research, collection of data and analysis of results?	☐
	▶ Will the *resources* be available to cover the costs of the research (e.g. travel, printing)?	☐
	▶ Will it be possible and practical to gain *access* to necessary data (people, events, documents)?	☐
Coverage Are the right things included?	▶ Will the questions cover the *full range of issues*?	☐
	▶ Will an adequate *number* and suitable *diversity* of people, events etc. be included?	☐
	▶ Will it be reasonable to make *generalizations* on the basis of the data collected?	☐
	▶ Is it likely that there will be an adequate *response rate*?	☐
Accuracy Will the research produce true and honest findings?	▶ Will the data be *precise* and detailed?	☐
	▶ Are respondents likely to give full and *honest answers*?	☐
	▶ Will the investigation manage to focus on the most *vital issues*?	☐
Objectivity What chance is there that the research will provide a fair and balanced picture?	▶ Can I avoid being *biased* because of my personal values, beliefs and background?	☐
	▶ Will the research be approached with *an open mind* about what the findings might show?	☐
	▶ Am I prepared to recognize the *limitations* of the research approach that is adopted?	☐
Ethics What about the rights and feelings of those affected by the research?	▶ Can I *avoid any deception* or misrepresentation in my dealings with the research subjects?	☐
	▶ Will the *identities* and the *interests* of those involved be protected?	☐
	▶ Can I guarantee the *confidentiality* of the information given to me during the research?	☐

1

SURVEYS

In one sense, the word 'survey' means 'to view comprehensively and in detail'. In another sense it refers specifically to the act of 'obtaining data for mapping'. These aspects of the definition of a survey, of course, derive from the classic versions of geographical surveys and ordnance surveys, which map out the landscape or the built environment of roads and buildings. The principles, though, have been used to good effect on mapping out the social world as well as the physical world and, indeed, surveys have emerged in the later parts of the twentieth century as one of the most popular and commonplace approaches to social research. Such *social* surveys share with their physical counterparts some crucial characteristics.

▶ *Wide and inclusive coverage.* Implicit in the notion of 'survey' is the idea that the research should have a wide coverage – a breadth of view. A survey, in principle, should take a panoramic view and 'take it all in'.

▶ *At a specific point in time.* The purpose of mapping surveys is generally to 'bring things up to date', and so it is with the notion of social surveys. Surveys usually relate to the present state of affairs and involve an attempt to provide a snapshot of how things are at the specific time at which the data are collected. Though there might be occasions when researchers will wish to do a retrospective study to show how things used to be, these remain more an exception than the rule.

▶ *Empirical research.* In the sense that 'to survey' carries with it the meaning 'to look', survey work inevitably brings with it the idea of empirical research. It involves the idea of getting out of the chair, going out of the office and purposefully seeking the necessary information 'out there'. The researcher who adopts a survey approach tends to buy in to a tradition of research which emphasizes the quest for details of tangible things – things that can be measured and recorded.

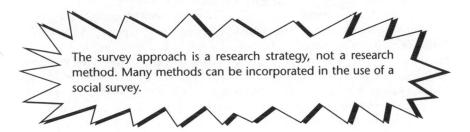

The survey approach is a research strategy, not a research method. Many methods can be incorporated in the use of a social survey.

These three characteristics of the survey approach involve no mention of specific research methods. It is important to recognize this point. The survey approach is a research *strategy*, not a method. Researchers who adopt the strategy are able to use a whole range of methods within the strategy: questionnaires, interviews, documents and observation. What is distinctive about the survey approach is its combination of a commitment to a breadth of study, a focus on the snapshot at a given point in time and a dependence on empirical data. That is not to deny that there are certain methods which are popularly associated with the use of surveys, nor that there are certain methods which sit more comfortably with the use of the strategy than others. This is true for each of the main research strategies outlined in the book. However, in essence, surveys are about a particular approach – not the methods – an approach in which there is empirical research pertaining to a given point in time which aims to incorporate as wide and as inclusive data as possible.

1 Types of survey

Surveys come in a wide variety of forms, and are used by researchers who can have very different aims and discipline backgrounds. A brief listing can never include all the possibilities, but it can help to establish the most common types of survey and give some indication about their application.

Postal questionnaires

Probably the best known kind of survey is that which involves sending 'self-completion' questionnaires through the post. This generally involves a large-scale mailing covering a wide geographical area.

Postal questionnaires are usually, though not always, received 'cold' by the respondent. This means that there is not usually any personal contact between the researcher and the respondent, and the respondent receives no prior notification of the arrival of the questionnaire.

Link up with **Response rates, p. 19**

The proportion of people who respond as requested to such 'cold' postal questionnaires is quite low. The actual proportion will depend on the nature of the topic(s) and the length of the questionnaire. As a rough guide, any social researcher will be lucky to get as many as 20 per cent of the questionnaires returned. As a result, this form of postal questionnaire tends to be used only with very large mailings, where a low response will still provide sufficient data for analysis. The small proportion that respond is unlikely to represent a true cross-section of those being surveyed in terms of age, sex, social class etc. Some types of people are more likely to fill in and return their questionnaires than others. However, the results can be 'weighted' according to what is already known about the composition of the people being surveyed (in terms of age, sex, social class etc.), so that the data which eventually get analysed are based on the actual proportions among those surveyed rather than the proportions that were returned to the researchers via the post.

Email surveys operate on basically the same principle as the postal questionnaire. In the case of email, though, the mail-shot tends to be more random. It is more difficult to calculate who or how many will be contacted through the mail-shot. The potential advantage is that vast numbers can be contacted with practically no costs involved. Responding to the questionnaire can be made less onerous for the respondent, and returning the completed questionnaire can be done at a keystroke without the need for an envelope or stamp.

Face-to-face interviews

As the name suggests, the face-to-face survey involves direct contact between the researcher and the respondent. This contact can arise through approaches made by the researcher 'in the street'. The sight of the market researcher with her clipboard and smile is familiar in town centres. Or the contact can be made by calling at people's homes. Sometimes these will be 'on spec' to see if the householder is willing and able to spare the time to help with the research. On other occasions, contact will be made in advance by letter or phone.

The face-to-face interview is a more expensive way of conducting the survey than the use of the post or the use of telephones to collect information. Interviewer time and interviewer travel costs are considerable. Weighed against this, researchers might expect the data obtained to be more detailed and rich, and the face-to-face contact offers some immediate means of validating the data. The researcher can sense if she is being given false information in the face-to-face context in a way that is not possible with questionnaires and less feasible with telephone surveys.

The response rate will be better than with other survey approaches. Part of the researcher's skill is to engage the potential respondent and quickly manoeuvre the person to get his or her cooperation. An armlock is not called for here; something a little more subtle. The point is, though, that the face-to-face contact allows the researcher the opportunity to 'sell' the thing to the potential respondent in a way that the use of questionnaires and telephones does not.

Face-to-face contact also allows researchers to select carefully their potential respondents so that they get responses from just those people needed to fill necessary quotas. A required number of males and females can be ensured. A suitable balance of age bands can be guaranteed. Appropriate numbers of ethnic groups and earnings categories can be incorporated with a minimum prospect of redundant material. There is an efficiency built into this form of data collection despite its expensive nature.

 Link up with **Quota sampling, p. 13**

Telephone interviews

Telephone surveys used to be considered a rather suspect research method, principally because it was felt that contacting people by phone led to a biased sample. There was a strong probability that the kind of people who could be contacted by phone were not representative of the wider population. In the past they tended to be the financially better off. However, telephone surveys are now in widespread use in social research, and there are three main reasons for this.

1   *Telephone interviewing is cheaper and quicker than face-to-face interviewing.* Researchers do not have to travel to all parts of the country to conduct the interviews – they only have to pick up a phone. This has always been recognized as an advantage but, until recently, there have been doubts about the reliability of the data gathered by telephone. Social researchers have not been willing to sacrifice the quality of data for the economies that telephone interviewing can bring. However . . .

2   *Question marks are now being placed against the assumption that face-to-face interviews produce better, more accurate, data.* The emerging evidence suggests that people are as honest in telephone interviews as they are with face-to-face type interviews. 'Initial doubts about the reliability of factual information obtained over the telephone and its comparability with information obtained face-to-face have largely been discounted . . . There is no general reason to think that the measures obtained by telephone are less valid (it has been claimed that in some situations they are more valid)' (Thomas and Purdon 1995: 4).

3   *There is now less chance of bias in the sample when conducting surveys by phone.* It is estimated that by the late 1990s researchers are able to contact 91 per cent of people aged over 18 years directly by telephone. So the old doubts about the ability of telephone interviews to reach a sufficiently *representative population* have faded somewhat. Developments in technology have further boosted the attractiveness of telephone surveying, because it has become easier to contact a truly *random sample* of the population using a 'random-digit dialling' technique. Researchers can select the area

they wish to survey and identify the relevant dialling code for that area. They can then contact phone numbers at random within that area using random-digit dialling, where the final digits of the phone numbers are produced by computer technology which automatically generates numbers at random.

 Link up with **Random sampling, p. 12**

Telephone contact brings with it some of the immediate one-to-one interaction associated with face-to-face interviews. Although it forfeits the visual contact of face-to-face interviewing, it retains the 'personal' element and the two-way interaction between the researcher and the respondent. It gives the researcher some brief opportunity to explain the purpose of the phone call and to cajole the respondent into providing the required information: 'Or perhaps I can call back at a later time if that is more convenient.' On the other hand, the telephone contact is more intrusive than the postal questionnaire, intruding on people's quality time at home in a way that a postal questionnaire does not. But, perhaps, more than this, it confronts the problem of having to contend with the 'double-glazing' sales pitch which comes over the phone in the guise of research. *The methods of genuine research can be used and abused to sell products rather than collect information.*

The net result of all this is that, although telephone interviewing reduces the level of non-responses through non-contact, it actually suffers a higher non-response rate overall – by some 10 per cent. This is owing to a *higher refusal rate over the phone*. People evidently feel less inhibited about saying 'no' to the researcher over the phone.

Documents

All too often in writing about social surveys, the attention is focused solely on surveys of people. Yet, in practice, the strategy of the survey can be applied to documents as well as living people. The social researcher can undertake empirical research based on documents which incorporates as wide and as inclusive data as possible, and which aims to 'bring things up to date'. The *literature survey*, of course, is a prime example. It is the basis for good research and it involves the use of survey principles applied to documents on the topic of the research. The idea is to encompass as much as possible of the existing material – equivalent to getting the panoramic view of the landscape.

 Link up with **Literature review, p. 158**

The literature review may be the kind of document survey with which most researchers are familiar. It is not, however, the only kind of document survey.

Economists and business analysts rely heavily on surveys which use documents as their base data. They use records rather than people as their source of data. Company reports, financial records, employment statistics, records of imports and exports and the like provide the foundation for *business surveys and economic forecasts,* which are heavily used by governments and the world of commerce. And social policy developments would hardly be viable without the use of *demographic surveys* based on official statistics covering areas of residence, service provision, profile of the population etc.

Observations

Classic social surveys involved observations of things like poverty and living conditions. Such observation followed the tradition of geographical and ordnance surveys, with their emphasis on looking at the landscape. Although the practice of conducting a survey through observing events and conditions is less common as a feature of social research as we enter the twenty-first century, it serves to remind us that the survey strategy can use a range of specific methods to collect data and that we should not get hung up on the idea of a social survey as meaning the same thing as a postal questionnaire survey. As well as asking people what they do and what they think, surveys can also *look* at what they actually do.

2 Surveys and sampling

Social researchers are frequently faced with the fact that they cannot collect data from everyone who is in the category being researched. As a result, they rely on getting evidence from a portion of the whole in the expectation and hope that what is found in that portion applies equally to the rest of the 'population'.

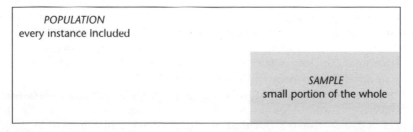

It is not good enough, though, to *assume* that findings for the sample will be replicated in the rest of the population. The sample in the first place needs to be carefully selected if there is to be any confidence that the findings from the sample are similar to those found among the rest of the category under investigation.

Basically, there are two kinds of sampling techniques that can be used by social researchers. The first is known as 'probability' sampling, the second as 'non-probability' sampling. Probability sampling, as the name suggests, is based on the idea that the people or events that are chosen as the sample are chosen because the researcher has some notion of the probability that these will be a representative cross-section of people or events in the whole population being studied. Non-probability sampling is conducted without such knowledge about whether those included in the sample are representative of the overall population.

Probability sampling

Random sampling

This approach to sampling involves the selection of people or events literally 'at random'. Behind the use of random sampling lies the assumption that,

▶ if there are a sufficiently large number of examples selected and

▶ if their selection has genuinely been 'at random',

then the resulting sample is likely to provide a *representative* cross-section of the whole. To illustrate the idea, with a random sampling approach the researcher might decide to select the sample from a telephone directory. The researcher might use a random set of digits (produced specifically for the purpose) to choose the page and the line on the page to select a person for inclusion in the sample. The list of random digits ensures the choice is genuinely 'random'.

Link up with **Sampling frame, p. 17**

Systematic sampling

Systematic sampling is a variant of random sampling. It operates on the same principles but introduces some system into the selection of people or events. With the systematic sampling approach, the researcher's choice of people from the telephone directory is based on choosing every '*n*th' case. This could be every hundredth person listed in the directory, for instance.

If the researcher knows that there are something like 100,000 people listed in the directory and he or she wants to identify about 1,000 people for the sample, it is easy to work out that by choosing every hundreth person this number can be reached quite accurately – selecting across the alphabetical range of surnames from A to Z.

Stratified sampling

A stratified sample can be defined as one in which every member of the population has an equal chance of being selected *in relation to their proportion within the total population.* In the first instance, then, stratified sampling continues to adhere to the underlying principle of randomness. However, it adds some boundaries to the process of selection and applies the principle of randomness *within* these boundaries. It is something of a mixture of random selection and selecting on the basis of specific identity or purpose.

To illustrate the point, a researcher who wishes to collect information about voting behaviour will know in advance, from demographic data, that the population of voters from whom data are to be collected will include a given proportion of males and females, and will include given proportions of different age bands from 18 years up. The researcher should also realize from a review of the literature that sex and age are factors linked with voting behaviour. When constructing the sample, then, the researcher could wisely choose to adopt a stratified sampling approach in which:

▶ *all relevant categories* of sex and age are included;

▶ the numbers included for each category are *directly in proportion* to those in the wider population (all voters).

In this way, the voting intentions displayed by the sample are likely to correspond with the voting intentions in the wider population of voters.

The significant advantage of stratified sampling over pure random sampling is that the social researcher can assert some control over the selection of the sample in order to guarantee that crucial people or crucial factors are covered by it, and in proportion to the way they exist in the wider population. This obviously helps the researcher when it comes to generalizing from the findings of the research.

Quota sampling

Quota sampling is widely used in market research. It operates on very similar principles to stratified sampling. It establishes certain categories (or strata) which are considered to be vital for inclusion in the sample, and also seeks to fill these categories in proportion to their existence in the population. There is, though, one distinctive difference between stratified and quota sampling. With quota sampling, the method of choosing the people or events that make up the required number within each category is not a matter of strict random selection. In effect, it is left up to the researcher to choose who fills the quota. It might be on a 'first to hand' basis – as when market researchers stop people in the street. The people might be appropriate but were chosen because they just happened to be there, not as part of a random selection from a known population. The technical difference here excites statisticians but need not trouble the project researcher too much. The crucial point is that, like stratified sampling, it has the advantage of ensuring the representation of all crucial categories in the sample in proportion to their existence in the wider population. It does so without waste. Because the quotas are set in advance, no people or events that subsequently become 'surplus to requirements' are incorporated into the research. Quota sampling, then, has particular advantages when it comes to costs – especially when used with face-to-face interviewing. Its main *disadvantage* is that the numbers needed in each category in order to be in proportion with the wider population can turn out to be quite small – small enough indeed to put a question mark against their use for statistical analysis. The more strata that are used – age, sex, ethnicity, social class, area of residence etc. – the more likely it is that the quotas for specific categories will be small.

Link up with **Face-to-face interviews, p. 8**

Cluster sampling

The question of resources needs to be taken seriously when it comes to the selection of samples. Identifying units to be included, contacting relevant respondents and travelling to locations can all entail considerable time and expense. The virtues of a purely random selection, then, can be weighed against the savings to be made by using alternative approaches which, while they retain some commitment to the principles of random selection and the laws of probability, try to do so in cost-effective ways.

Cluster sampling is a typical example of this. The logic behind it is that, in reality, it is possible to get a good enough sample by focusing on naturally occurring clusters of the particular thing that the researcher wishes to study. By focusing on such clusters, the researcher can save a great deal of time and money that would otherwise have been spent on travelling to and fro visiting research sites scattered throughout the length and breadth of the land. The selection of clusters as appropriate sites for research follows the principles of probability sampling outlined above. The underlying aim is to get a representative cluster, and the means for getting it rely on random choice or stratified sampling.

A good example of a naturally occurring cluster is a school. If the researcher wishes to study young people aged between 11 and 16 years, then secondary schools offer the possibility of using cluster sampling because they contain a concentration of such people on one site. The researcher does not need to organize the grouping of all the young people on one site – they are there anyway – and it is in this sense that the school offers a naturally occurring cluster.

Multi-stage sampling

Multi-stage sampling, as the name suggests, involves selecting samples from samples, each sample being drawn from within the previously selected sample. For example, departments might be sampled within schools which, themselves, have already been selected as a suitable cluster or chosen through some process of random sampling. Having identified the initial sample (possibly a cluster, possibly not), the researcher then proceeds to choose a sample from among those in the initial level sample. The researcher might even go on to select a further sample from the second level sample. In principle, multi-stage sampling can go on through any number of levels, each level involving a sample drawn from the previous level.

Non-probability sampling

There are often occasions when researchers find it difficult or undesirable to choose their sample on the basis of probability sampling. The reasons for this are varied but, in the main, will be because:

▶ The researcher feels it is not feasible to include a sufficiently large number of examples in the study.

▶ The researcher does not have sufficient information about the *population* to undertake probability sampling. The researcher may not know who, or how many people or events, make up the *population*.

▶ It may prove exceedingly difficult to contact a sample selected through conventional probability sampling techniques. For example, research on drug addicts or the homeless would not lend itself to normal forms of probability sampling.

Under such circumstances, the social researcher can turn to forms of non-probability sampling as the basis for selecting the sample. When one does so, there is a departure from the principle which underlies probability sampling: that each member of the research population stands an equal chance of being included in the sample. With non-probability sampling this is certainly not the case. A different set of criteria come into play, in terms of how and why people or events get included in the study. The crucial and defining characteristic of non-probability sampling, whatever form it takes, is that the choice of people or events to be included in the sample is definitely *not* a random selection.

Purposive sampling

With *purposive sampling* the sample is 'hand picked' for the research. The term is applied to those situations where the researcher already knows something about the specific people or events and deliberately selects particular ones because they are seen as instances that are likely to produce the most valuable data. In effect, they are selected with a specific purpose in mind, and that purpose reflects the particular qualities of the people or events chosen and their relevance to the topic of the investigation. From the researcher's point of view, the question to ask is this: 'Given what I already know about the research topic and about the range of people or events being studied, who or what is likely to provide the best information?'

The advantage of purposive sampling is that it allows the researcher to home in on people or events which there are good grounds for believing will be critical for the research. Instead of going for the typical instances, a cross-section or a balanced choice, the researcher can concentrate on instances which will display a wide variety – possibly even a focus on extreme cases – to illuminate the research question at hand. In this sense it might not only be economical but might also be informative in a way that conventional probability sampling cannot be.

Snowball sampling

With *snowballing*, the sample emerges through a process of reference from one person to the next. At the start, the research might involve, for example, just a few people. Each can be asked to nominate two other people who would be relevant for the purposes of the research. These nominations are then contacted and, it is hoped, included in the sample. The sample thus snowballs in size as each of the nominees is asked, in turn, to nominate two or more further persons who might be included in the sample.

Snowballing is an effective technique for building up a reasonable-sized sample, especially when used as part of a small-scale research project. One advantage is that the accumulation of numbers is quite quick, using the multiplier effect of one person nominating two or more others. Added to this, the researcher can approach each new person, having been, in a sense, sponsored by the person who had named him or her. The researcher can use the nominator as some kind of reference to enhance his or her *bona fides* and credibility, rather than approach the new person cold. And, of course, the snowball technique is completely compatible with purposive sampling. People can be asked to nominate others who meet certain criteria for choice, certain conditions related to the research project and certain characteristics such as age, sex, ethnicity, qualifications, residence, state of health or leisure pursuits. In a nutshell, snowballing can be very useful for developing the numbers involved in the sample and the issues linked to the research.

Theoretical sampling

With theoretical sampling, the selection of instances follows a route of discovery based on the development of a theory which is 'grounded' in evidence. At each stage, new evidence is used to modify or confirm a 'theory', which then points to an appropriate choice of instances for research in the next phase.

Link up with **Grounded theory, p. 214**

Convenience sampling

Convenience sampling is built upon selections which suit the convenience of the researcher and which are 'first to hand'. Now some words of caution are needed in relation to this. To be honest, an element of convenience is likely to enter into sampling procedures of most research. Because researchers have limited money and limited time at their disposal, it is quite reasonable that where there is scope for choice between two or more equally valid possibilities for inclusion in the sample, the researcher should choose the most convenient. As Stake makes the point, 'Our time and access for fieldwork are almost always limited. If we can, we need to pick cases which are easy to get to and hospitable to our inquiry' (Stake 1995: 4). If two or more clusters are equally suitable as research sites, it would be crazy to opt for ones that were the furthest away without some good reason to do so.

 **Caution**

Convenience itself offers nothing by way of justification for the inclusion of people or events in the sample. It might be a reasonable practical criterion to apply when faced with equally viable alternatives but, in its own right, is not a factor that should be used by researchers to select the sample. Choosing things on the basis of convenience runs counter to the rigour of scientific research. It suggests a lazy approach to the work. Good research selects its items for study not on the basis that they are the *easiest* to obtain but for specific reasons linked to the subject matter of the research and the requirements of the investigation. For this reason, *the practice of convenience sampling is hard to equate with good research*.

3 The sampling frame

The use of a sampling frame is very important. A sampling frame is an objective list of 'the population' from which the researcher can make his or her selections.

A sampling frame should ideally contain a complete, up-to-date list of all those that comprise the population for research. As far as surveys of people are concerned, various registers are the most usual basis for the sampling frame. Examples of a sampling frame would be the voting register, the telephone directory or a school attendance list. These supply a list of the residents or school children. The researcher could then either select the required sample size purely at random, or do it more systematically by choosing every tenth, hundredth or whatever case.

Constructing a sampling frame

Researchers wishing to conduct a survey will need to search for a suitable sampling frame. However, it is quite possible that there may not be one that actually meets the needs of the researcher. In this case, he or she will have to produce one. When constructing a sampling frame, it is worth bearing in mind that there are specialist companies supplying lists of addresses. Some companies are able to supply *private addresses* within given postcode or zipcode areas. Usually, they will extract sections from a huge national data-base which contains 98 per cent of all private addresses in the country. It is also possible to obtain precise address lists of businesses, schools, hospitals, charities and other organizations. Researchers can obtain mailing lists which can be all-encompassing (e.g. all schools in Australia, all hospitals in California), or companies will supply much smaller lists for particular purposes. There is no need to buy a list of all schools, for instance, because the researcher can specify just those kinds of school relevant for research – possibly just secondary schools in the London area, or just primary schools in Wales. Such specific lists tend to suit the needs of small-scale research projects, not least because they can be supplied at relatively low cost. The lists supplied can come in the form of gummed labels for posting, or the researcher can purchase the addresses in the form of a computer database that can be reused as many times as needed for mailing purposes. Generally, mailing lists supplied by commercial companies are kept up-to-date and are as complete as it reasonably possible to be.

Bias in sampling frames

There is a danger with the use of any sampling frame that it might be incomplete or out of date. A list of private addresses will not lead the researcher to those who are homeless and live on the streets. An electoral register will not include those under 18 years of age or those who, for whatever reason, have not registered to vote. Things omitted might well be different in some important respects from the things which actually exist on the list, and overlooking them as part of the research can lead to a biased sample. Just as damaging for the purposes of research, registers can include certain items that should not be there. They can contain names of people who have passed on – in either a geographical or a mortal sense. People move home, people die, and unless the register is regularly and carefully updated on a routine basis there is the likelihood that it will be out of date and include items it should not. Either way, the impact can be significant as far as research is concerned. If the sampling frame systematically excludes things that should be in, or systematically includes things which should be out, the sample will almost inevitably be biased. So it is vital that the researcher should check on the completeness and up-to-dateness of any sample frame that is considered for use.

 Caution

Since it unlikely that any sampling frame will be perfect, deficiencies ought to be acknowledged. Good research does not depend on trying to hide limitations in matters like this. It is far better to recognize any ways in which the sampling frame might be less than perfect and to discuss the possible impact on the nature of the sample and the results obtained by the research. There

> ### A good sampling frame
>
> A good sampling should be:
>
> ▶ *Relevant:* it should contain things directly linked to the research topic.
>
> ▶ *Complete:* it should cover all relevant items.
>
> ▶ *Precise:* it should exclude all the items that are not relevant.
>
> ▶ *Up-to-date:* it should incorporate recent additions and changes, and have redundant items cleansed from the list.

needs to be a brief discussion as part of the research methodology about who is likely to have been missed from the frame and what impact this might have. Any measure to compensate for missing items should be explained.

4 Response rates

When researchers talk of the 'response rate' they are referring to the proportion of the total number of questionnaires distributed which are completed and returned as requested. The assumption is that not everyone will do so. As a rule, good research tries to minimize its non-responses.

The willingness of people to go along with the research is affected principally by the following factors.

▶ *Nature of respondents* (age, sex, disability, literacy, employment status etc.). Certain kinds of people are less inclined than others to spare the time and make the effort to comply with requests to help with research. Busy people can ill afford the time. Others with more time on their hands, those who are retired for instance, might be more inclined to get involved. People with communication disadvantages, those with reading or hearing difficulties, are less likely than others to get involved unless there is special attention devoted to their needs.

▶ *Subject of research* (sex, race, religion, politics, income). Certain subjects are taboo and others are sensitive. If the investigation touches on intimate matters or embarrassing topics, there is every likelihood that the response rate will be low. To a lesser extent, where research delves into matters of religion, politics and income there tends to be a lower response rate.

▶ *Interviewer appearance* (age, sex, social class, ethnicity, clothes, accent). Where the research involves face-to-face contact between the researcher and the respondent, physical appearance has an effect on the response rate. The general adage is that respondents need to feel 'comfortable' with the presence of the researcher. Such comfort, of course, depends on the topic being investigated and the prejudices of the respondent. Within that context, however, the researcher needs to avoid, as far as is possible, presenting himself or herself in a way that will be perceived as threatening or unwholesome by the potential respondent.

Link up with **The interviewer effect, p. 116**

▶ *Social climate* (free speech). The right to free speech is obviously a factor that will influence people's willingness to collaborate with research and to supply honest and full answers. But this is not simply a matter of legal rights in a democratic society. There are situations in organizations and other social settings where potential respondents may not *feel* free to speak their thoughts. A threatening climate, wherever it exists and whatever its cause, can reduce the response rate.

Bias from non-responses

The main problem with a high non-response rate is that the researcher has no way of knowing whether those who did not respond were in some way different from those who did respond. If the non-respondents are indeed different from the respondents in some significant and relevant way (e.g. in terms of age, sex, gender, social class, religion) the data available to the researcher will be biased, because they systematically overlook facts or opinions from the non-response group. This potential bias arising from non-responses is critical.

There are two types of non-response, both of which can lead to bias in the sample. First, there is *non-response through refusal*. As we have already made the point, if there are grounds for believing that those who refuse are consistently of a different type from those who tend to provide responses, and this difference is relevant to the matter at hand for the research, then there is the likelihood of a bias in the results. Second, there is *non-response stemming from non-contact*. If the sampling frame is used to identify a number of people, items or locations for inclusion in the sample, the researcher needs to be sure that these are indeed contacted and included. Or, perhaps more pertinently, the researcher needs to be sure that any non-contact with those identified through the frame is more or less a random occurrence. If there is any element of a *systematic non-contact* the researcher faces the prospect of having a biased sample. If, for example, the sample is based on household addresses, researchers calling at these addresses between 9 a.m. and 5 p.m. will tend to miss contact with those who are at work. To avoid this they would need to make contact in the evenings as well as during the day.

Response rates will vary markedly within social research depending on the methods being used, the nature of the respondents and the type of issues being investigated. So there is no hard and fast rule about what constitutes an acceptable response rate. With large-scale postal questionnaire surveys, for instance, it will not be uncommon to get a response rate as low as 15 per cent. Interviews, arranged by personal contact between the researcher and the interviewee, are the kind of approach at the other end of the spectrum where very high response rates can be expected – possibly even 100 per cent. Rather than look for a figure above which a response rate is acceptable and below which the results become suspect, it is *more productive to evaluate the response rate that is actually achieved in terms of the following questions.*

▶ *Is the level of response reasonable and in line with comparable surveys?* The researcher can look to similar studies as a way of gauging whether the response rate is acceptable. The methods, the target group, the topic of research, the sponsor of the research and the use of prior contact are all important factors here. Each has a bearing on the level of response. The benchmark, then, needs to be set by the experience of *similar* surveys.

▶ *Have appropriate measures been adopted to minimize the likelihood of non-responses, and have suitable steps been taken to follow up non-respondents to encourage them to collaborate with the research?* With any style of research there are practical measures which can be taken to reduce to a minimum the things that deter people from participating in research. These, obviously, will depend on the methods being used and the people being targeted. It is with large-scale questionnaire-type surveys that the measures are generally associated. In such surveys, the research should always build in some tactics for capturing those who do not respond at the initial contact. After a tactful delay, such people should be reminded, and possibly even cajoled into responding.

▶ Most importantly, *do the non-respondents differ in any systematic and relevant fashion from those who have responded?* Of course, to answer this question the researcher needs to have some information about those who have been targeted but not responded. This may prove difficult. None the less, it is good practice to endeavour to get some data about the non-respondents and to assess whether they are different from the respondents in any way that will have a bearing on the representativeness of the findings.

5 Size of the sample

In order to generalize from the findings of a survey, the sample must not only be carefully selected to be representative of the population: it also needs to include a sufficient number. The sample needs to be of an adequate size. This, of course, begs the question 'What is an adequate size for a sample?' – a straightforward and perfectly reasonable question. However, it is a question which does not lend itself to a correspondingly straightforward answer. The answer, in fact, depends on a number of factors connected with the research which need to be borne in mind and weighed up by the researcher in the process of reaching a decision about the necessary size of the sample.

Big is beautiful(?)

The 'big is beautiful' stance on survey size is based on the principle that the more instances that are covered the less likely it is that the findings will be biased. With a large sample, the researcher is more assured that:

▶ *all aspects of relevance to the research* question will have been covered and included in the findings;

▶ there will be some balance between the proportions within the sample and the proportions which occur in the overall population being investigated.

Both factors enhance the representativeness of the sample and, in turn, this allows greater confidence about making generalizations based on findings from the sample.

However, while this provides a good starting point for judging an adequate sample size, it still side-steps the issue of exactly what number of people or events needs to be included in the sample in order for it to be 'adequate'. The researcher still needs to know 'how many'. And for this, statisticians point out that the following points need to be considered.

The accuracy of the results

Any sample, by its very nature, might produce results which are different from the 'true' results based on a survey of the total population. Inevitably, there is an element of luck in terms of who gets included in the sample and who gets excluded, and this can affect the accuracy of the findings which emerge from the sample. Two different samples of 100 people, chosen from the same population and using the same basic method, will produce results that are likely to be slightly different. This is not so much a fault with the sample as a built-in feature of sampling. It is known as the *sampling error*.

To achieve greater accuracy, the researcher might need to increase the size of the sample. Statistical procedures can be used to calculate what specific sample size will be necessary in order to achieve a given level of accuracy. However, there is an interesting point that springs from statistical estimates and sample size. It is that there is relatively little advantage to be gained in terms of accuracy once a sample has reached a given size. There are diminishing returns to increases in the size of samples. In effect, this means that *the crucial factor to be considered in relation to sample size is not the proportion of the population which gets included in the survey, but the absolute size of the sample.* This runs contrary to common sense, which would probably say to us that the degree of accuracy of results would depend on what proportion of the population is included in the sample. Common sense might say that a sample of

25 per cent of cases will produce better results than a sample of 10 per cent. Statistics would say that where the population size is large, there is hardly any increase in accuracy to be obtained by incorporating another 15 per cent.

The absolute size of the sample will depend on the complexity of the population and the research questions being investigated. But, to give an illustration, market research companies will often limit their national samples to around 2,000 to give accurate enough results, and opinion polls in Britain tend to be based on stratified samples of something over 1,000 people. Adding another 5,000 to the sample would not appreciably increase the accuracy of the findings, which are used to generalize about the opinions of over 50 million people.

The number of subdivisions likely to be made within the data

When calculating the number of people or events to include in the sample the researcher needs to take into consideration the complexity of the data that are likely to emerge. A sample size which initially looks quite large might produce only very small returns in relation to specific subdivisions. So, for example, a sample of 100 people used to investigate earnings and occupational status might need to be subdivided according to the age, sex, ethnicity, marital status and qualifications of the people, and according to whether they are full-time, part-time, unemployed, child-rearing or retired. This simple investigation would need a cross-tabulation of five personal factors by five occupational factors, i.e. 25 subdivisions of the data. If the data were equally distributed, this means that there would be only four cases in each of the subdivisions, which is hardly an adequate basis for making generalizations.

In practice, of course, we know that the data would not be evenly distributed and that many of the subdivisions would end up with no cases in them at all. The researcher therefore needs to think ahead when planning the size of the sample to ensure that the subdivisions entailed in the analysis are adequately catered for.

The likely response rate

A survey rarely achieves a response from every contact. Especially when using postal questionnaires and the like, the rate of response from those contacted

In practice, the complexity of the competing factors of resources and accuracy means that the decision on a sample size tends to be based on experience and good judgement rather than relying on a strict mathematical formula.

(Hoinville et al. 1978)

is likely to be pretty low. As far as sample size is concerned, though, the important thing for the researcher to consider is that the number in the original sample may not equal the number of responses that are finally obtained which can be used in the research. The researcher needs to predict the kind of response rate he or she is likely to achieve, based on the kind of survey being done, and build into the sample size an allowance for non-responses. If the researcher wants to use a sample of some 100 people for research and is using a postal questionnaire survey for which a response rate of 30 per cent is anticipated, the original sample size needs to be 334.

Resources available

Research in the real world does not take place with infinite time and resources. In practice, social research is tailored to meet the constraints of the time and money available for it. Commercial research companies actually advise potential customers that for a given sum of money they can be supplied with results within a given level of accuracy; a greater level of accuracy will cost more. The customer and the commercial researcher need to agree about whether results will be accurate *enough* in relation to the money available to do the research and, in terms of survey research, much of the cost will reflect the chosen size of the sample. This means that *there is a general tendency to choose the minimum sample size that is feasible in light of the level of accuracy demanded of the findings.*

Sample size and small-scale research

The use of surveys in social research does not necessarily have to involve samples of 1,000 or 2,000 people or events. Whatever the theoretical issues, the simple fact is that surveys and sampling are frequently used in small-scale research involving **between 30 and 250** cases.

Four points need to be stressed in relation to the use of smaller sample sizes.

► Extra attention needs to be paid to the issue of how representative the sample is and special caution is needed about the extent to which generalizations can be made on the basis of the research findings. Provided that the limitations are acknowledged and taken into account, the limited size of the sample need not invalidate the findings.

► The smaller the sample, the simpler the analysis should be, in the sense that the data should be subjected to fewer subdivisions. Keeping the analysis down to four factors, for instance, greatly increases the prospect of having a reasonable number of cases in each category.

► *Samples should not involve fewer than 30 people or events.* Certainly, it is a mistake to use statistical analyses on samples of fewer than 30 without exceptional care about the procedures involved. Further, it is not acceptable to present the findings of small surveys as percentages without specifying the actual numbers involved. To write that 10 per cent of respondents held a particular opinion when commenting on a survey of 30 people is to attempt to disguise the very low number (i.e. three) on which the comment is based. At best this is naive; at worst it is deceptive.

▶ *In the case of qualitative research there is a different logic for the size of the sample* and the selection of cases to be included. A small sample size is quite in keeping with the nature of qualitative data.

6 Sampling and qualitative research

Traditionally, it is probability sampling which has set the standard for social research. It follows statistical laws and is well suited to the selection of samples in large-scale surveys designed to produce quantitative data. However, researchers who conduct small-scale research, especially qualitative researchers, find it difficult to adhere to the principles and procedures of probability sampling for selecting their people or events. Either it is not possible to include all types to be found in the population within a small sample, or not enough is known about the characteristics of the population to decide which people or events are suitable for inclusion in the sample. Some researchers have even attacked the principles of probability sampling as altogether inappropriate for smaller-scale, qualitative research. For these researchers, the selection of people or events for inclusion in the sample tends to be based on non-probability sampling.

The word 'tends' is quite important here. There is no absolute reason why qualitative research cannot use principles of randomness, or operate with large numbers. There are, however, some sound theoretical reasons why most qualitative research uses *non-probability sampling techniques* and good practical reasons why qualitative research deals with *small numbers* of instances to be researched.

One justification for non-probability sampling techniques stems from the idea that the research process is one of *'discovery'* rather than the testing of hypotheses. This approach was popularized by Glaser and Strauss (1967) and, in various reformulations, provides a foundation for the distinct approach to sampling which characterizes qualitative research. In this approach, the selection of people, texts or events to include in the research follows a path of discovery in which the sample emerges as a sequence of decisions based on the outcomes of earlier stages of the research. It is a strategy which Lincoln and Guba (1985) describe as 'emergent and sequential'. Almost like a detective, the researcher follows a trail of clues. As each clue is followed up it points the researcher in a particular direction and throws up new questions that need to be answered. Sometimes the clues can lead the researcher up blind alleys. Ultimately, though, the researcher should pursue his or her investigation until the questions have been answered and things can be explained.

Link up with **Grounded theory, p. 214**

This process can be exciting. It can also prove frustrating. Certainly, it tends to be *time-consuming* in a way that the snapshot survey approach is not. The research necessarily takes place over a period of time as the sequence of 'clues' is investigated. And the process also confounds efforts to specify at the beginning of a research project exactly what the sample to be studied will entail. To the horror of those who are committed to conventional survey approaches, *the size and composition of the sample is not completely predictable at the outset.* This does not mean that the qualitative researcher has no idea of which or how many people, texts or events will be included. A shrewd look at the time and resources available, and some reading of similar studies, will help to give a reasonable indication before the research starts. However, such an estimate of which and how many must remain exactly that – an estimate. It cannot be treated as a rigid and inflexible part of the research design if the qualitative research is to adhere to the 'discovery' route.

Another difference between the sampling which tends to be associated with quantitative research and the sampling which tends to be associated with qualitative research concerns the issue of 'representativeness'. With qualitative research, people, texts or events are not necessarily selected as being representative or normal instances. It is more likely than is the case with quantitative approaches that the selection will try to include *special instances* – ones that are extreme, unusual, best or worse. This allows the qualitative researcher to get 'maximum variation' in the data that are collected, a broad spectrum rather than a narrowly focused source of information. This, of course, accords with the spirit of qualitative research and its quest for explanations which encompass complexity, subtlety and even contradictions. It also allows a check on the findings based on the 'mainstream'. Miles and Huberman (1994) call these special instances 'outliers', and commend their inclusion in the process of discovery as a check which explores rival possible explanations and tests any explanation based on mainstream findings, by seeing if they can work with instances which are distinctly *not* mainstream. As they argue:

> Outliers are not only people; they can be discrepant *cases*, atypical *settings*, unique *treatments*, or unusual *events* . . .
>
> But *the outlier is your friend*. A good look at the exceptions, or the ends of a distribution, can test and strengthen the basic finding. It not only tests the generality of the finding but also protects you against self-selecting biases, and may help you build a better explanation.
>
> (Miles and Huberman 1994: 269, emphasis in the original)

Qualitative research, then, tends to adopt an approach to sampling which is based on *sequential discovery* of instances to be studied and which emphasizes the inclusion of *special instances* more than is generally the case with quantitative research. These two features tend to lead qualitative researchers towards non-probability sampling strategies such as 'purposive sampling', '*snowballing*' and '*theoretical sampling*', rather than strategies based on principles of randomness and probability.

Sample size

There are two things which can be said about the sample size in qualitative research. First, it is unlikely to be known with precision or certainty at the start of a research project. Second, the sample size will generally be relatively small. Both points can prove unnerving. They go against the grain as far as conventional survey approaches are concerned, and open up the prospect of accusations of sloppy and biased research design. The qualitative researcher, therefore, needs to be quite explicit about the use of non-probability sampling and its roots in the work of people such as Glaser and Strauss (1967), Lincoln and Guba (1985) and Miles and Huberman (1994).

7 Advantages of surveys

▶ *Empirical data*. As an approach to social research, the emphasis tends to be on producing data based on real-world observations. The very notion of a survey suggests that the research has involved an active attempt by the researcher to go out and look and to search. Surveys are associated with getting information 'straight from the horse's mouth'. And, more than this, the search is purposeful and structured. As a consequence, survey research tends to *focus on data more than theory* – although, of course, good survey research is not entirely devoid of theory. It is a matter of emphasis.

▶ *Wide and inclusive coverage*. Surveys are easily associated with large-scale research covering many people or events but, as we have seen, surveys can also be used with small-scale qualitative research projects. The crucial point is not so much the number of people or events involved as the breadth of coverage. The notion of a survey involves the idea of a span of vision which is wide and inclusive. Here lies the key to a major advantage of the survey approach. Its breadth of coverage means that it is more likely than some other approaches to get data based on a representative sample. This, in turn, means that the findings from good survey research score well when it comes to *generalizability*. If the coverage is suitably wide and inclusive it gives credibility to generalized statements made on the basis of the research.

▶ *Surveys lend themselves to quantitative data*. Researchers who find that quantitative data will suit their needs will find themselves drawn to the survey approach. The survey approach lends itself to being used with particular methods, such as the postal questionnaire, which can generate large volumes of quantitative data that can be subject to statistical analysis. There is nothing which inherently excludes the use of surveys with qualitative research, as we have seen, but it can prove particularly attractive for the researcher wishing to use quantitative data.

▶ *Costs and time*. Surveys are not necessarily cheap but, relative to strategies such as experiments and ethnography, they can produce a mountain of data in a short time for a fairly low cost. The *costs are perhaps more predictable* than is the case with other strategies. Added to this, the results, though they are not instant, can be obtained over a fairly short period of time. The researcher can set a finite time-span for this, which is very useful when it comes to planning the research and delivering the end-product.

8 Disadvantages of surveys

▶ *Tendency to empiricism*. There is nothing inevitable about this, but there is none the less a danger that a user of the survey approach, with its focus on producing data based on a wide and inclusive coverage, can become obsessed with the data to the exclusion of an adequate account of the implications of those data for relevant issues, problems or theories. There is a danger that the 'data are left to speak for themselves'. The *significance* of the data can become neglected.

▶ *Detail and depth of the data*. To the extent that the survey approach gets associated with large-scale research using methods such as the postal questionnaire, the data that are produced are likely to lack much by way of detail or depth on the topic being investigated. This is almost inevitable. If the researcher wants detail and depth, then the case study approach might be more beneficial. This should not blind us to the point that surveys tend to forfeit depth in favour of breadth when it comes to the data that are produced.

▶ *Accuracy and honesty of responses*. The survey approach has advantages when it comes to the representativeness of the data that it can produce, but the other side of the coin is that the emphasis on wide and inclusive coverage limits the degree to which the researcher can check on the accuracy of the responses. Again, the use of the survey approach, as such, does not prevent researchers checking on the accuracy or honesty of the responses, but resourcing generally places severe constraints on the prospects of actually doing so. Most vividly, this is illustrated by the use of postal questionnaires with a survey approach.

Checklist for surveys and sampling

When undertaking research which involves surveys and sampling you should feel confident about answering 'yes' to the following questions:

1 Is the research aiming at a wide and inclusive coverage of the relevant people/events? ☐

2 Is it clear which sampling technique(s) is being used in the research?
- ▶ random sampling ☐
- ▶ systematic sampling ☐
- ▶ stratified sampling ☐
- ▶ quota sampling ☐
- ▶ cluster sampling ☐
- ▶ multi-stage sampling ☐
- ▶ purposive sampling ☐
- ▶ snowball sampling ☐
- ▶ theoretical sampling ☐

3 When choosing a sample size have I taken account of:
- ▶ the desired level of accuracy? ☐
- ▶ the likely non-response rate? ☐
- ▶ the sub-divisions in the data? ☐

4 Is the sample size larger than 30? ☐
If not, have the implications of this for statistical analysis been recognized in the research? ☐

5 Have I assessed the sampling frame in terms of how far it is:
- ▶ complete and inclusive? ☐
- ▶ up-to-date? ☐
- ▶ relevant for the research topic? ☐
Have any deficiencies been acknowledged and their implications taken into account? ☐

6 Is the response rate comparable with that obtained by other similar surveys? ☐

7 Have efforts been made to see if there are significant differences between the respondents and the non-respondents? ☐

2

CASE STUDIES

The use of case studies has become extremely widespread in social research, particularly with small-scale research. When researchers opt for a case study approach they buy into a set of related ideas and preferences which, when combined, give the approach its distinctive character. True, many of the features associated with the case study approach can be found elsewhere and are not necessarily unique to this strategy. However, when brought together they form a broad approach to social research, with an underlying rationale for the direction and planning of an investigation that separates it from the rationale for survey research or the rationale for experimental research.

▶ *Spotlight on one instance.* The starting point, and arguably the defining characteristic, of the case study approach, is its *focus on just one instance of the thing that is to be investigated.* Occasionally, researchers use two or more instances but, in principle, the idea of a case study is that a spotlight is focused on individual instances rather than a wide spectrum. The case study approach, then, is quite the opposite of any mass study. The logic behind concentrating efforts on one case rather than many is that there may be insights to be gained from looking at the individual case that can have wider implications and, importantly, that would not have come to light through the use of a research strategy that tried to cover a large number of instances – a survey approach. The aim is to illuminate the general by looking at the particular.

▶ *In-depth study.* The prospects of getting some valuable and unique insight depends on being able to investigate things in a way that is different from, and in some senses better than, what is possible using other approaches. What a case study can do that a survey normally cannot is to study things in detail. When a researcher takes the strategic decision to devote all his or her efforts to researching just one instance, there is obviously far greater opportunity to delve into things in more detail and discover things that might not have become apparent through more superficial research.

▶ *Focus on relationships and processes*. Relationships and processes within social settings tend to be interconnected and interrelated. To understand one thing it is necessary to understand many others and, crucially, how the various parts are linked. The case study approach works well here because it offers more chance than the survey approach of going into sufficient detail to unravel the complexities of a given situation. It can deal with the case as a whole, in its entirety, and thus have some chance of being able to discover how the many parts affect one another. In this respect, *case studies tend to be 'holistic' rather than deal with 'isolated factors'*. It follows from this that within case studies there is a tendency to emphasize the detailed workings of the relationships and social processes, rather than to restrict attention to the outcomes from these. Quite rightly, *a good case study plays to its strengths*. End-products, outcomes and results all remain of interest to the case study researcher, but if attention were not given to the processes which led to those outcomes then the value of the case study would be lost. The real value of a case study is that it offers the opportunity to explain *why* certain outcomes might happen – more than just find out what those outcomes are. For example, when one is looking at the turnover of labour in an organization, the strength of a case study approach would be that it could investigate the processes that explain the actual level of turnover – the intricate details of the recruitment policy, staff development, nature of the work, levels of pay, background of the workers etc., and how all these are interrelated – all this over and above giving a detailed description of what the facts of the situation are with respect to labour turnover (the outcome).

▶ *Natural setting*. 'The case' that forms the basis of the investigation is normally something that already exists. It is not a situation that is artificially generated specifically for the purposes of the research. It is not like an experiment where the research design is dedicated to imposing controls on variables so that the impact of a specific ingredient can be measured. As Yin (1994) stresses, the case is a 'naturally occurring' phenomenon. It exists prior to the research project and, it is hoped, continues to exist once the research has finished.

▶ *Multiple sources and multiple methods*. One of the strengths of the case study approach is that it allows the researcher to use a variety of sources, a variety of types of data and a variety of research methods as part of the investigation. It not only allows this, it actually invites and encourages the researcher to do so. Observations of events within the case study setting can be combined with the collection of documents from official meetings and informal interviews with people involved. Questionnaires might be used to provide information on a particular point of interest. Whatever is appropriate can be used for investigating the relationships and processes that are of interest.

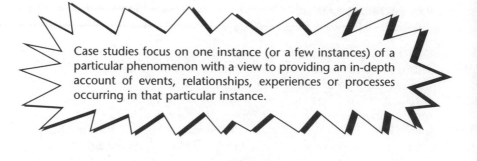

Case studies focus on one instance (or a few instances) of a particular phenomenon with a view to providing an in-depth account of events, relationships, experiences or processes occurring in that particular instance.

Case study research characteristically emphasizes		
Depth of study	rather than	Breadth of study
The particular	rather than	The general
Relationships/processes	rather than	Outcomes and end-products
Holistic view	rather than	Isolated factors
Natural settings	rather than	Artificial situations
Multiple sources	rather than	One research method

 Caution

The decision to use a case study approach is a strategic decision that relates to the scale and scope of an investigation, and it does not, at least in principle, dictate which method or methods must be used. Indeed, a strength of the case study approach is just this – that it allows for the use of a variety of methods depending on the circumstances and the specific needs of the situation.

Any impression that case study research is a *method* for collecting data is wrong. Properly conceived, case study research is a matter of research *strategy*, not research methods. As Hammersley (1992: 184–5) makes the point:

> The concept of case study captures an important aspect of the decisions we face in research. It highlights, in particular, the choices that we have to make about how many cases to investigate and how these are to be selected.

Whereas the survey approach tends to go for large numbers, the case study approach tends to *prefer small numbers*, which are investigated in depth. Whereas experiments place great emphasis on the manipulation of variables, the case study tends to opt for *studying things as they naturally occur*, without introducing artificial changes or controls.

1 The selection of cases

The case study approach generally calls for the researcher to make choices from among a number of possible events, people, organizations etc. The researcher needs to pick out one example (or just a few) from a wider range of examples of the class of thing that is being investigated: the choice of one school for a case study from among the thousands that could have been chosen; the choice of one sexually transmitted disease (STD) clinic from among the many in hospitals across the country; the focus on one bus company from among the hundreds throughout the nation which provide local public transport services. Whatever the subject matter, the case study normally depends on a conscious and explicit choice about which case to select from among a large number of possibilities. *This selection needs to be justified.*

Selection on the basis of 'suitability'

A good case study requires the researcher to defend the decision by arguing that the particular case selected is *suitable* for the purposes of the research, and there are broadly speaking four grounds on which this can be justified.

Typical instance

The most common justification to be offered for the selection of a particular case is that it is typical. The logic being invoked here is that the particular case is similar in crucial respects with the others that might have been chosen, and that the findings from the case study are therefore likely to apply elsewhere. Because the case study is like most of the rest, the findings can be generalized to the whole class of thing.

Extreme instance

A case might be selected on the grounds that, far from being typical, it provides something of a contrast with the norm. An illustration of this would be the selection of an organization which is notably smaller or notably larger than usual. Among local authorities in the country, a very small one might be chosen for a case study, and the logic for doing so would be that this would allow the influence of the factor (size) to be more easily seen than it would be in the average size authority. In an extreme instance, a specified factor is seen in relief – highlighted in its effect.

Test-site for theory

The logic for the selection of a particular case can be based on the relevance of the case for previous theory. This is a point Yin (1994) stresses. Case studies can be used for the purposes of 'theory-testing' as well as 'theory-building', to use Layder's (1993) distinction. The rationale for choosing a specific case, then, can be that it contains crucial elements that are especially significant, and that the researcher should be able to predict certain outcomes if the theory holds true.

Least likely instance

Following the idea of test-sites for theory, a case might be selected to test the validity of 'theory' by seeing if it occurs in an instance where it might be least expected. So, for example, a researcher who wants to test the 'theory' that school teachers place a high value on their autonomy could deliberately select a situation where such autonomy would seem to be least valued: a school with team teaching in open plan classrooms. If there is evidence supporting the 'theory' even under such 'least likely' conditions, then the 'theory' has all the more credibility.

Selection on a 'pragmatic' basis

There are times when case studies are selected for reasons which seem to fall short of the high ideals of scientific research. The newcomer to research should be warned against relying on any such pragmatic reasons as the principal or the sole criterion for selecting a case. Having said this, in the real world of social research there are often elements of such pragmatism which can be detected just beneath the veneer of scientific justification. They are in the background and, as such, deserve some attention.

A matter of convenience

In the practical world of research, with its limits to time and resources, the selection of cases is quite likely to include a consideration of convenience. Faced with alternatives which are equally suitable, it is reasonable for the researcher to select the one(s) which involves the least travel, the least expense and the least difficulty when it comes to gaining access. The crucial point here, though, is that convenience should only come into play when deciding between equally suitable alternatives. Selection on the basis of 'the first to hand', 'the easiest' or 'the cheapest' is not a criterion in its own right which can be used to justify the selection of cases. If used on its own, if fact, it would almost certainly be a symptom of poor social research. Used properly, it is subordinate to the other criteria.

Intrinsically interesting

If a case is intrinsically interesting then it can prove an attractive proposition. The findings are likely to reach a wider audience and the research itself is likely to be a more exciting experience. There are even some experts in the field who would go as far as to argue that selection on the basis of being intrinsically interesting is a sufficient justification in its own right (Stake 1995). This hits at the heart of the debate about whether cases are studied 'in their own right', as Stake would maintain, or for what they reveal about others of the kind, and, in light of its controversial nature, it would be rather foolhardy for the new-comer or project researcher to use this as the sole criterion for selecting a case. The vast majority of social researchers would not see it as a justification for selection in its own right. It might work for journalism, but social research by most definitions calls for more than just this (Ragin 1994). It is far wiser, there-fore, to regard any intrinsic interest of the case as a criterion to be used when deciding between instances that in all other crucial respects are equally suit-able, and as a bonus.

Selection on the basis of 'no real choice'

On some occasions, researchers do not really have a great deal of choice when it comes to the selection of suitable cases for inclusion in the investigation. The choice is more or less dictated by circumstances beyond their control. This happens in the following two circumstances.

The study is part of commissioned research

Commissioned research might leave the researcher with little leeway in the selection of cases. The funder is quite likely to stipulate that the research must be linked to a specified organization or activity, leaving no discretion on the matter to the researchers themselves. Under such circumstances, there is *no real choice in the selection of cases.*

There are unique opportunities

There are times when events occur which provide the researcher with unique opportunities. The events themselves, of course, will not be unique; they will be instances of a class of such events. The opportunity to study such events, however, may be unique. Situations which could not be planned or created present themselves as 'one-off chances'. At one level, this could take the form of social catastrophes, such as war, famine or natural disaster. At a more mundane level, the unique opportunities could reflect the unpredictable or rare nature of the events. Strikes, for example, might be the kind of class of events that could be illuminated through the depth study of individual cases. Researchers, though, will have little choice over which instances they select as their cases and will necessarily find themselves homing in on such events as and when they occur. As a consequence, *there is no real element of choice in the selection of the cases.*

2 Can you generalize from a case study?

The value of a case study approach is that is has the potential to deal with the subtleties and intricacies of complex social situations. This potential comes from the strategic decision to restrict the range of the study to just one or a few cases. When opting for this approach, however, the social researcher is likely to confront scepticism about the findings – scepticism which arises from doubts about how far it is reasonable to generalize from the findings of one case. The researcher will probably find people asking questions such as:

▶ How *representative* is the case?

▶ Isn't it possible that the findings, though interesting, are *unique* to the particular circumstances of the case?

▶ How can you *generalize* on the basis of research into one instance?

These are reasonable questions. They reflect the key issue of generalization in social research and need to be addressed by anyone who decides to adopt a case study approach. They should not be ignored in the hope that readers of the research report will overlook the point. Indeed, it is good practice for any researcher who decides to choose a case study approach to pre-empt possible criticism by addressing the issue head-on. There should be an explicit defence against the allegation that you cannot generalize from case study findings, and this can use the following line of reasoning.

Although each case is in some respects unique, it is also a single example of a broader class of things

If, for example, the study is based on a small primary school this is to be treated as an instance of other schools which are small and which are in the primary sector. It is one of a type (Hammersley 1992; Ragin and Becker 1992; Yin 1994).

The extent to which findings from the case study can be generalized to other examples in the class depends on how far the case study example is similar to others of its type

To pursue the example of the small primary school, the applicability of the findings from the case study to other small primary schools will depend on how far the case study example shares with other schools in the class (small size, primary sector) features which are significant as far as the operation of such schools are concerned. Its catchment area, the ethnic origins of the pupils and the amount of staff turnover might be regarded as vital factors. If so, the generalizability of the findings from the particular case study school to small primary schools in general will depend on the extent to which its profile on these factors is typical of those found elsewhere. Equally, the case study researcher might wish to stress the extent to which the particular example being investigated is unusual, and thus emphasize the limits to how far the findings should be generalized to others in the class.

Either way, the crucial tasks for the case study researcher are:

Comparing a case with others of its type

Comparison might call for the inclusion of details on the following factors.

Physical location	geographical area, town, building, room, furniture, decor
Historical location	developments and changes
Social location	catchment area, ethnic grouping, social class, age, sex and other background information about the participants
Institutional location	type of organization, size of organization, official policies and procedures

---

(a) to identify significant features on which comparison with others in the class can be made; and
(b) to show how the case study compares with others in the class in terms of these significant features.

With the example of the small primary school, this means that the researcher must obtain data on the significant features (catchment area, the ethnic origins of the pupils and the amount of staff turnover) for primary schools in general, and then demonstrate where the case study example fits in relation to the overall picture.

When reporting the case study findings, the researcher needs to include sufficient detail about how the case compares with others in the class for the reader to make an informed judgement about how far the findings have relevance to other instances

When it comes to making generalizations on the basis of case studies, then, some of the responsibility falls to the reader. The *reader* of the findings will use the information to make some assessment of how far the findings have implications across the board for all others of the type, or how far they are restricted to just the case study example. The reader, though, must be provided with the necessary information on which to make an informed judgement on this matter.

3 Boundaries to case studies

The use of a case study approach assumes that the researcher is able to separate some aspect of social life so that it is distinct from other things of the same kind and distinct from its social context. Without some notion of a *boundary*, it becomes impossible to state what the case is. If the case has no end-point, no outside, then it bleeds into other social phenomena and ceases to have any distinct identity. The notion of a 'case', then, must carry with it some idea of a boundary which is sufficiently clear and obvious to allow the researcher to see what is contained within the case (and to be incorporated into the investigation) and what is outside the case (and therefore to be excluded from the focus of the study). In principle,

▶ a 'case' needs to be a fairly *self-contained entity*;

▶ a 'case' needs to have fairly *distinct boundaries*.

It follows that *good case study research needs to contain a clear vision of the boundaries to the case and provide an explicit account of what they are*. This may sound basic and rather obvious. However, in practice, the identification of clear and consistent boundaries can pose quite a hard task for the social researcher. It is just not as easy as it seems.

Physical boundaries

For social researchers, the outside limits of a case are hardly ever defined by a geographical area, a line on a map or a ring fence. The nearest the social researcher gets to such straightforward boundaries is likely to come in the form of organizations whose boundaries might coincide with the areas covered by land and property – buildings such as factories and office blocks offering nice examples. In similar vein, a hospital ward, a school classroom, a personnel department, a warehouse and the like all suggest that case studies conducted within their confines would have easily identified boundaries based on space, area, geography and location. But such simplicity is something of an illusion. The fact is that a case study, for the purpose of *social* research, will not actually be based on an office block or a school classroom. The case study will actually be on the activities, processes and relationships that go on within those physical areas. And this is where the trouble begins. At a superficial level, it might seem reasonable to say that the case study will concern itself with only those activities, processes and relationships that occur within the physically defined boundaries. Certainly, this offers a boundary definition which is practical. It is, though, almost certainly going to be an *artificial boundary*. For the purposes of the case study it will exclude those things happening outside the physical boundary that have a bearing on what happens inside the case study boundary.

Social and historical boundaries

More authentic boundaries are likely to be identified when case studies focus on 'naturally occurring' social or historical phenomena. As Ragin and Becker (1992) indicate, case studies in social research normally deal with 'objects' with fairly *well established boundaries prior* to any investigation. Since they exist prior to the research, the cases must have some boundaries built around them which are widely recognized and which do not need to be generated by the researcher. The study of an organization, for instance, can use factors such as membership (employment) and formal structure (span of operations) as boundaries – things which define the organization as a distinct unit yet which exist quite independently of any involvement of the researcher in conducting a case study. The researcher's task is just to identify the boundaries that already exist, not to create boundaries anew or to define them into existence.

But, as with the use of physical boundaries, things are not quite as clear-cut as they might at first appear and, just the same as with physical boundaries, the root of the problem lies with the possibility that *when a researcher specifies the boundaries to a case there is an in-built tendency to create an artificially 'closed system'*. There is the danger of treating the case as a sealed unit, impervious to the influence of outside factors. The problem with most boundaries is that they are rather too rigid and inflexible to reflect the permeable nature of boundaries in real life. But this is not an easy problem to overcome. If definitions of the boundary become fuzzy at the edges and more like 'open' systems in the way that they allow for influences to pass to and from the case to the wider context in which it exists, then it raises questions about what the case is. The more flexible the boundaries become, the more loose and woolly the entity becomes in terms of the kind of precision and rigour expected of research.

The *best advice on boundaries*, then, is that they should be explicitly identified but that, when defining the boundaries to a case, researchers should be sensitive to the potential of such boundaries:

▶ to exclude factors occurring outside the boundaries which have a genuine impact on activities, processes and relationships within the case study;

▶ to ignore the things that happen to those involved when they are away from the defined area;

▶ to have difficulty in dealing with those occasions when outsider factors temporarily intrude on the zone of the research.

4 Advantages of the case study approach

▶ The main benefit of using a case study approach is that the focus on one or a few instances allows the researcher to *deal with the subtleties and intricacies* of complex social situations. In particular, it enables the researcher to grapple with relationships and social processes in a way that is denied to the survey approach. The analysis is holistic rather than based on isolated factors.

▶ The case study approach allows the use of a variety of research methods. More than this, it more or less encourages the use of *multiple methods* in order to capture the complex reality under scrutiny.

Link up with **Triangulation, p. 83**

▶ In parallel with the use of multiple methods, the case study approach fosters the use of *multiple sources* of data. This, in turn, facilitates the validation of data through *triangulation*.

▶ The case study approach is particularly suitable where the researcher has little control over events. Because the approach is concerned with investigating phenomena as they naturally occur, there is *no pressure on the researcher to impose controls* or to change circumstances.

▶ The case study approach can fit in well with the needs of small-scale research through *concentrating effort on one research site* (or just a few sites).

▶ Theory-building and theory-testing research can both use the case study approach to good effect.

5 Disadvantages of the case study approach

▶ The point at which the case study approach is most vulnerable to criticism is in relation to the *credibility of generalizations* made from its findings. The case study researcher needs to be particularly careful to allay suspicions and to demonstrate the extent to which the case is similar to, or contrasts with, others of its type.

▶ Unwarranted though it may be, case studies are often *perceived as producing 'soft' data*. The approach gets accused of lacking the degree of rigour expected of social science research. This tends to go alongside the view of case study research as focusing on processes rather than measurable end-products, as relying on qualitative data and interpretive methods rather than quantitative data and statistical procedures. Often, case studies are regarded as all right in terms of providing descriptive accounts of the situation but rather ill-suited to analyses or evaluations. None of this is necessarily justified, but it is a preconception which the case study researcher needs to be aware of, and one which needs to be challenged by careful attention to detail and rigour in the use of the approach.

▶ On the technical side, the *boundaries* of the case can prove difficult to define in an absolute and clear-cut fashion. This poses difficulties in terms of deciding what sources of data to incorporate in the case study and which to exclude.

▶ *Negotiating access* to case study settings can be a demanding part of the research process. Research can flounder if permission is withheld or withdrawn. In case studies, access to documents, people and settings can generate ethical problems in terms of things like confidentiality.

▶ It is hard for case study researchers to achieve their aim of investigating situations as they naturally occur without any effect arising from their presence. Because case study research tends to involve protracted involvement over a period of time, there is the possibility that the presence of the research can lead to *the observer effect*. Those being researched might behave differently from normal owing to the knowledge that they are 'under the microscope' and being observed in some way.

Link up with **The observer effect, p. 47**

Checklist for the case study approach

When undertaking research which involves a case study approach you should feel confident about answering 'yes' to the following questions:

1. Have the *criteria for selection* of the case (or cases) been described and justified? ☐

2. Has the case (or cases) been identified as a particular *instance of a type* of social phenomenon? (e.g. kind of event, type of organization) ☐

3. Is the case a fairly *self-contained entity*? ☐

4. Is the research based on a '*naturally occurring*' situation? ☐

5. Have the *boundaries* to the case been described and their implications considered? ☐

6. Has careful consideration been given to the issue of *generalizations* stemming from research? ☐

7. Have the *significant features* of the case been described and have they been compared with those to be found elsewhere amongst the type of thing being studied? ☐

8. Does the research make suitable use of *multiple methods* and *multiple sources* of data? ☐

9. Does the research give due attention to *relationships and processes*, and provide a 'holistic' perspective? ☐

© M. Denscombe, *The Good Research Guide*. Open University Press.

▶ ▷ ▷ **3**

EXPERIMENTS

The idea of an experiment tends to be linked with white-coated scientists working in a laboratory, possibly using highly sophisticated equipment to measure things with extreme precision. The point of conducting an experiment is to isolate individual factors and observe their effect in detail. The purpose is to discover new relationships or properties associated with the materials being investigated, or to test existing theories.

Now, although this draws on a rather idealized image of the way experiments are conducted in the natural sciences, it is not entirely irrelevant for the *social* sciences. It largely succeeds in capturing the essence of the notion and provides something of a benchmark for social researchers wishing to use experiments. It incorporates the three things that lie at the heart of conducting an experiment:

▶ *Controls*. Experiments involve the manipulation of circumstances. The researcher needs to identify factors which are significant and then introduce them to or exclude them from the situation so that their effect can be observed.

▶ *The identification of causal factors*. The introduction or exclusion of factors to or from the situation enables the researcher to pinpoint which factor actually causes the observed outcome to occur.

▶ *Observation and measurement*. Experiments rely on precise and detailed *observation* of outcomes and changes that occur following the introduction or exclusion of potentially relevant factors. They also involve close attention to the measurement of what is observed.

These essential features of 'the experiment', it is worth noting, are concerned with the aims of the investigation and its design. They do not say anything about *how* exactly the data are to be collected. This is why experiments are better

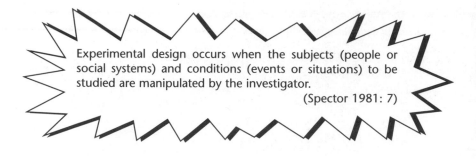

Experimental design occurs when the subjects (people or social systems) and conditions (events or situations) to be studied are manipulated by the investigator.

(Spector 1981: 7)

seen as a strategy for research rather than a method. Especially in the social sciences, the decision to use an experimental approach is a strategic one, in which the researcher decides to investigate the topic under controlled conditions, paying careful attention to the meticulous measurement of what goes on.

1 Controls

In experiments, the researcher attempts to control the situation in a way that manipulates the range of variables that might have any impact, so that it will be possible ultimately to eliminate interference in the cause–effect chain by any other factor. The aim is to control variables, all at once or in a sequence of experiments, so that only the one factor at the end remains as a viable *cause* of the observed change. Introducing controls into the design of a piece of research can be achieved in a variety of ways.

Eliminate the factor from the experiment

This is the most direct way of controlling for factors which might have a bearing on the outcome from an experiment, and it can operate in either of two ways. It can be used to eliminate things which might interfere with the clear and precise measurement of the key factor. Or it can be used as *the* experimental change itself. Rather than *introduce* a new factor to the situation, the researcher might find it easier to eliminate one factor. So, for instance, a study of the link between hyperactivity and diet in children might see the researcher deliberately excluding all artificial colourings from the subjects' diets and then observing any change in behaviour. If other factors remain unaltered, it would be logical to deduce that any observed change was due to the absence of this factor.

Hold the factor constant

In social science, a large number of the key relevant variables come in the form of attributes that cannot be written out of the equation through eliminating them from the situation altogether. Things like income, weight and age are attributes that cannot be eliminated. However, they can be controlled for by 'holding the factor constant'. To prevent the factors from having an unwanted intrusion on the outcome of the experiment, the researcher can devise a situation in which the subjects are all of the same income or of the same weight. Observed outcomes from the experiment, as a result, can be deduced to stem from some factor other than income or weight.

Balance groups

When we can predict that the factor has an effect we can try to 'balance out' the effect. So, for example, if age is suspected to be a factor, we can make a point of incorporating all age bands into the group involved in the experiment. In this way, the effect should cancel itself out.

Random selection of groups

If the research subjects are chosen on a random basis there should be a tendency for those factors which are not crucial to cancel themselves out. The principle here is that by the choice of a large enough group of subjects on a random basis, any interference with the results through factors like income or weight would have a nil effect overall, because the random nature of the selection would ensure that all the individual effects would cancel themselves out in terms of the results for the whole research group.

Use of control groups

This is the most used and established way of exercising control over significant variables. The principle is simple. First, it is necessary to identify two groups of people for the experiment. The two groups should be similar in terms of their composition. The start point for the experiment, then, is *two matched groups or samples*. The experiment involves introducing a factor to the experimental group and leaving the other group with no artificially induced changes. Having added the new factor, the experimenter can then look at the two groups again with the belief that any *difference* between the groups can be attributed to the factor which was artificially induced. Note here that it is not the *change* in the experiment group as such which is important. Certain changes over time are likely to happen irrespective of whether an experiment had taken place. Time moves on for all of us. But, if the two groups were as identical as possible at the outset, any change of this kind in one group will also occur in the other group. So, instead of measuring the change from time 1 to time 2, we measure the difference between the control group and the experimental group at the end of the experiment at time 2. Any differences we observe can be logically deduced to come from the factor which was artificially induced in the experiment.

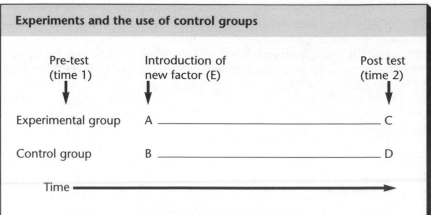

Experiments and the use of control groups

Pre-test (time 1)	Introduction of new factor (E)	Post test (time 2)

Experimental group   A _____ C

Control group   B _____ D

Time ➤

Experimental group and control group are matched groups or samples. Factor E causes a change in the experimental group of (C – A) – (D – B).

 **Caution**

In the case of social research, there are certain limitations to the extent to which circumstances can be manipulated. Basically, a researcher can do things to chemicals and plants that cannot be contemplated with fellow human beings. For the purposes of doing an experiment it may be neither feasible nor, indeed, ethical to manipulate people's lives in order to provide the controlled conditions necessary for a 'social science experiment'. People have feelings, people have rights.

2 Cause and effect

Experiments are generally concerned with determining the *cause* of any changes that occur to the thing being studied. It is not normally enough to show that two things that occur are linked; that they always occur at the same time or they always happen in sequence. Useful though it is to know about such a relationship, experiments usually aim to discover which of the factors is the cause. In practice, the control of factors in the experiment centres on the distinction between *dependent and independent variables*. It is vital that the researcher has a clear vision of which is which, and sets up the experiment in a way which produces results that show the distinction between the two.

▶ The independent variable is the one that has the effect on the dependent variable. Its size, number, structure, volume or whatever exists autonomously, owing nothing to the other variable. A change in the independent variable affects the dependent variable.

Example

Tobacco smoking is related to the incidence of lung cancer. Both are variables and both appear to be linked to each other: more smoking, higher incidence of lung cancer; less smoking, lower incidence. Smoking increases the likelihood of lung cancer. Lung cancer does not increase the likelihood of smoking. In this example, there is clearly a dependent variable and an independent variable. Smoking tobacco is the independent variable, and lung cancer is the dependent variable.

▶ the dependent variable is the factor which changes as a result of changes to the independent variable. It literally 'depends' on the independent variable. A change in the dependent variable does not affect the independent variable.

3 Observation and measurement

It might be argued that any form of research involves observation and measurement, but the point about observation and measurement as they are associated with experiments is that they are conducted ideally under conditions which are artificially created to a greater or lesser extent. They take place under conditions which have been manipulated to allow the greatest rigour and precision. That is why the experiments generally take place in laboratories, because these are purpose-built contexts for the research. They enhance the possibility

The Observer effect

People are likely to alter their behaviour when they become aware that they are being observed.

Unlike atoms, people can become *aware* of being studied – conscious of it – and then react in a way that is not usual. They can:

▶ be embarrassed;
▶ disguise normal practice/be defensive.

To overcome the effect, researchers are generally advised to:

▶ spend time on site, so that researcher becomes 'part of the furniture';
▶ have minimal interaction with those being observed.

of precision. There are, though, two points that need to be borne in mind in relation to observations that form part of an experiment.

First, the artificial setting of an experiment can heighten people's sensitivity to being observed. Humans have self-awareness in a sense that makes them very different from the materials studied in other forms of research. When humans become aware that they are the focus of attention for research, there is the very real possibility that they will act differently from normal. They might possibly become self-conscious or alter their behaviour to take account of the purposes of the research. This is known as 'the halo effect'. Experimenters can take steps to overcome this. They can, for instance, make hidden observations from behind a one-way mirror. Or they can disguise the real purpose of the research to avoid getting altered behaviour in relation to the factor being investigated (see the account of Milgram's research below). But both solutions to the halo effect raise ethical problems and need very careful consideration before being used by the newcomer or project researcher.

4 Laboratory experiments

The use of controls, the search for causes and the emphasis on detailed observation and measurement are seen in their most extreme form in *'laboratory experiments'*. Such experiments are characteristically:

▶ of relatively *short* duration;

▶ located *'on site'* rather than 'in the field';

▶ involving *close control* of variables to isolate causal factors;

▶ with *meticulous observation* and measurements.

Although not necessarily typical of experiments conducted by psychologists, a series of experiments conducted by Stanley Milgram at Yale University between 1960 and 1963 offers an example that illustrates how such laboratory experiments might operate in the case of social research (Milgram 1974). The aim of the series of experiments was to shed more light on the apparent willingness of ordinary individuals to inflict cruel pain on others when instructed to do so by an authority figure. It formed part of an ongoing debate, prompted by Nazi atrocities during the Second World War, about whether those who inflicted the torture were psychologically different from normal people, or whether there is a normal psychological tendency to obey authority, even to the point of following instructions to hurt a fellow human being against whom you bear no personal animosity. Milgram's series of experiments sought to investigate this under strictly controlled conditions.

> The point of the experiment is to see how far a person will proceed in a concrete and measurable situation in which he is ordered to inflict increasing pain on a protesting victim. At what point will the subject refuse to obey the experimenter?
>
> (Milgram 1974: 3–4)

An advertisement was put in a local newspaper inviting people aged 20 to 50 to participate in 'a scientific study of memory and learning'. The advertisement offered $4 plus 50 cents car fare for those willing to give up one hour of their time. Those who took up the offer were met at the university department by a person who said he was in charge of the experiment – a smart looking young man in a laboratory coat. The 'subject' was then introduced to a man who, he was led to believe, was another participant in the experiment. This person was in his late fifties, very mild-mannered and inoffensive, and slightly overweight: not the kind of person you would want to harm. The whole thing, however, was a 'set-up'. The 'experimenter' and the other subject were colleagues of Milgram, and they were actually taking part in a carefully scripted sequence of events. Their words and actions were part of the experiment and in accord with a strict plan which was followed with each new volunteer who came in off the street. This meant that the only real variable was the action of each subject who had volunteered to help. As far as was possible, all other aspects of what happened were controlled to be the same on each occasion.

The subjects were told that they were to take part in a study of the effects of punishment on learning. One of the two participants was to take the role of the 'teacher' administering the punishment, the other was to be the 'learner'. It was rigged so that when drawing a piece of paper out of a hat to determine which subject took which role, Milgram's colleague always got the role of the learner, ensuring that the real subject was left to undertake the teacher role. At this point the late-fifties, mild-mannered, slightly overweight 'learner' was taken to a room and sat in a chair. He was strapped down and electrodes were attached to his arm. The whole thing was deliberately set up to resemble the 'electric chair'. In an adjoining room, from which this could be seen, the unsuspecting subject and the 'experimenter' in his lab coat went to an 'impressive shock generator'. The subject was given a 45 volt shock from this generator to make the whole performance that followed convincing. In fact, it was the only real electric shock administered throughout the whole experiment – but the subject was not to know this. The learning experiment consisted of the 'teacher' (the subject) reading out a series of paired words (e.g. fat–neck, blue–girl, nice–day). A stimulus word was then read out, followed by five others, among which was the actual paired word read out in the original series. The learner had to identify which was the correct word out of the five. Each time he made a mistake, the subject had to deliver an electric shock by way of punishment – purportedly to see if this would encourage better learning. Each time a mistake was made, an electric shock 15 volts higher than the one before was apparently administered.

The learner put on a performance. Although he actually received no electric shock at all, he acted as though he did. As the voltage of the shocks was increased he began to moan and protest – all, of course, to a precise script that went with each increase. At 150 volts Milgram's colleague would cry out, 'Experimenter, get me out of here! I won't be in the experiment any more! I refuse to go on!' At 180 volts he would shout, 'I can't stand the pain!' and by 270 volts he would let out an agonized scream. After 330 volts the learner fell silent. The lab-coated experimenter continued to coax the subject to give the electric shocks, and each time the 'learner' protested he gave a carefully scripted reassurance to the real subject: 'No permanent tissue damage is caused; he has to go on because it is part of the experiment.'

The experimental conditions were altered through the series of experiments. The proximity of the subject to the learner was altered, for example, and the nature of the complaints that could be heard by the subject emanating from the pained learner, but the basic design continued. Milgram found that ordinary volunteers were remarkably willing to give dangerously high voltages to a person they believed to be another 'off-the-street' volunteer, a person who was apparently vulnerable to heart attack, an inoffensive person, a person who was quite evidently suffering extreme pain and demanding to be released. Depending on the specifics of the experiment, between half and two-thirds of subjects went on to administer up to 450 volts! They did not do so with glee; they often protested and expressed disquiet about the whole thing. But this proportion of ordinary people could be persuaded by the authority of the scientific experimenter in his lab coat to deliver what by any standards is an extremely dangerous and painful 'punishment' to a vulnerable fellow being.

The psychological explanation for this level of obedience to authority is discussed in detail by Milgram, but this is not the point of describing the experiment here. The point of describing it is to illustrate the way in which the use of an experiment relies on controlling as many of the variables as possible to allow an uncontaminated measurement of the factor that is of prime interest and involves precise measurements. It is very unlikely that these could have been achieved had the research not taken place in the laboratory, on home territory where the researchers are able to set things up in a very meticulous fashion and repeat the experiment time and again without interference from outside factors.

Admittedly, most laboratory experiments in the social sciences do not achieve the fame and notoriety of the Milgram experiments, for obvious reasons. They tend to be less provocative in their topic and design. The principles, none the less, remain the same.

5 Tests

The use of tests to measure things like knowledge and ability is commonplace. Just about everyone who has been through a formal education system will have been 'tested' at some time or another, in the form of progress tests and examinations. Then there are eye tests, driving tests and a whole host of other ways in which particular aptitudes and abilities are measured. Questions are posed and answers are given. Tasks are requested and actions follow. The process is very familiar.

Such tests, of course, are not usually given as part of what we would consider to be 'research'. *For the most part, tests are used as diagnostic tools rather than research tools*. The optician who tests our eyes is not likely to be engaged in pushing back the frontiers of knowledge through the systematic study of eye defects. There is a far greater likelihood that he or she will be primarily concerned with measuring a customer's eyesight so that an appropriate lens can be dispensed to compensate for any deficiency from 20:20 vision. In school, a science test for 15-year-olds will, in the vast majority of cases, be carried out to assess the amount of knowledge the students have accumulated about science, not to investigate new ways of teaching the science curriculum.

None the less, *tests can have a role to play in research*, and this role stems from three features of tests. What tests have in common is:

▶ *The application of a uniform procedure.* A test procedure relies on giving the same questions or the same tasks to all people. It is, in effect, administered under *controlled conditions*. The logic of this is that any variation in the responses given to the test are the result of differences in the aptitude or task being measured, not differences in the nature of the test itself. Candidates sitting an examination, we would suppose, should all be given the same questions and the same amount of time to complete the answers. Only by adopting such a uniform procedure can we expect the grades to reflect variations in ability rather than differences in the questions.

▶ *An emphasis on measuring a specific trait.* In accord with experiments, there is a strong emphasis on rigorous observation and meticulous measurement as key facets of the approach. Tests involve a process of classifying, categorizing and enumerating specific traits, such as people's knowledge or skills, with the aim of then measuring such traits in terms of numbers (e.g. 8 out of 10) or in terms of categories (satisfactory/unsatisfactory).

▶ *A comparison with some 'universal' standard.* Tests are generally designed to produce results which allow comparisons to be made. For this reason, there are advantages to the use of 'off-the-shelf' ready-made tests, so-called *standardized tests*. The reason they are called standardized tests is that such tests have been thoroughly trialled with a representative sample of the appropriate population. This trialling not only establishes the reliability of the test, but also allows the producers of the test to supply objective benchmarks against which the individual user of the test can compare his or her results. This means that the person using the test has a predefined expectation of what the 'normal' results might look like. It allows comparisons between the results from any single use of the test and results that are standard for the particular population. Such tests are frequently available via commercial publishers who market the tests on the basis of the fact that the test is widely accepted.

Advantages of standardized tests

▶ It is *faster* to use a ready-made test than to devise a new one.

▶ The standardized test will be of *better quality*, having been devised and checked out by experts.

▶ Standardized tests tend to be well tried and have a good reputation.

▶ Standardized tests offer an *'objective' referent point* that allows comparison within groups, between groups and over time.

▶ They allow wider generalizations and more certain interpretations from the results.

Disadvantages of standardized tests

▶ They can be expensive to purchase.

▶ Some tests have *restricted accessibility*. Only those with an appropriate professional qualification are allowed to administer certain tests, a restriction aimed at making sure that proper procedures are followed and that the tests are not used or interpreted in a cavalier fashion, bringing them into disrepute.

▶ It is difficult to assess the extent to which the test results reflect the respondent's experience of the test situation itself rather than the specific ability or aptitude under investigation. Tests can prove stressful, and this can affect performance – the experience of taking a driving test should emphasize this point!

6 Field experiments

The use of experiments by social researchers would appear to be restricted to those situations where they are able to manipulate the situation and impose controls on crucial variables. Laboratories clearly are designed to aid this. There is, though, something of a dilemma here.

> It is often argued that laboratory experiments are of little use because the settings in which they take place are artificial and so the results of the ensuing findings have little validity beyond the confines of the laboratory.
> (Bryman 1989: 90)

It is not just that the data are generated under artificial conditions: they are actually shaped to some degree by those artificial conditions. Yet, if researchers move outside the laboratories in order to gather data in more natural settings, they are, of course, likely to pay a high price in terms of their ability to control the variables. Beyond the laboratory, the social researcher has far less prospect of managing to manipulate things for the express purpose of a social experiment. Sociologists cannot control levels of incomes in order to conduct experiments on things like poverty. Nor can health educators manipulate levels of smoking among adolescent girls in order to study it. Economists cannot generate a recession in order to investigate its consequences. It is simply not possible to manipulate circumstances like these. It is not feasible, nor would it be ethical.

There are, however, approaches within social research which recognize that it is neither feasible nor ethical to attempt to impose controls on all the relevant factors, yet which strive to retain the logic of the experimental approach, albeit in a watered down version, beyond the bounds of the laboratory. Because they cannot always control all the variables, some social scientists have resorted to a *'quasi-experimental'* approach as a realistic possibility. The quasi *('as if')* experimental approach is conducted in the spirit of the classic laboratory experiment, but recognizes that the researcher cannot dictate circumstances and needs to take the role of observing events 'as they naturally occur'. Much like weather forecasters, these social scientists tend to rely on observing events which occur in circumstances over which they have little or no control. Researchers in this case are on the lookout for 'naturally occurring' experiments – situations in which they can see the possibility of observing and measuring the impact of isolated variables through circumstances as they happen, without imposing artificial controls.

Naturally occurring experiments are part of the logic of anthropological studies of simple, 'primitive' societies. As Margaret Mead made the point:

> The study of human development in a primitive society has ... two advantages: contrast with our own social environment which brings out different aspects of human nature and often demonstrates that behaviour which occurs almost invariably in individuals within our own society is nevertheless due not to original nature but to social environment; and a homogeneous and simple social background, easily mastered, against which the development of the individual may be studied.
>
> The anthropologist submits the findings of the psychologist who works within our society to the test of observation within other societies.
>
> (Mead 1963: 212)

Another example of quasi-experimental research comes in the form of *ex post facto experiments*. In this instance, the starting point for the investigation is the 'effect', and the researcher sets out to deduce what factors could be held to account for this outcome. The idea is to work backwards from the effect to find the cause. For example, the researcher might ask, 'Does imprisonment affect earnings after release from detention?' The research design here would be to identify a number of people who had been to prison. This *independent* variable – imprisonment – is not something the research can or should manipulate. It is a *fait accompli*, existing prior to and quite separate from the research. However, by comparing ex-prisoners with people who in most other respects match them it is possible to deduce whether or not that factor has had a direct effect on the *dependent* variable: earnings. Or, to give another illustration, the starting point for the research might be the discovery of lung cancer in particular people. *Ex post facto* research then sets about trying to identify variables that might explain the incidence of lung cancer in these people. It might be discovered that, compared with the population as a whole, a higher proportion of those with lung cancer smoke tobacco. Controlling for other factors to discount them as possible causes, the researcher might eventually deduce that smoking tobacco is the cause of the higher incidence of lung cancer.

Experimental research

Laboratory experiments	Field experiments
Located 'on site'	Located 'in the field'
Close control of variables	Use available possibilities
Meticulous measurements	Structured observations
Shorter duration	Longer duration

---

7 Advantages of experiments

▶ *Repeatable.* In the case of laboratory experiments, there is every chance that the research will be repeatable. The procedures should have been carefully recorded and the variables controlled for. It is in line with the spirit of scientific research, lending itself to being checked by being repeated by other researchers using identical procedures.

▶ *Precision.* Again, in the case of laboratory experiments, the context for the research permits the highest possible level of precision when it comes to the measurements that form the basis of the data.

▶ *Convenience.* In the laboratory, the researcher is on 'home territory'. This has advantages in terms of setting up the research, and there are also some positive benefits when it comes to costs. The researcher does not need to go out into the field and incur the travel costs and the loss of time spent going to research sites.

8 Disadvantages of experiments

▶ *Deception and ethics.* There are a number of ethical considerations to be borne in mind when one is considering the use of experimental research. For instance, if the research design employs the use of control groups, which it is likely to, will there be any advantage or disadvantage experienced by those in the respective groups? Is it possible that adverse comparisons might result through different treatments of experimental and control groups? If there is a significant difference, this could pose both ethical and practical/political problems for the researcher. Equally, the experiment's success might depend on keeping its purpose secret from the research subjects. This raises a question about the ethics of deception when used in social research.

▶ *Artificial settings.* With laboratory experiments there are question marks about whether the experimental situation creates conditions comparable with the 'real-world' situations in which the behaviour/decisions would be made, or whether it encourages artificial responses in line with the artificial setting.

▶ *Representativeness of the research subjects.* For most purposes, experimental researchers will want to use a control group. To use a control group in a valid fashion, the researcher needs to be sure that the experimental group and the control group constitute a 'matched pair'. They need to be very closely matched in terms of those features which are relevant to the experiment and to the broader population from which the research subjects are drawn. This can be difficult to achieve. Are the research subjects typical of the 'population' being studied? Do the subjects share the same prior experiences? Has there been an element of self-selection?

▶ *Control of the relevant variables.* Being able to control the relevant variables lies at the heart of the experimental method. However, this places a burden on the would-be experimenter to be sure that he or she can do so. And, even if it is practically possible, is it ethical?

Checklist for the experimental approach

✓

When undertaking research which involves experiments you should feel confident about answering 'yes' to the following questions:

1 Have control groups been used?
   If so, are the control group and the experimental
   group closely matched in all key respects? ☐ ☐

2 Have the key variables been identified? ☐

3 Has a clear distinction been drawn between
   dependent and independent variables? ☐

4 Is it practical to manipulate the independent variable? ☐

5 Does the experimental situation create conditions
   comparable to the 'real-world' situations in which the
   behaviour/decisions would be made? ☐

6 Am I satisfied that neither the control group nor the
   experimental group will have been disadvantaged in any
   significant way as a consequence of the experiment? ☐

7 Does the experiment *explain* the *causal* relationship
   it observes? ☐

8 Did the research subjects know their true involvement?
   If yes, has the effect of this on the subjects' responses
   been taken into consideration? ☐ ☐

9 Is the research ethical in terms of its treatment of those
   involved in the experiment? ☐

© M. Denscombe, *The Good Research Guide*. Open University Press.

▶ ▷ ▷ **4**

ACTION RESEARCH

Action research is normally associated with 'hands-on', small-scale research projects. Its origins can be traced back to the work of social scientists in the late 1940s on both sides of the Atlantic, who advocated closer ties between social theory and the solving of immediate social problems. More recently, action research has been used in a variety of settings within the social sciences, but its growing popularity as a research approach perhaps owes most to its use in areas such as organizational development, education, health and social care. In these areas it has a particular niche among professionals who want to use research to improve their practices.

Action research, from the start, was involved with *practical* issues – the kind of issues and problems, concerns and needs, that arose as a routine part of activity 'in the real world'. This specifically practical orientation has remained a defining characteristic of action research. Early on, action research was also seen as research specifically geared to *changing* matters, and this too has remained a core feature of the notion of action research. The thinking here is that research should not only be used to gain a better understanding of the problems which arise in everyday practice, but actually set out to alter things – to do so as part and parcel of the research process rather than tag it on as an afterthought which follows the conclusion of the research. This, in fact, points towards a third defining characteristic of action research: its commitment to a process of research in which the application of findings and an evaluation of their impact on practice become part of a *cycle of research*. This process, further, has become associated with a trend towards involving those affected by the research in the design and implementation of the research – to encourage them to *participate* as collaborators in the research rather than being subjects of it.

Together, these provide the *four defining characteristics of action research.*

▶ *Practical*. It is aimed at dealing with real-world problems and issues, typically at work and in organizational settings.

▶ *Change*. Both as a way of dealing with practical problems and as a means of discovering more about phenomena, change is regarded as an integral part of research.

▶ *Cyclical process*. Research involves a feedback loop in which initial findings generate possibilities for change which are then implemented and evaluated as a prelude to further investigation.

▶ *Participation*. Practitioners are the crucial people in the research process. Their participation is active, not passive.

Action research quite clearly is a *strategy* for social research rather than a specific method. It is concerned with the aims of research and the design of the research, but does not specify any constraints when it comes to the means for data collection that might be adopted by the action researcher. This point is captured by Susman and Evered:

> Action research can use different techniques for data collection . . . Action researchers with a background in psychology tend to prefer questionnaires for such purposes . . . while action researchers with a background in applied anthropology, psychoanalysis or socio-technical systems tend to prefer direct observation and/or in-depth interviewing . . . Action researchers with any of these backgrounds may also retrieve data from the records, memos and reports that the client system routinely produces.
>
> (Susman and Evered 1978: 589)

1 The practical nature of action research

Action research is essentially practical and applied. It is driven by the need to solve practical, real-world problems. It operates on the premise, as Kurt Lewin put it, that 'Research that produces nothing but books will not suffice' (Lewin 1946: 35).

But being practical would not be enough to set it apart from other approaches to research. After all, many approaches can lay claim to this territory. Many can claim with justification to offer applied research. While it

Action research [rejects] the concept of a two-stage process in which research is carried out first by researchers and then in a separate second stage the knowledge generated from the research is applied by practitioners. Instead, the two processes of research and action are integrated.

(Somekh 1995: 34)

certainly does embrace this aim, being 'practical' has a second sense as far as action research is concerned, and it is this which helps to give it a unique identity as a research strategy. The research needs to be undertaken *as part of practice* rather than a bolt-on addition to it.

Clearly, if the processes of research and action are integrated, then action research must involve 'the practitioner' very closely. And this provides a further meaning which can be added to the practical nature of action research: *practitioner research*. However, although it may be linked with the notion of practitioner research, it is important to appreciate that action research is not exactly the same thing as practitioner research. Edwards and Talbot stress this point:

> Practitioner research can only be designated action research if it is carried out by professionals who are engaged in researching, through structured self-reflection, *aspects of their own practice as they engage in that practice.*
>   (Edwards and Talbot 1994: 52, emphasis added)

It is not enough simply for the research to be undertaken as part of the job, because this could include all kinds of data gathering and analysis to do with remote people and systems, the findings from which might have no bearing on the practitioner's own activity. To accord with the spirit of action research, the researcher needs to investigate his or her *own* practices with a view to altering these in a beneficial way.

2 Change and professional self-development

Action research is wedded to the idea that change is good. Initially, this is because studying change is seen as a useful *way of learning more about the way a thing works* (Bryman 1989). Change, in this sense, is regarded as a valuable enhancer of knowledge in its own right, rather than something that is undertaken after the results of the research have been obtained. But, of course, the scale and the scope of changes introduced through action research will not be grand. The scale of the research is constrained by the need for the action researchers to focus on *aspects of their own practice as they engage in that practice.* So change as envisaged by action research is not likely to be a wide-scale major alteration to an organization. The element of change will not be in the order of a large-scale experiment such as changes in the bonus schemes of production workers at Ford's car assembly plants. No. Because, action research tends to be localized and small-scale, it usually focuses on change at the micro level.

One of the most common kinds of change involved in action research is at the level of *professional self-development.* It is in keeping with the notion of professional self-development that a person should want to improve practices and that this should involve a continual quest for ways in which to change practice for the better. Action research provides a way forward for the professional which, while it entails a certain degree of reflection, adds the systematic and rigorous collection of data to the resources the professional can use to achieve the improvement in practice.

It is important to recognize that reflection may be of itself insufficient to make the professional's endeavour 'action research'. The reflection needs to be systematic if it is to qualify as action *research*. Merely *thinking* about your own practice – though possibly a valuable basis for improving practice – is not the same as researching that action. And here a distinction needs to be made between the 'reflective practitioner' (Schön 1983) as one who strives for professional self-development through a critical consideration of his or her practices, and the action researcher who, while also being a reflective practitioner, adds to this by using research techniques to enhance and systematize that reflection.

3 Action research as a cyclical process

The vision of action research as a cyclical process fits in nicely with the quest for perpetual development built into the idea of professionalism. The purpose of research, though it might be prompted by a specific problem, is seen as part of a broader enterprise in which the aim is to improve practice through a rolling programme of research.

The crucial points about the cycle of inquiry in action research are (a) that *research feeds back directly into practice*, and (b) that *the process is ongoing*. The critical reflection of the practitioner is not only directed to the identification of 'problems' worthy of investigation with a view to improving practice, but can also involve an evaluation of changes just instigated, which can, in their own right, prompt further research. It is fair to point out, however, that this is something of an ideal and that, in reality, action research often limits itself to discrete, one-off pieces of research.

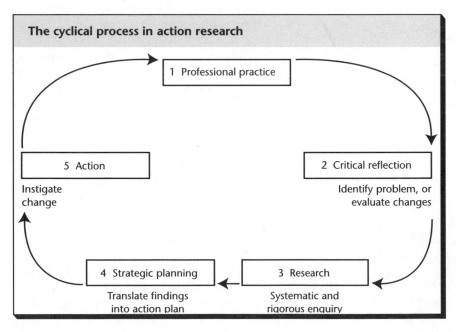

The cyclical process in action research

1 Professional practice

5 Action
Instigate
change

2 Critical reflection
Identify problem, or
evaluate changes

4 Strategic planning
Translate findings
into action plan

3 Research
Systematic and
rigorous enquiry

4 Participation in the research process

The participatory nature of action research is probably its most distinctive feature, since, in some ways, it hits at the heart of conventions associated with formal social research. Conventionally, research is the province of the expert; the outside authority who is a professional. This researcher more often than not initiates the process of research, sets the agenda and designs the collection and analysis of data. After the research is concluded, those involved might receive some feedback in the form of results from the research. They may, or may not, instigate changes on the basis of such findings. Broadly speaking, the act of doing research is separated from the act of making changes (Boutilier *et al.* 1997). Action research, by contrast, insists that practitioners must be participants, not just in the sense of taking part in the research but in the sense of being *a partner in the research.*

Partnerships, of course, take many forms. Grundy and Kemmis (1988: 7) argue that 'in action research, all actors involved in the research process are equal participants, and must be involved in every stage of the research.' With action research it can be the practitioner, not some outside professional researcher, who wants to instigate a change and who consequently initiates the research (Elliott 1991). The research, in this sense, is practitioner-driven, with the practitioner not just an equal partner but a sponsor and director of the research process. And if this sounds radical, there are others who would push the matter further, insisting that the practitioner should be the dominant partner – calling the shots at all stages and in all aspects of the research.

Even in less radical revisions to the conventional relationship between researcher and practitioners, the inclusion of participation as a fundamental feature of action research brings with it a shift in the direction of *democratizing the research process.* Control is transferred away from the professional researcher and towards the practitioner. Power shifts towards the insider who is the practitioner. There is, of course, still a role for the outside expert, but that role shifts in the direction of mutual collaboration in the research process, or even to the position where the outside expert has the role of *facilitator* of the practitioner's own project, a resource to be drawn upon as and when the practitioner sees fit.

Behind this shift in the relationship there rests a *respect for the practitioner's knowledge.* Again, this respect may not be unique to action research, but it is an aspect of action research which is distinctive and built into an approach which is broadly sympathetic to democratizing the research process by challenging the separation of expert from lay person in research.

There can be an explicitly political angle to the participatory aspect of action research, with its 'democratization' of the research process and 'respect for practitioner knowledge'. Zuber-Skerritt (1996) refers to this as *'emancipatory'* action research. This type of action research is quite clear about the nature of the change which is brought about through action research; it is change which challenges the existing system. It is change which goes beyond *technical* matters that can have a bearing on the effectiveness or efficiency of the professional's current practice. It is change which goes beyond *practical* matters that can have a bearing on the way practitioners interpret the task at hand. For sure, emancipatory action research incorporates these, but it also challenges the fundamental framework within which the practice occurs.

Three approaches to action research

1. *Technical* action research aims to improve effectiveness of educational or managerial practice. The practitioners are co-opted and depend greatly on the researcher as a facilitator.

2. *Practical* action research, in addition to effectiveness, aims at the practitioners' understanding and professional development. The researcher's role is . . . to encourage practical deliberation and self-reflection on the part of the practitioners.

3. Action research is *emancipating* when it aims not only at technical and practical improvement and the participant's better understanding, along with transformation and change within the existing boundaries and conditions, but also at changing the system itself of those conditions which impede desired improvement in the system/organisation.

(Zuber-Skerritt 1996: 4–5)

---

5 Issues connected with the use of action research

'Ownership' of the research

The participatory nature of action research brings with it a question mark concerning who owns the research and its outcomes. With conventional approaches to research this tends to be less complicated. To offer something of a caricature, the outsider research initiates the process and approaches practitioners to gain their permission for the research to be conducted (by the outsider). Having obtained authorization from relevant people, research proceeds, with the outsider 'owning' the data collected and having full rights over the analysis and publication of findings. Of course, complications arise with various forms of sponsored research and consultancy, where authorization might include certain restrictions on the rights of the two parties over the research and its findings. However, these are likely to be *explicitly* recognized as a result of negotiating access.

In the case of action research, the *partnership* nature of work can make matters rather less clear cut. Who is in charge? Who calls the shots? Who decides on appropriate action? Who owns the data? These and similar issues need to be worked out sensitively and carefully by the partners to *ensure that there are shared expectations about the nature of participation* in action research.

Ethical issues associated with action research

The distinct ethical problem for action research is that, although the research centres on the activity of the practitioner, it is almost inevitable that the activity of colleagues will also come under the microscope at some stage or other, as their activity interlinks with that of the practitioner who instigates the research. Practitioners are not 'islands' – isolated from routine contact with colleagues and clients. Their practice and the changes they seek to make can hardly be put in place without some knock-on effect for others who operate close-by in organizational terms.

The idea that the action researcher is exempt from the need to gain authorization, as a consequence, evaporates. Because the activity of action research almost inevitably affects others, it is important to have a clear idea of when and where the action research necessarily steps outside the bounds of collecting information which is purely personal and relating to the practitioners alone. Where it does so, the usual standards of research ethics must be observed: permissions obtained, confidentiality maintained, identities protected.

Two things follow. First, there is a case for arguing that those who engage in action research should be open about the research aspect of their practice. It should not be hidden or disguised. Second, the need for informed consent from those involved in the research should be recognized.

Ethics in action research

▶ The development of the work must remain visible and open to suggestions from others.

▶ Permission must be obtained before making observations or examining documents produced for other purposes.

▶ Description of others' work and points of view must be negotiated with those concerned before being published.

▶ The researcher must accept responsibility for maintaining confidentiality.
(Winter 1996: 17)

Reflexivity and action research

Practitioners who engage in action research have a privileged insight into the way things operate in their particular 'work-sites'. They have *'insider knowledge'*. This can be a genuine bonus for research. However, it can also pose problems. The outsider – 'the stranger' – might be better placed to see the kind of thing which, to the insider, is too mundane, too obvious, to register as an important factor. Because the practitioner cannot escape the web of meanings that the 'insider' knows, he or she is constrained by the web of meanings. The outsider 'expert' may not have the 'right' answer, but can possibly offer an alternative perspective which can help the practitioner to gain new insights into the nature of the practical problem.

 Link up with **Ethnography and reflexivity, p. 73**

So, although action research respects the knowledge of the practitioners, it would be rather naive to assume that practitioners' knowledge – of itself – provides all the answers. Particularly in relation to *practical* action research, and *emancipatory* action research, their aim is to enhance practitioner understanding and this is likely to call upon some modicum of outsider advice.

Resources and action research

The action researcher's investigation is necessarily fairly localized and relatively small-scale. None the less, the action researcher faces the difficulty of trying to combine a probably demanding workload with systematic and rigorous research. *Time constraints*, alone, make this hard to accomplish. Even if, as should be the case, action research is integrated with practice rather than tagged on top of practice, the routine demands of the job are unlikely to be reduced by way of compensation. In the short run, prior to positive benefits emerging, the action researcher is likely to face extra work.

Generalizability and action research

Given the constraints on the scope of action research projects, it might be argued that their findings will rarely contribute to broader insights. Located as they are in the practitioner's work-site, there are not very good prospects for the *representativeness* of the data in action research. The setting and constituent features are 'givens' rather than factors which can be controlled or varied, and the research is generally focused on the one site rather than spread across a range of examples. Action research, therefore, is vulnerable to the criticism that the findings relate to one instance and should not be generalized beyond this specific 'case'.

Link up with **Case studies, p. 30**

In one sense this reservation needs to be acknowledged. Surely, practice-driven research in local settings hardly lends itself to conclusions with universal application. New truths and new theories will be unlikely to find foundation in such studies alone. And this caution is worth taking to heart for the action researcher: beware of making grandiose claims on the basis of action research projects. However, it can rightly be argued that action research, while practice-driven and small-scale, should not lose anything by way of rigour. Like any other small-scale research, it can draw on existing theories, apply and test research propositions, use suitable methods and, importantly, offer some evaluation of existing knowledge (without making unwarranted claims). It is the rigour, rather than the size of the project or its purpose, by which the research should be judged.

6 Advantages of action research

▶ It addresses practical problems in a positive way, feeding the results of research directly back into practice. In the words of Somekh (1995: 340), 'It directly addresses the knotty problem of the persistent failure of research in the social sciences to make a difference in terms of bringing about actual improvements in practice.'

▶ It has personal benefits for the practitioner, as it contributes to professional self-development.

▶ It should entail a continuous cycle of development and change via on-site research in the workplace, which has benefits for the organization to the extent that it is geared to improving practice and resolving problems.

▶ It involves participation in the research for practitioners. This can democratize the research process, depending on the nature of the partnership, and generally involves a greater appreciation of, and respect for, practitioner knowledge.

7 Disadvantages of action research

▶ The necessary involvement of the practitioner limits the scope and scale of research. The 'work-site' approach affects the representativeness of the findings and the extent to which generalizations can be made on the basis of the results.

▶ The integration of research with practice limits the feasibility of exercising controls over factors of relevance to the research. The setting for the research generally does not allow for the variables to be manipulated or for controls to be put in place, because the research is conducted not alongside routine activity but actually as part of that activity.

▶ The nature of the research is constrained by what is permissible and ethical within the workplace setting.

▶ Ownership of the research process becomes contestable within the framework of the partnership relationship between practitioner and researcher.

▶ Action research tends to involve an extra burden of work for the practitioners, particularly at the early stages before any benefits feed back into
improved effectiveness.

▶ The action researcher is unlikely to be detached and impartial in his or her
approach to the research. In this respect, action research stands in marked
contrast to positivistic approaches, as Susman and Evered (1978) point out.
It is clearly geared to resolving problems which confront people in their
routine, everyday (work) activity, and these people therefore have a vested
interest in the findings. They cannot be entirely detached or impartial in
accord with the classic image of science.

Checklist for action research

When undertaking action research you should feel confident about answering 'yes' to the following questions:

1. Does the research project address a concrete issue or *practical problem*? ☐

2. Is there *participation* by the practitioner in all stages of the research project? ☐

3. Have the grounds for the *partnership* between practitioner and any outside expert been explicitly negotiated and agreed? ☐

4. Is the research part of a *continuous cycle* of development (rather than a one-off project)? ☐

5. Is there a clear view of how the research findings will *feed back* directly into practice? ☐

6. Is it clear *which kind* of action research is being used – 'technical', 'practical' or 'emancipatory'? ☐

7. Has *insider knowledge* been acknowledged as having disadvantages as well as advantages for the research? ☐

8. Is the research sufficiently *small-scale* to be combined with a routine workload? ☐

9. Have *ethical* matters been taken into consideration? ☐

© M. Denscombe, *The Good Research Guide*. Open University Press.

▶ ▷ ▷ 5

ETHNOGRAPHY

The term *ethnography* literally means a description of peoples or cultures. It has its origins as a research strategy in the works of the early social anthropologists, whose aim was to provide a detailed and permanent account of the cultures and lives of small, isolated tribes. Such tribes were seen, with some justification, as 'endangered species', and the social anthropologists saw the need to map out those cultures before they became contaminated by contact with the industrial world or withered away to extinction.

The image of the pith-helmeted outsider dressed in khaki shorts arriving on the shores of some remote and exotic palm tree island to set up camp and study the lives of the 'native' has become legendary – largely through the works of people like Bronislaw Malinowski (1922) and Margaret Mead (1943). The concerns of such social anthropologists and the research strategy they employed set the scene for much of what is undertaken as 'ethnography' today.

Ethnography, based on the early anthropological origins of the term and on subsequent developments by influential classics in the field (e.g. Whyte 1981), has the following characteristics.

▶ It requires the researcher to spend considerable *time in the field* among the people whose lives and culture are being studied. The ethnographer needs to share in the lives rather than observe from a position of detachment. Extended fieldwork allows for a *journey of discovery* in which the explanations for what is being witnessed emerge over a period of time.

▶ Routine and normal aspects of *everyday life* are regarded as worthy of consideration as research data. The mundane and the ordinary parts of social life are just as valid as the special events and ceremonies which can all too easily capture our attention.

▶ There is special attention given to the way the people being studied see their world. Quite distinct from the researcher's analysis of the situation, the ethnographer is generally concerned to find out *how the members of the group/culture being studied understand things,* the meanings *they* attach to happenings, the way *they* perceive their reality. 'To grasp the native's point of view, his relation to life, to realize *his* vision of *his* world' (Malinowski 1922: 25).

▶ There is an emphasis on the need to look at the interlinkages between the various features of the culture and to avoid isolating facets of the culture from the wider context within which it exists. Ethnography generally prefers a *holistic approach* which stresses processes, relationships, connections and interdependency among the component parts.

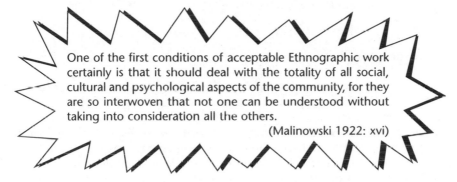

One of the first conditions of acceptable Ethnographic work certainly is that it should deal with the totality of all social, cultural and psychological aspects of the community, for they are so interwoven that not one can be understood without taking into consideration all the others.

(Malinowski 1922: xvi)

▶ There is some acknowledgement that the ethnographer's final account of the culture or group being studied is more than just a description – it is a *construction*. It is not a direct 'reproduction', a literal photograph of the situation. It is, rather, a crafted construction which employs particular writing skills (rhetoric) and which inevitably owes something to the ethnographer's own experiences.

1 Ethnography as a topic

Lifestyles and meanings

As a topic, ethnography refers to the study of cultures and groups – their lifestyle, understandings and beliefs. In doing so, ethnography tends to emphasize the importance of *understanding things from the point of view of those involved*. Rather than explaining things from the outsider's point of view, there is a concern to see things as those involved see things – 'to grasp the native's point of view'.

Comparison and contrast

Early anthropologists used to study relatively small groups in societies which were *different* from their own. They hoped the comparison would illuminate aspects of their own society as well as explain the 'primitive' society where their fieldwork was based. Ethnography, in this respect, resembles an anthropological approach, but it does not restrict its attention to remote tribes in distant lands. Indeed, the most popular development of ethnography in recent times has been its application to lifestyles, understandings and beliefs within 'our own' society. The element of *comparison and contrast*, though, is retained as an underlying facet of ethnographic research. Ethnography, for its part, thrives on being able to compare and contrast lifestyles, understandings and beliefs within a society, rather than between societies.

Link up with **Field experiments, p. 62**

The exotic and the routine

In its early days, ethnography 'within our own society' tended to focus on groups who were relatively small in number, and tended to be somewhat alien to the mainstream of society. The anthropological stance was applied to deviant subgroups, oddball cultures that stood out as different from the norm. And, just as with the study of 'natives' in far off lands, there was an immediate attraction for studying such groups. They offered something intrinsically interesting in the way their lifestyles seemed quaint, crazy, even exotic compared with the everyday experience of those who studied the groups and those who read the resulting books. The title of one of the classics illustrates the point. Margaret Mead's (1943) study, originally published in 1928, was titled *Coming of Age in Samoa: a Study of Adolescence and Sex in Primitive Societies*. Such a style of research, in a sense, pandered to a certain voyeurism. When applied to 'our own' society, the focus was on 'deviant' groups, such as drug users, religious sects, street gangs and the like. There remains, it is true, legacies of an interest in the exotic and the special, ceremonies and the unusual features of social life within the realms of ethnography. However, the routine and the mundane, the normal and the unspectacular facets of social life have become recognized as equally valid topics for ethnographic enquiry. In recent times, attention has been refocused on to more routine, mainstream aspects of social life – for example, life in classrooms (Woods 1979) or life on a building site (Reimer 1979).

2 Ethnography as description

At first glance it would seem easy to associate ethnography with the task of providing straightforward descriptions of things witnessed first hand in the field by the researcher. The crucial factor, from this position, is the depth and detail of the description, the accuracy of what it portrays and the insights it offers to readers about the situation being studied. The purpose of the ethnographic research is to produce detailed pictures of events or cultures –

descriptions which stand in their own right without the need to worry about how representative the situation is or what the broader implications might be in terms of other events or cultures of the type, or of contributing to wider theories. The ethnography, from this stance, is a stand-alone 'one-off' that is to be judged by the depth of its portrayal and the intricacy of its description. This is an *idiographic* approach to ethnography.

> In ethnographic terms ... the concept of 'naturalism' implies a commitment to the observation and description of social phenomena in much the manner that naturalists in biology have studied flora and fauna and their geographical distribution.
>
> (Hammersley 1983: 5)

In order to produce a pure and detailed description, ethnographers will wish to avoid disrupting the situation by their very presence as observers in the field. They will wish to preserve the natural state of affairs. And this is why *naturalism* is a key concern of ethnography. The ethnographer's concern with naturalism derives from the wish to study things in their natural state – undisturbed by the intrusion of research tools or the disruption of experimental designs. Going 'into the field' to witness events first hand in their natural habitat lies at the very heart of what it means to do ethnography.

Link up with **Participant observation, p. 148**

3 Ethnography and theory

There is another side to ethnography. As Woods argues,

> There are two different approaches to ethnography. Some see it as exclusively idiographic, that is to say, descriptive of particular situations; these emphasize the holistic nature of ethnography and the distinctive nature of information discovered ... It does not in itself, therefore, permit generalization, though it might serve as a basis.
>
> On the other hand there are those who prefer to see it as nomothetic, that is to say, generalizing, comparative, theoretical.
>
> (Woods 1979: 267)

A challenge to the idiographic stance within ethnography comes from those who question the value of producing numerous stand-alone descriptions if there is no attempt to derive something from them which goes beyond the specifics of the situation and which can, in some way or other, link to broader issues. If each ethnographic study produces a one-off, isolated piece of information, these pieces cannot contribute to the building up of any generalized knowledge about human societies, it is alleged. They take the position that ethnographic research should be initiated quite deliberately to develop some theory *grounded* in the detailed observation undertaken.

> Ethnography is directed towards producing what are referred to as 'theoretical', 'analytical', or 'thick' descriptions (whether of societies, small communities, organizations, spatial locations, or social worlds). These descriptions must remain close to the concrete reality of particular events but at the same time reveal general features of human social life.
>
> (Hammersley 1990: 598)

Some researchers would go still further. They would argue that the purpose of ethnographic research should be to shed some light on an area of life whose significance depends on a theory; to elaborate on a theory or even check on whether the theory really does hold true and explain things as they happen in 'real life' (Porter 1993).

At one end of the spectrum there are those who regard the main purpose of ethnography as providing rich and detailed descriptions of real-life situations as they really are. At the other end of the spectrum there are those who see the role of ethnographic fieldwork as a test-bed for theories – a means of developing theories by checking them out in small-scale scenarios.

Somewhere towards the middle of the spectrum lies the view 'that "idiographic" and "nomothetic" approaches are not mutually exclusive, and that we can have both rich and intensive description *and* generalizability' (Woods 1979: 268). Advocates of the middle position are keen to hold on to the idiographic aspect of ethnographic research in as much as it provides a valuable and distinct kind of data – the *detailed descriptions of specifics based on first hand observation in naturally occurring situations*. They also recognize the need for theory within ethnography. They recognize the need to *locate the ethnography within a theoretical context*.

To accommodate the need for ethnography to have some theoretical basis the social researcher should give:

▶ explicit consideration of how the findings tie in with, or contradict, existing relevant theories and generalizations about human social behaviour (extrapolation from the particular);

▶ explicit consideration of how the choice of setting might reflect social concerns in the researcher's culture and in the situation being studied (explanation of why the event or culture was selected for study);

▶ explicit consideration of how the findings compare with those of other similar ethnographies (comparison with other descriptions).

4 Ethnographers as part of the world they seek to describe: the issue of reflexivity

Ethnographers tend to be very sensitive to the matter of reflexivity and the way it affects their perception of the culture or events they wish to describe. What concerns them is that the conceptual tools they use to understand the cultures or events being studied are not, and can never be, neutral and passive instruments of discovery.

As researchers, the meanings we attach to things that happen and the language we use to describe them are the product of our own culture, social background and personal experiences. Making sense of what is observed during fieldwork observation is a process that relies on what the researcher already knows and already believes, and it is not a voyage of discovery which starts with a clean sheet. We can only make sense of the world in a way that we have learnt to do using conceptual tools which are based on our own culture and our own experiences. We have no way of standing outside these to reach some objective and neutral vantage point from which to view things 'as they really are'. To an extent, we can describe them only 'as we see them', and this is shaped by *our* culture, not theirs.

The question that taxes ethnographers is this: 'How far can my description of the culture or event depict things from the point of view of those involved when I can only use my own way of seeing things, my own conceptual tools, to make sense of what is happening?'

Broadly, ethnographers are conscious of the way in which their account of any particular lifestyle or beliefs is a construction based upon the researcher's interpretation of events. Even when it comes to writing up the ethnography, there are deep-rooted doubts about claims to objectivity. The outcome of ethnographic research is generally recognized by those who write it as being a creative work in its own right – the outcome of interpretation, editing and skilful writing techniques as well as a reflection of the reality of the situation they set out to study. Inescapably, the account is partial – an edited and abridged version – which owes something to the ethnographer as well as the culture or events observed. There is nothing new to this. Malinowski appreciated the point many years ago.

> In ethnography, the distance is often enormous between the brute material of information – as it is presented to the student in his own observations, in native statement, in the kaleidoscope of tribal life – and the final authoritative presentations of the results. The ethnographer has to traverse this distance in the laborious years between the moment when he sets foot upon a native beach, and makes his first attempts to get into touch with the natives, and the time when he writes down the final version of his results.
>
> (Malinowski 1922: 4)

⚠ **Caution**

There is something of a contradiction between these concerns for naturalism and reflexivity. On the one hand there is the belief that the best way of getting to grips with reality is through direct contact and observation. By being part of the action, the ethnographer is able to 'see things as they *really* are'. On the other hand, there is the awareness that people construct the social world. Ethnographers, like others, interpret social events and are an integral part of the social world they seek to describe. They have no super-human privileged understanding of the social world that is 'objective' and immune to the influence of past experiences.

> Justifications offered for ethnography often involve the argument that it enables us to capture social reality more accurately than other approaches. On the other hand, it is intrinsic to ethnography that the people studied are viewed as constructing distinct social worlds. And if that idea is applied to ethnographers themselves it may seem that, rather than representing reality, ethnographic accounts simply construct versions of reality.
>
> (Hammersley 1992: 4–5)

5 Putting the researcher's 'self' into ethnographic research

One of the characteristic features of ethnography is the significance it attaches to the role of the researcher's 'self' in the process of research. The researcher's identity, values and beliefs become part of the equation – a built-in component that cannot be eliminated as an influence on the end-product findings of the project (Ball 1990).

Ethnographic research, therefore, calls for a certain degree of introspection on the part of the researcher. He or she needs to reflect upon the way that background factors associated with personal experiences, personal beliefs and social values may have shaped the way that events and cultures were interpreted.

However, the ethnographic researcher needs to go beyond mere reflection. This is, in a sense, a private activity. Necessary though it is, it needs to be portrayed more publicly if it is to support the research outcomes. Researchers need to *supply their readers* with some insights into the possible influence of the researcher's self on the interpretation of events or cultures. *There needs to be a public account of the self which explores the role of the researcher's self.*

The need for a 'public account of the role of the self' means it is necessary to include in the methodology section, and possibly in the preface or introduction, some information about the self and its perceived influence. This account of the self will vary in the amount of detail it provides, depending on

▶ the nature of the research topic;

▶ the kind of methods used;

▶ the audience for whom the ethnography is written.

There is obviously a matter of judgement here about the extent to which the account should delve to the depths of detail about researchers' personal matters, and the amount of detail that the readership needs to know in order to arrive at a reasonable evaluation of the likely impact of the 'self' on the research.

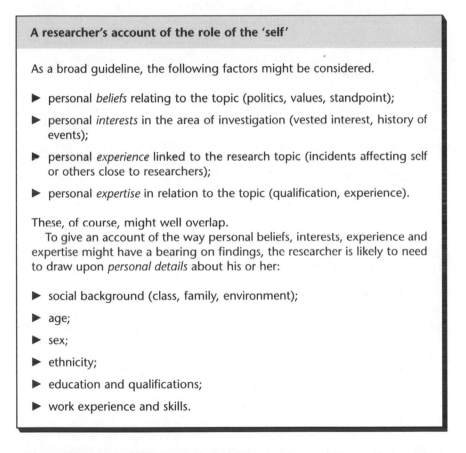

A researcher's account of the role of the 'self'

As a broad guideline, the following factors might be considered.

▶ personal *beliefs* relating to the topic (politics, values, standpoint);

▶ personal *interests* in the area of investigation (vested interest, history of events);

▶ personal *experience* linked to the research topic (incidents affecting self or others close to researchers);

▶ personal *expertise* in relation to the topic (qualification, experience).

These, of course, might well overlap.
   To give an account of the way personal beliefs, interests, experience and expertise might have a bearing on findings, the researcher is likely to need to draw upon *personal details* about his or her:

▶ social background (class, family, environment);

▶ age;

▶ sex;

▶ ethnicity;

▶ education and qualifications;

▶ work experience and skills.

The account of self, developed quite fully, can even take the form of a mini-autobiography. Peter Woods (1996), for example, devotes eleven pages to this in his book on ethnographic research and the 'art' of teaching.

I begin with myself, and some reflections on my life and research career which seem relevant to my current thoughts and actions.

I was born in the 1930s. My father was a jobbing bricklayer by trade . . .

After the war, I passed the eleven plus and went to the grammar school . . .

When I began to do research, it was invariably into subjects about individuals' struggles within and against [the more formal aspects of heavily
structured and bureaucratized worlds], like deviance and disruption, sur-
vival strategies, stress and burnout, teacher and pupil careers . . .

My own experiences, background and personality dispose me towards
principles of freedom, equality and justice as they are understood in moderate left-wing politics. I am fascinated by the struggle of human agency
against the forces of structure and society. I have empathy for those
labelled as 'deviants' or 'delinquents', and an interest in the circumstances
that produce such actions and reactions.

(Woods 1996: 1–9)

 **Caution**

It is worth stressing that this developed exploration of the self – running to
eleven pages – is appropriate in the context of a book of around 200 pages,
specifically concerned with the contribution of ethnography, and written by
a senior researcher with an international reputation and very many publications. Within the confines of shorter research reports by those for whom
there might be less intrinsic interest in autobiographical details, the best
advice is to encapsulate such information as is relevant within a statement of
a *couple of hundred words*.

6 Access to fieldwork settings

Gaining access to people, places and events is a crucial part of successful
ethnographic research. For field researchers this access cannot be taken for
granted. Researchers need to set about gaining access, and to do this they need
to engage in negotiations that have political, ethical and practical implications.

Covert research

It is sometimes possible for an ethnographer to conduct fieldwork without
people knowing that they have a researcher in their midst. The researcher can
blend into the background by adopting a role that fits in with the normal
situation. The researcher can go *undercover* and carry out the research in a
clandestine manner. This has benefits as far as ethnography is concerned
because (a) it preserves the naturalness of the setting and (b) it generally side-
steps any need to get authorization to conduct the research. However, it gives
rise to a different type of problem. The decision to undertake covert research
means that the researcher cannot also have 'informed consent' on the part of

the subjects of his or her research, and this raises substantial ethical problems (see Humphreys 1970).

Link up with **participant observation, p. 148**

Gatekeepers

Ethnographers do not always work in a covert manner. Indeed, it is fair to say that most ethnographies actually involve some degree of openness about the role of the researcher; that is, *overt* research. When this is the case, the ethical problems cease to be the sole concern. Added to this, ethnographers are faced with the possibility that their explicit research role might disrupt the naturalness of the situation. Most of all, though, an overt research role will most probably bring with it a call for the researcher to make contact with 'gatekeepers' who can help the researcher with the vital business of gaining access to the necessary fieldwork settings.

Link up with **The observer effect, p. 47**

Identifying key people who can grant permission, and successfully negotiating with them for access to people, places and events, is often a prerequisite without which the fieldwork cannot begin. In informal settings, such sponsors act as guarantors who vouch for the *bona fide* status of researcher. They use their informal status and relationship with subjects as a currency facilitating both contact and trust between researcher and subject or group (e.g. Polsky 1967; Whyte 1981).

Sponsors and gatekeepers, however, cannot be disregarded once their initial approval has been obtained. In reality, they exercise *continued* influence over the nature of the research. Their influence persists in terms of both:

▶ the kind of initial agreement established about access (influencing the nature of eventual research findings); and

▶ the access relationship necessitated by emergent needs of access.

The influence of such gatekeepers, then, goes beyond a simple granting or denial of contact with research subjects. As Burgess (1984) argues, access is a continual *process* in fieldwork research. It is a process because research is generally conducted over a period of time and it is a process, perhaps more importantly, because access needs to be sought to new people, places and events as new lines of inquiry become incorporated in the research. Since field research, especially ethnographic work, tends to evolve and develop in terms of its focus

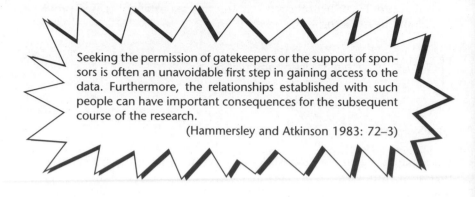

Seeking the permission of gatekeepers or the support of sponsors is often an unavoidable first step in gaining access to the
data. Furthermore, the relationships established with such
people can have important consequences for the subsequent
course of the research.

(Hammersley and Atkinson 1983: 72–3)

of enquiry, it is unlikely that the researcher could state at the outset of research
the precise nature and extent of access that will be required (see Glaser and
Strauss 1967). Access, in the sense of permission from a gatekeeper, is necessarily renewable and renegotiable, and should be viewed as an 'access relationship' rather than a one-off event.

Gatekeepers' authority to grant or withhold access varies, of course, depending on the degree to which the people, places and events being studied are
part of a formal environment. Whereas in the educational context head-
teachers have formal jurisdiction over entry to school premises and can withhold or grant access to teachers and pupils, in less formal settings the role of
the gatekeeper is different. As Whyte illustrated so graphically in his research
(Whyte 1981), the role of gatekeeper can become more akin to a guarantor for
the *bona fide* status of the researcher. 'Doc', Whyte's gatekeeper had no formal
authority to grant or deny access; he used his status with the group to open
up the possibility of Whyte making contact with the young men in question,
and acted as a sponsor/guarantor to enable some trust relationship to develop.
This is an important point. As Hammersley and Atkinson (1983) argue, access
is not simply a matter of physical presence or absence. It is far more than a
matter of granting or withholding of permission for research to be conducted
(Hammersley and Atkinson 1983: 56). Worthwhile access to people, places and
events involves, as well, an opening up to allow the researcher into the world
of the persons involved. Being present is one hurdle, but 'access' also involves
being trusted with insights and insider knowledge.

7 Advantages of ethnography

▶ *Direct observation*. As a research strategy it is based on direct observation via
fieldwork, rather than relying on second hand data or statements made by
research subjects.

▶ *Empirical*. It is essentially grounded in empirical research involving direct
contact with relevant people and places.

▶ *Links with theory.* It can be used as a means for developing theory, and it can also be used for testing theories.

▶ *Detailed data.* It provides data which are relatively rich in depth and detail. Potentially, it can deal with intricate and subtle realities.

▶ *Holistic.* Ethnography aspires to holistic explanations which focus on processes and relationships that lie behind the surface events. Potentially, it puts things in context rather than abstracting specific aspects in isolation.

▶ *Contrast and comparison.* There is an element of contrast and comparison built into ethnographic research in the way the distinct culture or events being studied are 'anthropologically strange' – different from other cultures or events which the researcher and his or her audience to some degree share.

▶ *'Actors' perceptions'.* Ethnographic research is particularly well suited to dealing with the way members of a culture see events – as seen through their eyes. It describes and explores the 'actors' perceptions'.

▶ *Self-awareness.* It has an open and explicit awareness of the role of the researcher's *self* in the choice of topic, process of research and construction of the findings/conclusions. It acknowledges the inherent reflexivity of social knowledge.

▶ *Ecological validity.* It is strong in terms of ecological validity, to the extent that the act of researching should have relatively little impact on the setting – retaining things in their 'natural' form.

8 Disadvantages of ethnography

▶ *Tensions within the approach.* There is a tension within the realms of ethnography stemming from its twin concerns with naturalism and reflexivity. Ethnographies generally attempt to accommodate an internal contradiction between (a) 'realist' aspirations to provide full and detailed *descriptions* of events or cultures as they naturally exist, and (b) a 'relativist' awareness of the reflexive nature of social knowledge and the inevitable influence of the researcher's 'self' on the whole research endeavour. *Depending on how this tension is accommodated* and the degree to which the ethnography adopts a 'realist' or a 'relativist' position, certain other weaknesses can exist.

▶ *Stand-alone descriptions.* Ethnographic research has the potential to produce an array of 'pictures' which coexist, but which tend to remain as separate, isolated stories. There is arguably an in-built tendency to scatter these building-block pictures at random, rather than erecting a structure where each is a brick which serves as a base for further bricks to be layered upon it moving ever upwards. To avoid this, ethnographies need to be guided by (or to) a coherent theoretical framework.

▶ *Story-telling.* There is the potential to provide detailed descriptive accounts at the expense of developing an analytic insight or contributing to a theoretical position. The story-telling can become the sole purpose, leaving a research product which is atheoretical, non-analytic and non-critical.

▶ *Reliability.* There is a potential weakness of *poor reliability* and *little prospect of generalizing* from the ethnographic account of the culture or event.

▶ *Ethics.* There is also a greater potential than with most other approaches to face ethical problems associated with intrusions upon privacy and with gaining informed consent from research subjects.

▶ *Access.* Ethnographic research can pose particularly acute difficulties of gaining access to settings, access which avoids disrupting the naturalness of the setting.

▶ *Insider knowledge,* rather than being a straight advantage, can also cause a 'blind spot', obscuring a vision of 'the obvious'.

Checklist for ethnographic research ✓

When undertaking ethnographic research you should feel confident about answering 'yes' to the following questions:

1. Has the research managed to avoid disrupting the *naturalness* of the settings? ☐

2. Has the research been conducted *ethically* with due respect to the rights of those being studied? ☐

3. Have *lifestyles and meanings* been treated as the main interest of the research? ☐

4. Has *access* to the fieldwork settings been negotiated where and when necessary? ☐

5. Has the research involved sufficient *time* doing fieldwork, and collected enough *empirical* data? ☐

6. Has a *holistic approach* been adopted, linking all significant contributing factors? ☐

7. Does the research Involve an account of the role of the *researcher's 'self'*? ☐

8. Is there a description of how the ethnography *builds on* (or contradicts) existing explanations of the phenomenon? ☐

9. Are the findings *compared and contrasted* with other ethnographies on similar topics? ☐

10. Has due acknowledgement been given to the fact that the ethnography is a *researcher's construction* rather than a literal description of the situation? ☐

▶ ▷ ▷ **Part II**

METHODS OF SOCIAL RESEARCH

Horses for courses

When it comes to selecting a method for the collection of data, certain research strategies will tend to be associated with the use of certain research methods. Surveys tend to be linked with questionnaires as experiments tend to be linked with observation. And such links are not just a matter of luck or the legacy of long research traditions. There are some sound theoretical reasons which explain the tendency of some strategies to be linked with some methods – but these need not detain us here. From the position of the project researcher, the crucial thing to recognize is that within the various strategies for social research there still remains some element of choice about which methods to use. This choice will be influenced by the strategy itself, but it will also reflect *preferences* about the kind of data that the researcher wishes to obtain and *practical considerations* related to time, resources and access to the sources of data.

Each of the methods has its particular strengths and weaknesses, and some guidance on these is contained in the following chapters. However, when it comes to choosing a research method, researchers should be aware that it is a matter of deciding which is the *most appropriate method in practice*, not of deciding that one data collection method is superior to all others in any absolute sense. They should ask themselves which method is best suited to the task at hand and operate on the premise that, when *choosing a method for the collection of data, it is a matter of 'horses for courses'.*

Multi-methods and triangulation

In some senses the four research methods – questionnaires, interviews, observation and documents – can be seen as competing with each other. They vie with each other for selection by the researcher. They are different, and they are suited to some situations better than others. Yet, in another way, they can come to complement each other. They can be combined to produce differing but mutually supporting ways of collecting data.

The possibility of employing more than one method stems from the fact that the various methods contain their own set of assumptions about the nature of the social world and the kind of data that can be produced to increase knowledge about the world. Theoretical debate about the relative merits of their underlying premises has failed to establish any single method as the universally accepted 'best' for all situations. The 'epistemological' debate continues; the jury is still out. This means that for those engaged in practical research, particularly the small-scale project researcher, none of the possible methods for data collection can be regarded as perfect and none can be regarded as rubbish. None has the sole key to 'truth', and none can be dismissed as hopelessly irrelevant for enhancing knowledge. A far more profitable way to approach things, and one which is far more in tune with the mood of social research as we enter the twenty-first century, is to recognize that each method provides its own distinctive perspective. Each method approaches the collection of data with a certain set of assumptions and produces a kind of data which needs to be recognized as having certain inherent strengths and certain inherent weaknesses in relation to the aims of the particular research and the practical constraints (time, resources, access) faced by the researcher.

A new and exciting possibility is opened up. Different methods can be used to collect data on the same thing. Each can look at the thing from a different angle – from its own distinct perspective – and these perspectives can be used by the researcher as a means of comparison and contrast. Imagine a case study in which the focus of attention is on disruptive behaviour by pupils in a secondary school. The researcher could elect to use observation as the method for collecting data, and would, of course, want to justify this choice in relation to the kind of data desired and practical factors affecting the research. A more creative and ambitious approach, though, might entail the use of more than one method. After all, interviews with the staff and pupils involved could shed light on the topic. Questionnaires administered to all staff and pupils might gather other relevant information, and documents such as school records could supply a further avenue for exploring the topic.

Using multi-methods produces different kinds of data on the same topic. The initial and obvious benefit of this is that it will involve *more data*, thus being likely to improve the quality of the research. There is a cost to this, though, because the researcher will almost certainly need to sacrifice some areas of investigation which would have been included using one method in order to free up the resources to use a multi-method approach. The researcher might well decide that this is a price worth paying. What he or she gets instead are different kinds of data on the same topic, which allow the researcher to *see the thing from different perspectives* and to understand the topic in a more rounded and complete fashion than would be the case had the data been drawn from just one method.

Valuable though this is, the production of more and different kinds of data on a given topic is not necessarily the prime benefit of using more than method. From the researcher's point of view, an equal benefit springs from the way the alternative methods allow the findings from one method to be checked against the findings from another. The multi-method approach allows findings to be *corroborated* or questioned by comparing the data produced by different methods. If observation of disruptive behaviour suggests one possible explanation, this might be corroborated or discarded on the basis of findings from, say, interviews with those involved. School records might confirm or deny impressions given through interviews or questionnaires. Indeed, as the example suggests, the use of more than one method can be designed with the clear sequence in mind, so that lines of enquiry can be pursued and checked, rather than simply using more than one method simultaneously to investigate the same thing.

Seeing things from a different perspective and the opportunity to corroborate findings can enhance the *validity* of the data. They do not *prove* that the researcher has 'got it right', but they do give some confidence that the meaning of the data has some consistency across methods and that the findings are not too closely tied up with a particular method used to collect the data. Effectively, they lend support to the analysis. There is an analogy which is often used in this respect: *triangulation*. Triangulation involves locating a true position by referring to two or more other coordinates. It relies on the known properties of triangles (angles, length of sides, ratios) and, in the past, was used for navigation. Sailors could identify their true position at sea with reference to known fixed points, such as stars. To follow the analogy using the example above, a researcher wishing to know the 'truth' about disruptive

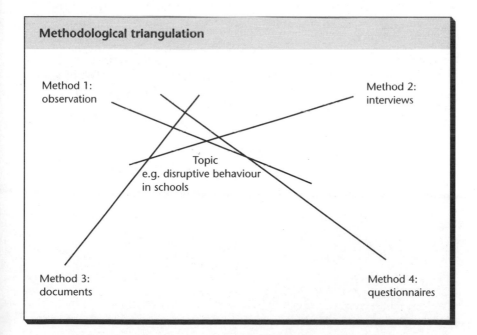

Methodological triangulation

Method 1:
observation

Method 2:
interviews

Topic
e.g. disruptive behaviour
in schools

Method 3:
documents

Method 4:
questionnaires

behaviour in school could use different methods of data collection to provide an angle on the topic. With two or three such referent points, the researcher will be able to know where the 'truth' lies.

The analogy with navigational triangulation can be taken too far. There is an assumption with navigation that there is a single true location which can be discovered using the known properties of triangles. With social science, there is a lot of controversy about whether such a comparable point exists. On the one hand there are positivists. They subscribe to the idea of a single truth and reality, and would ideally expect the lines from each method to converge on a single point of 'truth'. At the other extreme, constructivists dispute the idea that any single reality exists: it all depends on what angle you are coming from, what perspective you have. For them, the lines might hardly be expected to intersect at all.

In the context of this debate and uncertainty, then, what guidance can be offered to the newcomer or project researcher when it comes to the selection of research methods?

▶ The researcher should be encouraged, where possible, to use more than one method when investigating a topic.

▶ The researcher should recognize the value of using multi-methods for the corroboration of findings and for enhancing the validity of data.

▶ The researcher needs to recognize that the notion of a single social reality is controversial, and therefore adopt a cautious position which avoids any naive use of triangulation.

▶ The researcher should appreciate that different methods might point in a similar direction but are unlikely to meet at some precise, unequivocal point of reality.

▶ The researcher should avoid the presumption that use of methodological triangulation can *prove* that the data or analyses are absolutely correct.

QUESTIONNAIRES

There are no cast iron guarantees that following a set of practical guidelines will lead to the production of a good questionnaire. Guidelines, however, do help, and this chapter contains *checklists* which are based on 'good practice' and which spell out some fundamentals for avoiding the production of a bad questionnaire.

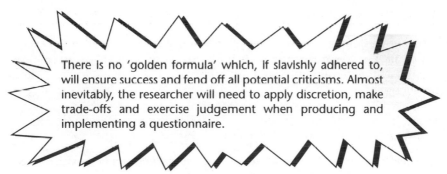

There is no 'golden formula' which, if slavishly adhered to, will ensure success and fend off all potential criticisms. Almost inevitably, the researcher will need to apply discretion, make trade-offs and exercise judgement when producing and implementing a questionnaire.

There are many types of questionnaires. They can vary enormously in terms of their purpose, their size and their appearance. To qualify as a *research* questionnaire, however, they should:

▶ *Be designed to collect information which can be used subsequently as data for analysis.* As a research tool, questionnaires do not set out to change people's attitudes or provide them with information. Though questionnaires are sometimes used for this purpose – for instance, as a way of marketing a product – it is not strictly in keeping with the spirit of a *research* questionnaire, whose purpose is to discover things.

▶ Consist of a *written list of questions.* The important point here is that each person who answers the particular questionnaire reads an identical set of questions. This allows for consistency and precision in terms of the wording of the questions, and makes the processing of the answers easier.

▶ *Gather information by asking people directly* about the points concerned with the research. Questionnaires work on the premise that if you want to find out something about people and their attitudes you simply go and ask them what it is you want to know, and get the information *'straight from the horse's mouth'*.

Questionnaires that are administered face-to-face with the respondent can be valuable for social research. They are widely used, especially in market research. However, the element of direct interaction between the researcher and the respondent introduces a number of considerations. For this reason, there is an assumption in this chapter that *the kind of research questionnaire being considered is the 'postal' type*. Whether or not it is actually posted, the questionnaire's data are collected without direct contact between the researcher and the respondent. By restricting the focus to this form of questionnaire, attention can be given to the design and administration of the questionnaire itself, rather than to the impact of face-to-face interaction. This is dealt with in Chapter 7. If a clipboard-style questionnaire is being considered, the effect of such interaction must be considered in addition to many of the points related to postal questionnaires.

1 When is it appropriate to use a questionnaire for research?

Different methods are better suited to different circumstances, and questionnaires are no exception. Although they can be used, perhaps ingeniously, across a wide spectrum of research situations, questionnaires are at their most productive:

▶ when used with *large numbers* of respondents in many locations, e.g. the postal questionnaire;

▶ when what is required tends to be fairly *straightforward information* – relatively brief and uncontroversial;

▶ when the *social climate is open* enough to allow full and honest answers;

▶ when there is a need for *standardized data* from identical questions – without requiring personal, face-to-face interaction;

▶ when *time allows for delays* caused by production, piloting, posting and procrastination before receipt of a response;

▶ when *resources allow for the costs* of printing, postage and data preparation;

▶ when the respondents can be expected to be *able to read and understand the questions* – the implications of age, intellect and eyesight need to be considered.

2 What kinds of data are collected by questionnaires?

Questionnaires rely on written information supplied directly by people in response to questions asked by the researcher. In this respect, the kind of data is distinct from that which could be obtained from interviews, observation or documents. The information from questionnaires tends to fall into two broad categories – 'facts' and 'opinions' – and it is vital that at all stages of using questionnaires the researcher is clear about whether the information being sought is to do with facts or to do with opinions.

Factual information does not require much in the way of judgement or personal attitudes on the part of respondents. It just requires respondents to reveal (accurately and honestly) information: their address, age, sex, marital status, number of children etc.

Opinions, attitudes, views, beliefs, preferences etc. can also be investigated using questionnaires. In this case, though, respondents are required to reveal information about feelings, to express values, to weigh up alternatives etc., in a way that calls for a judgement about things rather than the mere reporting of facts.

Example of a 'fact' question.

Q. Which TV programmes did you watch last night?

Example of an 'opinion' question.

Q. Which is your favourite TV programme?

It is worth stressing that, in practice, questionnaires are very likely to include questions about both facts and opinions. Political opinion polls, for instance, might include factual questions about how people actually voted at the last election as well as questions about feelings of support for particular political parties' policies, and market researchers might want to know factual information about the age, social class, sex etc. of the people whose opinions, attitudes and preferences they are investigating.

3 Planning the use of questionnaires

Questionnaires tend to be 'one-offs'. In general, researchers do not have the time or resources to repeat pieces of research which involve the use of questionnaires; nor do they have the opportunity to make amendments and corrections to the questionnaire once it has been printed and distributed. And the vast majority of respondents are likely to be less than sympathetic to a plea from the researcher to fill in the questionnaire a second time in order to overcome a mistake in the first version. There is, therefore, a lot of pressure to *get it right first time.*

Bearing this in mind, the successful use of questionnaires depends on devoting the right balance of effort to the planning stage, rather than rushing too early into distributing the questionnaire. If the questionnaire is to produce worthwhile results, the researcher needs to have a clear plan of action in mind and some reasonable idea of the costs and time-span involved in the venture.

 Link up with **Surveys, p. 6**

Planning, right from the start, involves the researcher in consideration of the following points:

Costs

What are the likely costs of producing, distributing, collecting and analysing the results of the questionnaire?

Production might entail printing costs. There might be postal charges and the need for envelopes (increased by the need to follow up non-respondents). Will the costs include supplying a stamped addressed envelope? Is there the intention to use a computer to analyse the results and, if so, what costs might emerge in terms of the necessary software, access to computers and data preparation? The shrewd researcher works out the resource implications before embarking on the use of questionnaires.

Production

There are technical questions to be considered in relation to the production of the questionnaire as well as the time and cost implications involved with production.

Access to a word processor and/or desktop publishing facilities can help the production of a professional-looking questionnaire. However, access is only part of the issue. To produce a high-quality appearance you need the skills to operate the software. Are these skills that will be acquired *en route* or is there someone else who will help? Either way, there can be considerable resource implications. The researcher will need to make an allowance for the time it will take him or her to learn how to operate the necessary software if the skills do not already exist. If outside help is to be used, this could cost money. With larger surveys, photocopying or printing facilities will be needed to mass-produce the questionnaires.

Access to such facilities for the production of the questionnaire may cost money and take time. In particular, the researcher needs to build into the schedule an allowance for delay if the questionnaire is being produced by someone else. Word processing and printing jobs may need to be booked in advance and some firm commitment needs to be obtained from the external agency about the turnaround time.

Organization

The process for distribution, collection and analysis of results from questionnaires demands an eye on organization. A fundamental skill of good research
is tight organization, and nowhere is this needed more than in the use of a
questionnaire survey.

From the outset the researcher must keep a record of how many questionnaires are sent out, to whom they are sent and when they were sent.
Unless the questionnaire is anonymous, responses can then be checked off
against the mailing list and an accurate follow-up survey of non-respondents
undertaken at an appropriate time. Obviously, a *filing system* of some sort is
vital.

Schedule

Questionnaires, especially when used as part of a broad postal survey, do not
supply instant results. The researcher, therefore, needs to consider what *time-
span* is likely to be involved before the results from the questionnaire are available for analysis.

The time-span for the research, it should be stressed, involves all the time
spent in the production, distribution and collection of the questionnaires. It
is not just the time between sending out the questionnaires and receiving the
completed returns; the planning should involve the whole period between the
conception of the research and the receipt of data. The researcher needs to be
aware of this and plan accordingly.

Permission

Depending on the nature of the questionnaire and the people to whom it is
being sent, there may be the need to gain permission from those in authority
to conduct the survey.

For example, if a questionnaire is being contemplated for use with young
people and it is intended to distribute the questionnaires via schools or youth
clubs, staff and the local authorities are likely to want to give approval before
allowing the survey to proceed using their facilities. The researcher needs to
be cautious on this score. It is dangerous to short-circuit proper channels of
authority. However, gaining permission from appropriate authorities can take
time and this consideration needs to be built into the schedule.

4 Routine essentials for questionnaire design

Designing a good questionnaire involves attention to certain almost routine
matters, quite separate from the more creative and taxing aspects, such as constructing the questions themselves (see below). However, such routine matters
are absolutely vital.

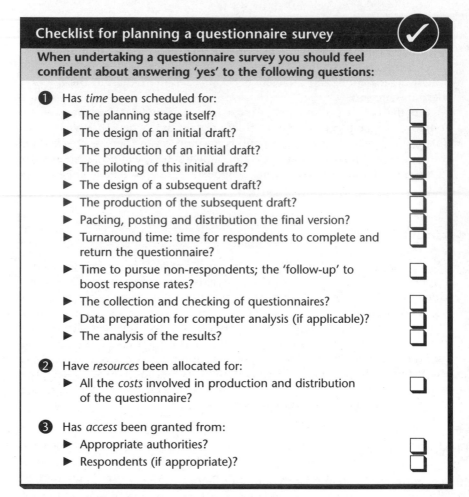

Checklist for planning a questionnaire survey

When undertaking a questionnaire survey you should feel confident about answering 'yes' to the following questions:

1 Has *time* been scheduled for:
- ▶ The planning stage itself?
- ▶ The design of an initial draft?
- ▶ The production of an initial draft?
- ▶ The piloting of this initial draft?
- ▶ The design of a subsequent draft?
- ▶ The production of the subsequent draft?
- ▶ Packing, posting and distribution the final version?
- ▶ Turnaround time: time for respondents to complete and return the questionnaire?
- ▶ Time to pursue non-respondents; the 'follow-up' to boost response rates?
- ▶ The collection and checking of questionnaires?
- ▶ Data preparation for computer analysis (if applicable)?
- ▶ The analysis of the results?

2 Have *resources* been allocated for:
- ▶ All the *costs* involved in production and distribution of the questionnaire?

3 Has *access* been granted from:
- ▶ Appropriate authorities?
- ▶ Respondents (if appropriate)?

© M. Denscombe, *The Good Research Guide.* Open University Press.

Background information about the questionnaire

From both an ethical and a practical point of view, the researcher needs to provide sufficient background information about the research and the questionnaire.

Each questionnaire should have a *cover page*, on which some information appears about:

▶ *The sponsor.* Under whose auspices is the research being undertaken? Is it individual research or does the research emanate from an institution? Headed notepaper is an obvious way to indicate the nature of the institution from which the questionnaire comes.

▶ *The purpose.* What is the questionnaire for, and how will the information be used? It is important here to reveal sufficient information to explain the purpose of the research without going too far and 'leading' the respondent into a line of answering. A brief paragraph should suffice.

▶ *Return address and date.* It is vital that the postal questionnaire contains in it somewhere quite visibly the name and address of the person(s) to whom the completed questionnaire is to be returned and the date by which it is required.

▶ *Confidentiality.* Assuming that the research is operating according to the normal code of ethics for social researchers, the information collected will not be made publicly available. Respondents should be reassured on this point. If the data are to be stored with respondents' names on computer, the Data Protection Act comes into play and respondents should be advised of their right to see their personal file on request.

▶ *Voluntary responses.* In the vast majority of cases, researchers collect information from respondents who volunteer to cooperate with the research. Rewards are not generally used (though in market research there may be some enticements offered), and people are not usually obliged to respond. Again, this point should be acknowledged on the cover page and respondents reassured that the questionnaire is to be completed voluntarily.

▶ *Thanks.* It follows from the fact that questionnaires are normally voluntarily completed that the researcher is beholden to those who cooperated. Courtesy suggests that some word of thanks from the researcher should appear either on the front cover or right at the end of the questionnaire.

Instructions to the respondent

It is very important that respondents are instructed on how to go about answering the questions. It is no good assuming that it is self-evident; experience will soon prove that wrong. Mistakes that occur can invalidate a whole questionnaire, so it is worth being meticulously careful in giving instructions on how to do the answers.

▶ *Example*. It is useful to *present an example at the start of the questionnaire*. This can set the respondent's mind at rest and indicate exactly what is expected of him or her.

▶ *Instructions*. *Specific instructions should be given for each question* where the style of question varies throughout the questionnaire (e.g. put a tick in the appropriate box, circle the relevant number, delete as appropriate).

The allocation of serial numbers

Whether dealing with small numbers or with thousands, the good researcher needs to keep good records. Each questionnaire, therefore, should be numbered so that it can be distinguished from others and located if necessary. The serial number can be used to identify the date of distribution, the place and possibly the person. But note; if the questionnaires are anonymous, such serial numbers should be added only after collection and should only allow general factors such as the date and location to be identified – not any individual. So, for example, a serial number might read 002 0198 0123, where 002 refers to a location, 0198 tells the researcher the questionnaire was completed in January 1998 and 0123 signifies that this is questionnaire number 123 of those collected at that place on that date.

Serial numbers of this kind are very useful in terms of computer analysis of results. The digits are suitable for inclusion in a data file and allow the results to be analysed according to factors such as the date and place of completion of the questionnaire.

The positioning of the serial number is worth considering. It is much easier to search for a specific questionnaire if the serial number is on the front cover rather than tucked away inside the back cover. So, when designing the questionnaire, make provision for the serial number to be visible without opening up each questionnaire to search for it.

Coding boxes

The advantage of questionnaires which use closed-ended answers is that the answers are tailor made for coding and analysis by computer. The closed-ended answers lend themselves to being given a numerical value which can be used for number-crunching, using one of a number of computer packages specifically designed for social science survey analysis.

When you are designing the questionnaire some forethought is necessary to prevent later complications which might arise at the coding stage. Note the following points:

▶ *Locate coding boxes neatly on the right-hand side of the page*. This allows the numbers in the boxes to be read off quickly and accurately as they are transferred to a computer data file.

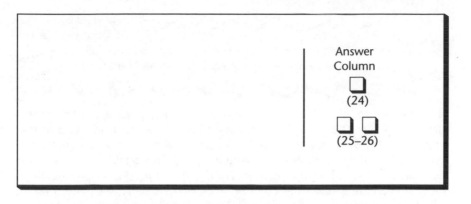

▶ *Allow one coding box for each answer.* This does not mean that, for example, a yes/no type answer requires two boxes. It does not. If yes is coded 1 and no is coded 2, just one box is needed and this box will contain either a 1 or a 2 once it is coded. Obviously, only when there are more than nine alternative answers offered to the respondent will two boxes be necessary, because the code might be in double figures (i.e. 10 or more).

▶ *Identify each column in the computer data file underneath the appropriate coding box in the questionnaire.* Again, this helps to prevent errors when transferring the coded data to a computer data file.

Note: researchers who have access to an *optical mark reader (OMR)* machine will want to design the questionnaire to meet the technical requirements of the machine. Basically, OMR questionnaires operate on the same basis as a lottery ticket. Boxes are marked on the questionnaire and when the questionnaires are fed into the OMR machine it reads those marks, translating them into an appropriate data file. These have certain benefits which really only come into effect on larger-scale distributions. For most project researchers it will not be worthwhile to use an OMR questionnaire.

5 Length and appearance of the questionnaire

The length of the questionnaire

There is no hard and fast rule about the number of questions that can be included in a questionnaire. This will depend on factors like the topic under investigation, how complex the questions are, the nature of the respondents who have been targeted and the time it takes to complete the questionnaire. Decisions about the size of a questionnaire are ultimately a matter of judgement on the part of the researcher, who needs to gauge how many questions can be included before the respondent is likely to run out of patience and consign the questionnaire to the waste paper bin.

In most cases, researchers do not get a second chance to follow up issues

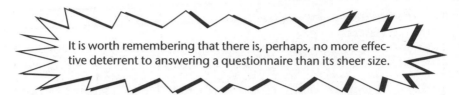

It is worth remembering that there is, perhaps, no more effective deterrent to answering a questionnaire than its sheer size.

they might have missed in the initial questionnaire. Conscious of this 'one-shot' constraint, there may be the temptation to ask about everything that might possibly be of relevance. It is, after all, vital to cover all key matters if the questionnaire is to supply data which permit a reasonable analysis by the researcher. But the shrewd researcher realizes that it is counter-productive to include everything that might *feasibly* have some relevance to the research issues. Every effort should be made to keep the questionnaire as brief as possible by restricting the scope of the questions to crucial issues related to the research, and avoiding any superfluous detail or non-essential topics. When designing a questionnaire, then, the researcher has to walk a tightrope between ensuring coverage of all the vital issues and ensuring the questionnaire is brief enough to encourage people to bother answering it.

To accomplish this balancing act there are certain rules to bear in mind.

▶ *Only ask those questions which are absolutely vital for the research.* The better the research is planned, the easier it will be to identify the absolutely crucial questions and discard the 'just in case I need this information later' questions.

▶ *Be rigorous in weeding out any duplication of questions.* For example, if a questionnaire contains as separate questions, 'What is your date of birth?' and 'How old are you?' we need to ask just how vital it is that both are included. A moment's reflection might lead the researcher to the conclusion that one or other will supply adequate information for the particular purposes of the investigation – or that one can be deduced from the other.

▶ *Make the task of responding to the questionnaire as straightforward and speedy as possible.*

▶ *Pilot the questionnaire to see how long it takes to answer* and then consider whether it is reasonable to expect the specific target group to spare this amount of time supplying the answers.

Remember, too, that a longer questionnaire is likely to cost more to have printed and is likely to weigh more, so that it costs more to post.

The visual appearance of the questionnaire

A questionnaire should be as user-friendly as possible. One positive way of making it user-friendly is to make it easy on the eye, because this encourages a more positive attitude to filling it in. A good layout also minimizes the possibility of errors arising through confusion about where answers should go and in which form they should be given. Third, an attractive visual layout makes life easier in terms of reading the results and transferring them, for instance, to the computer database.

A number of things can help the researcher to produce a visually attractive and, equally, highly functional questionnaire layout.

▶ *Single-sided paper*. Despite the resource implications, this is preferable from the researcher's point of view, because it is easier to read the results and allows faster data preparation. Arguably, respondents find it easier to deal with questions on one side of each sheet than to fold back each page as they plough their way through the document.

▶ *Use of space and size of print*. The questions should not be crowded too closely. Cramming plenty of questions on to one page might save on printing and postage costs, but it is also likely to make the questionnaire less clear and 'user-friendly'. Sufficient space must be left to insert answers without resorting to tiny writing.

▶ *Use of coloured paper*. Coloured paper may make the questionnaire more attractive. Two points, though, need to be borne in mind. First, the choice of colour needs to made carefully to avoid any misunderstandings about its significance. A questionnaire relating to gender, for example, would do well to avoid the use of either blue or pink paper. Second, coloured paper is more expensive than white paper – pushing up the printing costs.

▶ *Desktop publishing*. Where there is access to DTP equipment, it should normally be used. It helps to produce a clear document and the end-product looks more professional. A hand-written questionnaire would not normally convey an appropriate image for the research; it would be used only where a strategic decision was taken that the particular target group would be likely to respond better to a hand-written than typed/printed format.

▶ *Number the pages*. Although the question numbers should prove enough to locate any sheets that become detached, formal documents such as the research questionnaire ought to follow protocol and have each page sequentially numbered.

▶ *Answer column*. Be sure to leave adequate space on the right-hand side of the page for a column containing boxes for the coded answers. If the answer boxes are all located in such a column it makes it much easier to read off the answers and compile them in the database.

6 Constructing the questions

Identifying the key issues

A questionnaire needs to be crisp and concise, asking just those questions which are crucial to the research. This means that the researcher must have a clear vision of exactly what issues are at the heart of the research and what kind of information would enlighten those issues. *There is little room for vagueness or imprecision.*

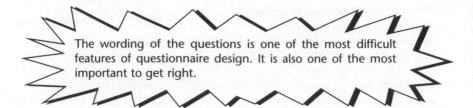

The wording of the questions is one of the most difficult features of questionnaire design. It is also one of the most important to get right.

Before focusing on the exact wording and structure of the questions, the researcher needs to consider a few broader points that will influence the style and direction of the questions. First of all, the researcher needs to consider whether the information being sought from the respondent is amenable to direct questions, or whether it will need to be measured by indirect means. This has a bearing on the matter of the 'validity' of the questionnaire. Yet again, the importance of the researcher having a clear conception of the issues under examination becomes evident. Where the information being sought is of an overt, factual nature, there is not normally a problem on this point. The questions will take the form of 'How many times . . . ? or 'When did you last . . . ? However, questionnaires are frequently geared to less straightforward matters, where a direct question would be inappropriate. If, for example, the researcher wishes to know what social class the respondent comes from, it would not be wise to ask the straightforward question, 'What is your social class?' Apart from the fact that some people might find this offensive, the term social class has different meanings for different people, and the question will produce inconsistent answers. In this case, the researcher needs to pinpoint exactly what he or she defines as social class and then devise questions that will supply the type of information which will allow the respondent's social class to be deduced. For this purpose, indirect questions will be used about occupation, income, education etc.

The wording of the questions

The researcher needs to be confident that:

▶ *The questions will not be irritating* or annoying for the respondents to answer. The success of the questionnaire depends on the willingness of the respondents to supply the answer voluntarily.

▶ *The respondents will have some information,* knowledge, experience or opinions on the topic of the questions. It is no good designing perfect questions where the responses are likely to be a series of 'don't knows' or 'not applicable'.

▶ *The proposed style of questions is suited to the target group.* Questions geared to 14-year-olds will need to be different in terms of conceptual complexity and wording from ones aimed at, for example, members of a professional association.

▶ *The questions require respondents to answer only about themselves* or matters of fact they can realistically answer for others. It is not good practice, generally speaking, to ask respondents to answer for other people. For example, it would be inappropriate to ask a parent to say which TV programmes were his or her children's favourite. The parent's perception might differ from the children's and, in any case, each child is likely to prefer something different. If we really wish to know the children's favourite TV programme we should devise a questionnaire that the children will answer.

▶ *The questions are on a topic and of a kind which the respondents will be willing to answer.* This point applies, in particular, where questions are on highly personal matters or moral/legal indiscretions.

There are some specific things the researcher needs to bear in mind when devising the questions:

▶ *Avoid the use of 'leading' questions.* These are questions which suggest an answer or which prompt the respondent to give a particular kind of answer (e.g. Would you agree that there should be controls on the emission of carbon dioxide from cars?).

▶ *Avoid asking the same question twice in a different fashion.*

▶ *Make sure the wording is completely unambiguous.*

▶ *Avoid vague questions.* The more specific and concrete the question, the easier it is to give a precise answer. And, in all probability, the answer will prove to be of more value to the researcher.

▶ *Be sure to include sufficient options in the answer.* If the list might prove too long, selecting the main possibilities and then tagging on the 'Other (please specify)' option is a good strategy.

▶ *Use only the minimum amount of technical jargon.* In terms of a questionnaire, the aim is not to see how clever people are.

▶ *Keep the questions as short and straightforward as possible.* This will avoid unnecessary confusion and wasted time re-reading questions or trying to decipher the meaning of the question.

▶ *Include only those questions which are absolutely vital for the research.*

▶ *Pay attention to the way the questions are numbered.* Obviously they should be sequential, but there are clever ways of using sub-questions (e.g. 4a, 4b and so on) which can help the respondent to map his or her way through the series of questions.

▶ *Don't make unwarranted presumptions in the questions.* It can be annoying to the respondent who does not match the presumption. For example, questions about people's reading habits should not start with something like 'How many novels have you read in the past 12 months?' This presumes that all respondents read novels. It would be better to ask first (1) 'Do you read novels?', and if the answer is yes, follow this up with a supplementary question: (1a) 'How many novels have you read in the past 12 months?'

▶ *Avoid words or phrases which might cause offence*. If, for example, the questionnaire involves ethnic minority issues, it is important to use the 'politically correct' terms.

The order of the questions

The ordering of the questions in a questionnaire is important for three reasons. First and foremost, questions asked at an earlier point in the questionnaire can affect the answers supplied at a later stage. This is evident in many commercial 'marketing/sales questionnaires', where there is a conscious attempt to make use of this feature of questionnaires.

The second way in which the ordering of questions can be important is that it can entice or deter the respondent from continuing with the exercise of providing answers. If the respondent is immediately faced with the most complex of the questions at the start of the questionnaire, this might deter him or her from going any further. However, if the questionnaire *starts with straightforward questions* and then gradually moves towards such questions at a later stage, there is a greater likelihood that the respondent will persevere. This same point is true for those questions which might be perceived as more personal and on sensitive issues. There will be a greater chance of success if such questions appear later in the questionnaire than if they appear right at the start.

Keypoints on the order of the questions

In a nutshell, the researcher should be sure that:

▶ the most straightforward questions come at the start;

▶ the least contentious questions and least sensitive issues are dealt with at the beginning of the questionnaire;

▶ the sequence of questions does not lead the respondents towards 'inevitable' answers, where the answers to later questions are effectively predicated on the answers to earlier ones.

---

7 Types of questions

There are *a variety of ways in which questions can be put* in a questionnaire. These are outlined below. However, from the outset it is worth giving some thought to whether the overall questionnaire will benefit from using a variety of kinds of questions, or whether it is better to aim for a consistent style throughout. Variety has two potential advantages. First, it stops the respondent becoming bored. Second, it stops the respondent falling into a 'pattern' of answers where, for example, on a scale of 1 to 5 he or she begins to put 4 down as the answer to all questions. Aiming for a consistent style of question, for its part, has the advantage of allowing the respondent to get used to the kind of questions so that they can be answered quickly and with less likelihood of confusion or misunderstanding. There is no hard and fast rule on this point: it is down to a judgement call on the part of the researcher.

'Open' and 'closed' questions

Open questions are those that leave the respondent to decide the wording of the answer, the length of the answer and the kind of matters to be raised in the answer. The questions tend to be short and the answers tend to be long. For example, the questionnaire might ask, 'How do you feel about the inclusion of nuclear arms as part of Britain's defence capability?' and then provide a number of empty lines which invite the respondent to enter his or her thoughts on the matter.

The advantage of 'open' questions is that the information gathered by way of the responses is more likely to reflect the full richness and complexity of the views held by the respondent. Respondents are allowed space to express themselves in their own words. Weighed against this, however, there are two disadvantages which are built into the use of open questions. First, they demand more effort on the part of the respondents (which might well reduce their willingness to take part in the research). Second, they leave the researcher with data which are quite 'raw' and require a lot of time-consuming analysis before they can be used.

Closed questions structure the answers by allowing only answers which fit into categories that have been established in advance by the researcher. The researcher, in this case, instructs the respondent to answer by selecting from a range of two or more options supplied on the questionnaire. The options can be restricted to as few as two (e.g. 'Yes' or 'No'; 'Male' or 'Female') or can include quite complex lists of alternatives from which the respondent can choose.

The advantages and disadvantages of the 'closed' question are more or less a mirror image of those connected with the open, unstructured approach. In a nutshell, the main advantage is that the structure imposed on the respondents' answers provides the researcher with information which is of uniform length and in a form that lends itself nicely to being quantified and compared. The answers, in fact, provide pre-coded data that can be easily analysed. Weighed against this, there are two disadvantages. First, there is less scope for respondents to supply answers which reflect the exact facts or true feelings on a topic if the facts or opinions happen to be complicated or do not exactly fit into the range of options supplied in the questionnaire. The closed question allows for less subtlety in the answers. Second, and largely as a result of the first disadvantage, the respondents might get frustrated by not being allowed to express their views fully in a way that accounts for any sophistication, intricacy or even inconsistencies in their views.

⚠ **Caution**

Closed questions, in general, lend themselves to the production of quantitative data. However, it is very important for the researcher to be clear *at the design stage* about which particular kind(s) of quantitative data will be collected (nominal, ordinal, etc.) and what specific statistical procedures will be used. Unless the researcher thinks ahead on this point there is a very real danger that the data collected will turn out to be inappropriate for the kind of analysis that the researcher eventually wants to undertake.

Link up with **Analysis of quantitative data, p. 177**

Nine types of question that can be used in a questionnaire

① A statement

Example:
What do you think about the UK's membership of the European Union?

_____

_____

_____

② A list

Example:
Please list the issues you feel are most important in relation to the UK's membership of the European Union:

_____

_____

_____

_____

③ A 'yes/no' answer

Example:
Have you travelled from the UK to another European country in the past 12 months?   Yes/No

Nine types of question that can be used in a questionnaire – *continued*

4 Agree/disagree with a statement

Example:
Would you agree or disagree with the following statement?
European economic unity carries economic advantages which outweigh
the political disadvantages.   Agree/Disagree

5 Choose from a list of options

Example:
Which ONE of the following list of European countries do you feel has
the strongest economy?

Spain	UK	Belgium	Netherlands
Ireland	France	Germany	Italy

6 Rank order

Example:
From the following list of European countries choose the THREE which
you feel have the strongest economies and put them in rank order: 1 =
strongest, 2 = second strongest, 3 = third strongest.

Spain	UK	Belgium	Netherlands
Ireland	France	Germany	Italy

7 Degree of agreement and disagreement: *the Likert Scale*

Example:
Membership of the European Union is a bad thing for the UK.

Strongly agree	Agree	Neutral	Disagree	Strongly disagree

8 Rate items

Example:
How significant would you rate the following factors in affecting further
European integration?

	Not significant						Very significant
political sovereignty	1	2	3	4	5	6	7
national currencies	1	2	3	4	5	6	7
past history	1	2	3	4	5	6	7
religious differences	1	2	3	4	5	6	7
language barriers	1	2	3	4	5	6	7

Nine types of question that can be used in a questionnaire – *continued*

9 **Feelings about a topic:** *the semantic differential*

Example:
European unity is:

Boring	1	2	3	4	5	Interesting
Unlikely	1	2	3	4	5	Likely
Risky	1	2	3	4	5	Safe
Important	1	2	3	4	5	Unimportant
Difficult	1	2	3	4	5	Easy

---

8 Evaluating questionnaires

There are five basic criteria for evaluating a research questionnaire. The first of these concerns an assessment of the likelihood that the questionnaire will provide *full information* on the particular topic(s) of research. The value of the questionnaire will depend in no small measure on the extent to which it includes coverage of all *vital* information pertaining to the area of research.

The second criterion concerns the likelihood that the questionnaire will provide *accurate information*. What confidence do we have that the responses on the questionnaires are as full and honest as they can be – free from mischievous attempts to scupper the research, errors arising through ambiguous questions etc.?

Third, the questionnaire can be evaluated according to its likelihood of achieving a decent *response rate*. In order to get a representative picture, the questionnaire needs to avoid 'turning people off' by being poorly presented, taking too long to complete, asking insensitive questions etc.

Fourth, the questionnaire needs to adopt an *ethical stance*, in which recognition is given to the respondents' rights to have the information they supply treated according to strict professional standards. Apart from legal requirements associated with data protection when personal information is stored on computer, there is some moral obligation on the researcher to protect the interests of those who supply information and to give them sufficient information about the nature of the research so that they can make an informed judgement about whether they wish to cooperate with the research.

These four criteria form the backdrop for a fifth criterion: the *feasibility* of the questionnaire. The issue of feasibility is two-sided. It draws attention initially to the amount of time and money available to the researcher, and whether or not the particular questionnaire is likely to supply enough information within a definite time-frame for it to provide worthwhile information. It is hardly worth embarking on a three-month postal questionnaire survey for a research report that needs to be completed in two months! The other side to feasibility is the likelihood that the questionnaire will reach appropriate respondents and that they will feel motivated to collaborate with the research by completing the questionnaires as honestly as possible and returning them to the researcher. This likelihood depends on a variety of factors.

Factors affecting the feasibility of using a questionnaire

Respondents	(who)
Location	(where)
Time	(when)
Topic	(what)
Number of questions	(how long)
Difficulty of questions	(how hard)

These will affect the *completion rate*, the *response rate* and the *accuracy* of the answers.

---

9 Advantages of questionnaires

▶ *Questionnaires are economical*, in the sense that they can supply a considerable amount of research data for a relatively low cost in terms of materials, money and time. This is particularly the case in relation to the *postal questionnaire*. Such costs should not be dismissed as negligible – but they are generally low in relation to the costs incurred by the amount of *researchers' time* involved. The costs of a postal survey need to be weighed against the savings made by the researcher not having to travel to meet people and spend time with them as they go through the questionnaire. A questionnaire that takes, perhaps, 40 minutes to complete might take a day of a researcher's time if the researcher has to travel some distance to deliver the questionnaire personally. The postal costs can seem well worth it when viewed against this alternative.

▶ *Easier to arrange*. The postal questionnaire is easier to arrange than, for example, personal interviews. There is no need to 'arrange' it at all, in fact, since the questionnaire may be simply sent unannounced to the respondent. (Some researchers, though, have sought to improve the response rate by contacting respondents before they send a questionnaire to them. This contact can be by phone or letter. However, it obviously increases the amount of time and money involved in conducting the research.)

▶ *Questionnaires supply standardized answers*, to the extent that all respondents are posed with exactly the same questions – with no scope for variation to slip in via face-to-face contact with the researcher. The data collected, then, are very unlikely to be contaminated through variations in the wording of the questions or the manner in which the question is asked. There is little scope for the data to be affected by '*interpersonal factors*'.

▶ *Pre-coded answers.* A further, and important, advantage of the questionnaire is that it encourages pre-coded answers. As we have seen, this is not an essential facet of questionnaires, because unstructured answers can be sought. However, particularly with postal questionnaires, the value of the data is likely to be greatest where respondents provide answers that fit into a range of options offered by the researcher. These allow for the speedy collation and analysis of data by the researcher. They also have an advantage for the respondents, who, instead of needing to think of how to express their ideas, are faced with the relatively easy task of needing to pick one or more answers which are spelt out for them.

10 Disadvantages of questionnaires

In many respects the potential disadvantages of questionnaires go hand in glove with the potential advantages. You can't have one without the other.

▶ *Pre-coded questions can be frustrating for respondents and, thus, deter them from answering.* The advantage for the researcher of using pre-coded answers set out in the questionnaire carries with it a possible disadvantage. While the respondents might find it less demanding merely to tick appropriate boxes they might, equally, find this *restricting and frustrating.* So, on the one hand, the 'ticking box' routine might encourage people to respond but, on the other hand, this same routine might be experienced as negative and put people off cooperating with the research.

Link up with **Response rates, p. 19**

▶ *Pre-coded questions can bias the findings towards the researcher's, rather than the respondent's, way of seeing things.* Questionnaires, by their very nature, can start to impose a structure on the answers and shape the nature of the responses in a way that reflects the researcher's thinking rather than the respondent's. Good research practice will minimize the prospect of this, but there is always the danger that the options open to the respondent when answering the questions will channel responses away from the respondent's perception of matters to fit in with a line of thinking established by the researcher.

▶ *Postal questionnaires offer little opportunity for the researcher to check the truthfulness of the answers given by the respondents.* Because the researcher does not meet the respondent and because the answers are given 'at a distance', the researcher cannot rely on a number of clues that an interviewer might have about whether the answers are genuine or not. The interviewer might see some incongruity between answers given by the same interviewee and be able to probe the matter. Or the interviewer might note a disparity between a given answer and some other factor (e.g. stated occupation and apparent level of income). In the case of the questionnaire, however, if a respondent states his or her occupation to be a 'dentist', it would seem at first glance that the researcher has little option but to accept this as true. Likewise, on matters of taste or opinion, if the respondent answers along a particular line, the questionnaire researcher would seem to have no solid grounds for challenging the answer. This is all the more true if the questionnaires are anonymous.

Keypoints: advantages and disadvantages of postal questionnaires

Advantages
▶ Wide coverage.
▶ Cheap.
▶ Pre-coded data.
▶ Eliminate effect of personal interaction with researcher.

Disadvantages
▶ Poor response rate.
▶ Incomplete or poorly completed answers
▶ Limit and shape nature of answers.
▶ Cannot check truth of answers.

Checklist for the production of a questionnaire

When producing a questionnaire for research you should feel confident about answering 'yes' to the following questions:

① Has the questionnaire been *piloted*? ☐

② Is the *layout* clear? ☐

③ Has the questionnaire got a suitable *cover page*? ☐

④ Is there an explanation of the *purpose* of the questionnaire? ☐

⑤ Is there a *return address* on the questionnaire? ☐

⑥ Have *thanks* been expressed to the respondents? ☐

⑦ Are there assurances about *confidentiality* of information or anonymity? ☐

⑧ Have *serial numbers* been given to the questionnaires? ☐

⑨ Are the *pages numbered*? ☐

⑩ Are the *coding boxes* neatly placed in an answer column? ☐

⑪ Are there clear and explicit *instructions* on how the questions are to be completed? ☐

⑫ Have the questions been *checked* to avoid any duplication? ☐

⑬ Are the questions *clear* and unambiguous? ☐

⑭ Are the essential questions included? ☐

⑮ Are the non-essential questions excluded? ☐

⑯ Are the questions in the *right order*? ☐

⑰ Has the questionnaire been *checked for spelling* and typographical errors? ☐

© M. Denscombe, *The Good Research Guide*. Open University Press.

▶ ▷ ▷ 7

INTERVIEWS

Interviews are an attractive proposition for the project researcher. At first glance, they do not involve much technical paraphernalia in order to collect the information – perhaps a notepad and a portable tape-recorder – and the basic technique draws on a skill that researchers already have – the ability to conduct a conversation. No complex equipment and no need to spend time learning new skills: this is a particularly enticing recipe.

The reality, though, is not quite so simple. Although there are a lot of superficial similarities between a conversation and an interview, interviews are actually something more than just a conversation. Interviews involve a set of assumptions and understandings about the situation which are not normally associated with a casual conversation (Denscombe 1983; Silverman 1985). When someone agrees to take part in a research interview:

▶ *There is consent to take part.* From the researcher's point of view this is particularly important in relation to research ethics. An agreement to be interviewed generally means that there is *informed consent.* The interview is not done by secret recording of discussions or the use of casual conversations as research data. It is openly a meeting intended to produce material that will be used for research purposes – and the interviewee understands this and agrees to it.

▶ *The interviewee's words can be treated as 'on the record' and 'for the record'.* In the research interview there is a general understanding (a) that the words can be used by the researcher at some later date and (b) that the talk can be taken as a genuine reflection of the person's thoughts, rather than being a joke or a 'wind up'. It is, of course, possible for the interviewee to stipulate that his or her words are *not* to be attributed to him or her, or *not* to be made publicly available. The point is, though, that unless the interviewee specifies to the contrary, the interview talk is 'on record' and 'for the record'. It is to be taken seriously.

▶ *The agenda for the discussion is set by the researcher.* There is a tacit agreement built into the notion of being interviewed that the proceedings and the agenda for the discussion will be controlled by the researcher. The degree of control exercised by the researcher will vary according to the style of interviewing, and there are occasions when interviewees might try to take control of proceedings, but there is none the less some implied agreement at the outset of the research interview that the researcher is given the right to control the proceedings and the direction of the discussion.

These assumptions do not apply during the course of a normal conversation. The research interview does not happen by chance; it is arranged. The discussion is not arbitrary or at the whim of one of the parties; it is dedicated to investigating a given topic. The flow of the discussion is rarely free form; it is normally monitored and follows an agenda set by the researcher.

⚠ Caution

The superficial similarity between an interview and a conversation can generate an illusion of simplicity. We all have conversations and it is likely that most of us do not have too much difficulty with them. So an interview should be fairly straightforward. As long as we know to whom we are going to talk and what we want to ask, the rest should be plain sailing. Here lies the problem. The researcher can be lulled into a sense of false security. The superficial similarity can encourage a relaxed attitude to the planning, preparation and conduct of the method that would be unlikely were it to involve questionnaires or experiments. In reality, interviewing is no easy option. It is fraught with hidden dangers and can fail miserably unless there is good planning, proper preparation and a sensitivity to the complex nature of interaction during the interview itself.

1 When is it appropriate to use interviews for research?

Whether it is large-scale research or small-scale research, the nature of the data collection depends on the amount of resources available. There are inevitably restrictions on the time and the money that can be used and, for the researcher, this means that choices need to be made – often difficult choices – about how to make the best use of the resources. In practice, the crucial choice as far as whether or not to use interviews is concerned is between, on the one hand, gathering more superficial information from a large number of people and, on the other hand, collecting more detailed information from a smaller number of people. The use of interviews normally means that the researcher has reached the decision that, for the purposes of the particular project in mind, the research would be better served by getting material which provides more of an in-depth insight into the topic, drawing on information provided by fewer informants.

To reach this decision, the social researcher needs to consider the following two questions and be persuaded that, overall, interviews are a reasonable option to pursue in terms of the desirability of the particular type of data they produce.

▶ Does the research really require the kind of *detailed information* that interviews supply?

▶ Is it reasonable to rely on information gathered from a small number of informants?

The researcher ought to be able to justify the decision to go for depth rather than breadth in the material as being best suited to the specific needs to the project. Such a justification is likely to incorporate reference to:

▶ *Data based on emotions, experiences and feelings.* If the researcher wishes to investigate emotions, experiences and feelings rather than more straightforward factual matters, then he or she may be justified in preferring interviews to the use of questionnaires. The nature of emotions, experiences and feelings is such that they need to be explored rather than simply reported in a word or two.

▶ *Data based on sensitive issues.* When the research covers issues that might be considered sensitive or rather personal, there is a case to be made for using interviews. Such things call for careful handling and perhaps some coaxing in order to get the informant to be open and honest. Any justification along these lines, however, will also need to recognize the problems that might arise from 'the interviewer effect' (see below) and argue that, on balance, the face-to-face approach will produce better data.

▶ *Data based on privileged information.* Here, the justification for interviews is based on the value of contact with key players in the field who can give privileged information. The depth of information provided by interviews can produce best 'value for money' if the informants are willing and able to give information that others could not – when what they offer is an insight they have as people in a special position 'to know'.

The decision to use interviews also needs to take account of their feasibility. Before embarking on a programme of interviews the researcher needs to feel assured about the following two questions.

▶ *Is it possible to gain direct access to the prospective interviewees?* There is obviously no point in pursuing the idea of conducting interviews unless there are good grounds for believing that the necessary people can be accessed, and that some agreement can be obtained from all the parties involved in the research.

▶ *Are the interviews viable in terms of the costs in time and travel involved?* With limited resources, the researcher needs to ensure that the people are not distributed too widely across a large geographical area and that conducting the interviews will not incur prohibitive costs.

2 What kinds of data are collected by interviews?

Interview data can be used in a variety of ways and for a variety of specialist purposes, depending on the background of the researcher and the context in which the interview occurs. For project researchers, by far the most common use will be as *a source of information*. Interviews can be a very effective method used in this way. For this purpose, the contents of the interview are more or less taken at face value for what they have to tell the researcher about the particular topic being discussed. Although the interviewer will want to cross-check for accuracy, the data themselves consist of the information conveyed in the informant's words.

As *an information-gathering tool*, the interview lends itself to being used alongside other methods as a way of supplementing their data – adding detail and depth. It is, indeed, frequently used by way of:

▶ *Preparation for a questionnaire.* To fine-tune the questions and concepts that will appear in a widely circulated questionnaire, researchers can use interviews to supply the detail and depth needed to ensure that the questionnaire asks valid questions.

▶ *Follow-up to a questionnaire.* Where the questionnaire might have thrown up some interesting lines of enquiry, researchers can use interviews to pursue these in greater detail and depth. The interview data complement the questionnaire data.

▶ *Triangulation with other methods.* Rather than interviews being regarded as competing with other methods, they can be combined in order to corroborate facts using a different approach.

3 Types of research interview

Structured interviews

Structured interviews involve tight control over the format of the questions and answers. In essence, the structured interview is like a questionnaire which is administered face to face with a respondent. The researcher has a predetermined list of questions, to which the respondent is invited to offer limited-option responses. The tight control over the wording of the questions, the order in which the questions occur and the range of answers that are on offer have the advantage of 'standardization'. Each respondent is faced with identical questions. And the range of pre-coded answers on offer to respondents ensures that data analysis is relatively easy. The structured interview, in this respect, lends itself to the collection of quantitative data.

Structured interviews are often associated with social surveys where researchers are trying to collect large volumes of data from a wide range of respondents. Here, we are witnessing the replacement of interviewers armed with clipboards and paper questionnaires with interviewers using laptop computers to input information direct into a suitable software program. Such *computer-assisted personal interviewing* (CAPI) has the advantage of using software with built-in checks to eliminate errors in the collection of data, and it · allows quick analysis of the data. However, its relatively large initial costs, caused by the purchase of the laptop computers, the development of suitable software and the training involved, means that CAPI is better suited to large-budget, large-number surveys than to small-scale research.

    Link up with **Questionnaires, p. 87**

Whether using a laptop computer, telephone or printed schedule of questions, the structured interview, in spirit, bears more resemblance to questionnaire methods than to the other types of interviews. For this reason, *this chapter focuses on semi-structured and unstructured interviews rather than structured questionnaires.*

Semi-structured interviews

With semi-structured interviews, the interviewer still has a clear list of issues to be addressed and questions to be answered. However, with the semi-structured interview the interviewer is prepared to be flexible in terms of the order in which the topics are considered, and, perhaps more significantly, to let the interviewee develop ideas and speak more widely on the issues raised by the researcher. The answers are open-ended, and there is more emphasis on the interviewee elaborating points of interest.

Unstructured interviews

Unstructured interviews go further in the extent to which emphasis is placed on the interviewee's thoughts. The researcher's role is to be as unintrusive as possible – to start the ball rolling by introducing a theme or topic and then letting the interviewee develop his or her ideas and pursue his or her train of thought.

Semi-structured and unstructured interviews are really on a continuum and, in practice, it is likely that any interview will slide back and forth along the scale. What they have in common, and what separates them from structured interviews, is their willingness to allow interviewees to use their own words and develop their own thoughts. Allowing interviewees to 'speak their minds' is a better way of discovering things about complex issues and, generally, semi-structured and unstructured interviews have as their aim 'discovery' rather then 'checking'. They lend themselves to in-depth investigations, particularly those which explore personal accounts of experiences and feelings.

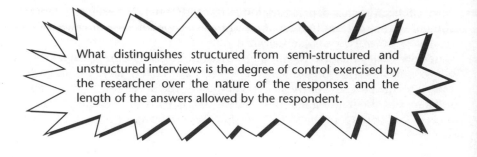

What distinguishes structured from semi-structured and unstructured interviews is the degree of control exercised by the researcher over the nature of the responses and the length of the answers allowed by the respondent.

One-to-one interviews

The most common form of semi-structured or unstructured interview is the one-to-one variety, which involves a meeting between one researcher and one informant. One reason for its popularity is that it is relatively easy to arrange. Only two people's diaries need to coincide. Another advantage is that the opinions and views expressed throughout the interview stem from one source: the interviewee. This makes it fairly straightforward for the researcher to locate specific ideas with specific people. A third advantage is that the one-to-one interview is relatively easy to control. The researcher only has one person's ideas to grasp and interrogate, and one person to guide through the interview agenda.

Group interviews

Sometimes research can involve the use of more than one informant. The numbers involved in such group interviewing, normally about four to six people, really reflect the practical matter of how difficult it is to get people together to discuss matters on one occasion, and how many voices can contribute to the discussion during any one interview. But the crucial thing to bear in mind here is that a group interview is not an opportunity for the researcher to pose questions to a sequence of individuals, taking turns around a table. The term 'group' is crucial here, because it tells us that those present during the interview will interact with one another and that the discussion will operate at the level of the group. As Lewis notes:

> Group interviews have several advantages over individual interviews. In particular, they help to reveal consensus views, may generate richer responses by allowing participants to challenge one another's views, may be used to verify research ideas of data gained through other methods and may enhance the reliability of . . . responses.
>
> (Lewis 1992: 413)

Weighed against this, of course, group interviews hold the prospect of drowning out certain views, especially those of 'quieter' people. Certain members of the group might dominate the talk, while others might struggle to get themselves heard. There is a gender issue here: it is men who tend to hog the centre stage in group discussions, it is women whose opinions might tend to get passed over in terms of data from such interviews.

Another potential disadvantage of group interviews is that the opinions that are expressed are ones that are perceived to be 'acceptable' within the group. Where group members regard their opinions as contrary to prevailing opinion within the group, they might be inclined to keep quiet, or moderate their views somewhat. The privacy of the one-to-one interview does not pose this difficulty.

Focus groups

Focus groups have become an extremely popular form of interview technique. Their extensive use in the worlds of market research and advertising has spread to social research more generally in recent years. Focus groups consist of a small group of people, usually between six and nine in number, who are brought together by a trained 'moderator' (the researcher) to explore attitudes and perceptions, feelings and ideas about a topic. The three distinctive and vital points about focus groups are that:

▶ the sessions usually revolve around a prompt, a trigger, some stimulus introduced by the moderator in order to 'focus' the discussion;

▶ there is less emphasis on the need for the moderator to adopt a neutral role in the proceedings than is normally the case with other interview techniques;

▶ they place particular value on the interaction within the group as a means for eliciting information, rather than just collecting each individual's point of view – there is a special value placed on the collective view, rather than the aggregate view.

Focus groups are generally regarded as a useful way of exploring attitudes on non-sensitive, non-controversial topics. They can excite contributions from interviewees who might otherwise be reluctant to contribute and, through their relatively informal interchanges, focus groups can lead to insights that might not otherwise have come to light through the one-to-one conventional interview. Weighed against this, it is difficult to record the discussion that takes place, as speakers interrupt one another and talk simultaneously. It should be recognized that, as with all group interviews, there is the possibility that people will be reluctant to disclose thoughts on sensitive, personal, political or emotional matters in the company of others, or that extrovert characters can dominate the proceedings and bully more timid members of the focus group into expressing opinions they would not admit to in private. Of course, the moderator ought to manage the event to avoid this happening, but this calls for experience on the part of the moderator and a judicious selection of people to participate in the focus group.

4 The interviewer effect

Personal identity

Research on interviewing has demonstrated fairly conclusively that people respond differently depending on how they perceive the person asking the questions.

In particular, the *sex*, the *age* and the *ethnic origins* of the interviewer have a bearing on the amount of information people are willing to divulge and their honesty about what they reveal. The data, in other words, are affected by the personal identity of the researcher.

The impact of the researcher's personal identity, of course, will depend on who is being interviewed. It is not, strictly speaking, the identity in its own right that affects the data, but what the researcher's identity means as far as the person being interviewed is concerned. *Interviewees, and interviewers come to that, have their own preferences and prejudices, and these are likely to have some impact on the chances of developing rapport and trust during an interview.*

The effect of the researcher's identity, of course, will also depend on the nature of the topic being discussed. On sensitive issues or on matters regarded as rather personal, the interviewer's identity assumes particular importance. If the research is dealing with religious beliefs, with earnings, with sexual relationships, with personal health or any of a host of similar issues, the sex, age and ethnicity of the interviewer in relation to the sex, age and ethnicity of the interviewee is very likely to influence the nature of the data that emerges – their fullness and their honesty. On some questions people can be embarrassed. They can feel awkward or defensive. Whenever this is the case, there is the possibility that interviewees might supply answers which they feel fit in with what the researcher expects from them – fulfilling the perceived expectations of the researcher. Or the answers might tend to be tailored to match what the interviewee suspects is the researcher's point of view, keeping the researcher happy. Either way, the quality of the data suffers.

From the perspective of the small-scale project researcher, there is a limit to

---

Questions a researcher should consider

▶ Is there likely to be an *age gap* between myself and the interviewee(s) and, if so, how will this affect the interview?

▶ In the light of the topic I propose to research, will interviewing someone of the *opposite sex or a different ethnic origin* have an impact on his or her willingness to respond?

▶ What are the *social status, educational qualifications and professional expertise* of the people I propose to interview, and how do these compare with my own? Is this likely to affect the interviewer–interviewee relationship in a positive or negative manner?

what can be done about this. There are limits to the extent that researchers can disguise their 'self' during interviews. We bring to interviews certain personal attributes which are 'givens' and which cannot be altered on whim to suit the needs of the research interview. *Our sex, our age, our ethnic origin, our accent, even our occupational status, all are aspects of our 'self' which, for practical purposes, cannot be changed.* We can make efforts to be polite and punctual, receptive and neutral, in order to encourage the right climate for an interviewee to feel comfortable and provide honest answers. What we cannot do is change these personal attributes.

Self-presentation

Conventional advice to researchers has been geared to minimizing the impact of researchers on the outcome of the research by having them adopt a passive and neutral stance. The idea is that the researcher:

▶ presents himself or herself in a light which is designed not to antagonize or upset the interviewee (conventional clothes, courtesy etc.);

▶ remains neutral and non-committal on the statements made during the interview by the interviewee.

Passivity and neutrality are the order of the day. The researcher's 'self', adopting this approach, is kept firmly hidden beneath a cloak of cordiality and receptiveness to the words of the interviewee. To a certain degree, this is sound advice. The researcher, after all, is there to listen and learn, not to preach. The point is to get the interviewee to open up, not to provoke hostility or put the interviewee on the defensive.

Questions a researcher should consider

▶ How should I adjust my appearance so that I best fit in with those being interviewed?

▶ How can I avoid being dragged into agreeing with views I find distasteful without antagonizing the interviewee or engaging in a debate?

Personal involvement

One line of reasoning argues that a cold and calculating style of interviewing reinforces a gulf between the researcher and the informant, and does little to help or empower the informant. Now, if the aims of the research are specifically to help or empower the people being researched, rather than dispassionately learn from them, then the approach of the interviewer will need to alter accordingly (Oakley 1981). Under these circumstances, the researcher will be

> **Questions a researcher should consider**
>
> ▶ Do I wish to adopt a style of interviewing which empowers or helps the people I hope to interview?
>
> ▶ Will those who read the research recognize and appreciate my involvement with the interviewees as a reasoned departure from the convention, rather than treat it as plain bad practice?

inclined to show emotion, to respond with feeling and to engage in a true dialogue with the interviewee. The researcher will become fully involved as a person with feelings, with experiences and with knowledge which can be shared with the interviewee. A word of warning, though. This style of interviewing remains 'unconventional', and the researcher needs to be confident and committed to make it work. The researcher also needs to feel sure that his or her audience understand and share the underlying logic of the approach rather than expecting the researcher to adopt the cool and dispassionate stance.

5 Planning and preparation for interviews

The topics for discussion

With the use of unstructured interviews, it might be argued that the researcher should not have preconceived ideas about the crucial issues and direction the interview should take. In practice, however, it is not very often that researchers operate at the extreme end of the continuum with unstructured interviews. In the vast majority of cases, researchers approach an interview with some agenda and with some game-plan in mind. In such cases it would be tempting fate to proceed to a research interview without having devoted considerable time to thinking through the key points that warrant attention. This does not necessarily mean that the researcher needs to have a rigid framework of questions and issues in mind – though this will be the case when using structured interviews. It does mean that there is likely to be more benefit from the interview if he or she is well informed about the topic and has done the necessary homework on the issues that are likely to arise during the interview.

Choice of informants

In principle, there is nothing to stop researchers from selecting informants on the basis of random sampling. In practice, though, this is unlikely to happen. Interviews are generally conducted with lower numbers than would be the case with questionnaire surveys, and this means that the selection of people to interview is more likely to be based on non-probability sampling. People tend to be chosen deliberately because they have some special contribution to make, because they have some unique insight or because of the position they hold. It is worth emphasizing, though, that there is no hard and fast rule on this. It depends on whether the overall aim of the research is to produce results which are generalizable (in which case the emphasis will be on choosing a representative sample of people to interview) or the aim is to delve in depth into a particular situation with a view to exploring the specifics (in which case the emphasis will be on choosing key players in the field).

In the case of group interviews, researchers can decide to select interviewees in order to get a cross-section of opinion within the group, or, perhaps, to ensure that group members hold opposing views on the topic for discussion.

Authorization

In many, if not most, research situations it will be necessary to get approval from relevant 'authorities'. This will be necessary in any instance of research where the people selected to participate in the interviews are either:

▶ working within an organization where they are *accountable to others* higher up the chain of command;

▶ or potentially vulnerable, and therefore *protected by responsible others* – the young, the infirm and some other groups are under the protection of others whose permission must be sought (e.g. school children).

Organizations or authorities that grant permission will wish to be persuaded that it is *bona fide* research, and they will also be influenced by the personal/research credentials of the researcher. Letters of contact, therefore, should spell out the range of factors which will *persuade the organization or authority that the researcher is both (a) trustworthy and (b) capable.* Research which can call on suitable referees or which will be conducted under the auspices of a suitable organization (e.g. a university) is at an advantage for these.

To emphasize what ought to be obvious, such authorization to conduct the interviews must be gained *before* the interviews take place.

Arranging the venue

Securing an agreement to be interviewed is often easier if the prospective interviewee is *contacted in advance*. This also allows both parties to arrange a mutually convenient time for the interview. At this point, of course, the researcher will probably be asked how long the interview will take, and should therefore be in a position to respond. It is most unlikely that busy people will feel comfortable with a suggestion that the interview will 'take as long as it takes'. The researcher needs to make a bid for an *agreed length of time* whether it be 15 minutes, half an hour, 45 minutes or an hour.

Where the interview is to take place in the field, the researcher loses much control over the arrangement. This means there is an added danger that things can go wrong. Through whatever means, though, the researcher needs to try to get a *location for the interview* in which they will not be disturbed, which offers privacy, which has fairly good acoustics and which is reasonably quiet. This can prove to be a pretty tall order in places like busy organizations, schools, hospitals and so on. But at least the desirability of such a venue should be conveyed to the person arranging the interview room.

Within the interview room, it is important to be able to set up the *seating arrangements* in a way that allows comfortable interaction between the researcher and the interviewee(s). In a one-to-one interview the researcher should try to arrange seating so that the two parties are at a 90 degree angle to each other. This allows for eye contact without the confrontational feeling arising from sitting directly opposite the other person. With group interviews, it is important to arrange the seating to allow contact between all parties without putting the researcher in a focal position and without hiding individuals at the back of the group or outside the group.

6 Recording the interview

The researcher wishing to capture the discussion that happened during the interview can rely on memory. However, the human memory is rather unreliable as a research instrument. It is prone to partial recall, bias and error, as any psychologist will testify. Interviewers, instead, can call on other more permanent records of what was said.

Field notes

Under certain circumstances researchers will need to rely on field notes written soon after the interview or actually during the interview. Sometimes interviewees will decline to be tape-recorded. This means that what was actually said will always remain a matter of recollection and interpretation. There will never be an objective record of the discussion. This suits the needs of certain interviewees, particularly where the discussion touches on sensitive issues, commercially, politically or even personally. Notes taken during the interview, however, offer a compromise in such situations. The interviewer is left with some permanent record of his or her interpretation of what was said, and can refer back to this at various later stages to refresh the memory. The notes also

Field notes
These can be made during the interview itself or, if the situation demands, immediately afterwards.

Checklist: preparation for interviews

When preparing to conduct interviews you should feel confident about answering 'yes' to the following questions:

1 Is the interview method appropriate in terms of:
- ▶ the *topic* of the research? ☐
- ▶ the need for detailed information? ☐
- ▶ access to informants? ☐
- ▶ necessary time and funding for the interviews? ☐

2 Do I have a clear vision of the *issues to be discussed* during the interview? ☐

3 Can the interviews be *scheduled in good time* to allow for the subsequent transcription and analysis of the data? ☐

4 Am I confident that 'self' and *personal identity* (age, sex etc.) will not prove a major obstacle to getting informants to respond openly and honestly during interviews? ☐

5 Have I obtained *authorization* from the appropriate authorities to conduct the interviews? ☐

6 Am I clear about what criterion has been used for *the selection of informants* (random selection, key informants)? ☐

7 Has a suitable *time and place for the interview* been arranged (privacy, acoustics etc.)? ☐

8 Is there a definite *time limit* for the interviews and are all parties to the interview aware of this limit? ☐

9 Has consideration been given to the most suitable mode of *self-presentation* (style of clothes, degree of formality etc.)? ☐

© M. Denscombe, *The Good Research Guide*. Open University Press.

act as some form of permanent record. However, from the interviewee's point of view, it is always possible to deny that certain things were said and to argue that the researcher might have 'misinterpreted' a point should the interviewee wish to dissociate himself or herself from the point as some later date. A crucial advantage of taking field notes at an interview, however, is that they can fill in some of the relevant information that the audio tape-recording alone might miss. Field notes can cover information relating to the context of the location, the climate and atmosphere under which the interview was conducted, clues about the intent behind the statements and comments on aspects of non-verbal communication as they were deemed relevant to the interview.

Tape-recording

Audio tape-recording offers a permanent record and one that is complete in terms of the speech that occurs. It lends itself to being checked by other researchers. However, it captures only speech, and misses non-verbal communication and other contextual factors.

Audio tape-recording
This is the standard method of capturing interview data.

Video tape-recording requires more bulky equipment and tends to be more intrusive in terms of the interview setting. It captures many non-verbal as well as verbal communications, and offers the most complete record of events during the interview. As with audio recording, it provides a permanent record which can be checked by other researchers.

In practice, most research interviewers rely on *audio tape-recording backed up by written field notes*. While some researchers can muster the resources and the enthusiasm to make video recordings, their use still tends to be the exception rather than the rule. It is not the cost factor which explains this, because video cameras are not prohibitively expensive. Generally, it is the intrusiveness of video recording on the setting. Audio tape-recording can be disconcerting enough for informants, and the researcher needs to proceed with caution when broaching the issue of using the tape-recorder during the interview. At first people can feel rather threatened by it. Most people ease up after an initial period of hesitancy and, when used sensitively, the audio tape does not pose too much of a disturbance to most interview situations. It is worth stressing, though, that the disturbance will depend on each distinct situation and the researcher needs to make an assessment of its feasibility before embarking on its use. Video recording has all the more potential to disturb the setting – especially where the interviews take place 'in the field'.

Equipment

It is a cardinal sin to start an interview without having thoroughly checked out the equipment. This sounds obvious, but in the run-up to an interview it is all too easy to overlook such a basic chore. Remember, an interview is a one-off situation. If the equipment fails you can hardly expect the interviewee to run through the whole discussion again!

If the equipment fails, the interview fails.

Audio tape-recorders and video cameras need a dependable power source. In most cases of conducting interviews, particularly in the field, it is not possible to rely on a mains supply. Unless you can be positive that there is a suitable mains socket close by, it is best to plan on using batteries. The researcher should have a good supply of batteries and, most importantly, be sure that the batteries are fully charged for each new interview.

The equipment itself needs to be of a good enough quality to give the best possible reproduction of sound (and picture). Efforts to transcribe a tape will be confounded where the recording is faint, fuzzy and full of hisses.

Audio tapes should be chosen so that they do not come to the end of a side in the middle of an interview. It is disconcerting and disruptive for the researcher to stop the interview so that he or she can change the tape. To do this also serves to remind the interviewee about the presence of the tape-recorder just at a stage when he or she might be relaxing and opening up. The advice here is to use tapes that are long enough *on each side* to cope with the planned duration of the interview. Dictaphone (miniature) tapes can pose a problem here. There is a case to be made for using equipment which uses the larger standard audio tapes that cover 45 minutes a side (i.e. 90-minute tapes).

Hard and fast advice on tapes and equipment is difficult to give, because technological advances can make such advice quickly out of date. What can be said at a general level is that the researcher should:

▶ use equipment which is good enough to supply adequate sound (and visual) reproduction;

▶ be certain that their equipment is functioning well before the interview;

▶ have a reliable power source plus back-up in case of emergency;

▶ choose tapes which are long enough on each side to cover the planned duration of the interview without the need to 'reload' the recorder.

The process of recording

At one level, the audio tape-recorder and the video camera are reliable research instruments. They capture the proceedings on a permanent record, and they provide an objective record of the proceedings in the sense that, in themselves, they have no values and no vested interest in the outcome of the interview. *These research instruments do not interpret the events, they simply store them.*

However, it would be naive to assume that they therefore have no impact on the nature of what emerges as the 'interview data'. They *do* have an impact, in two ways. First, they are selective in terms of what they capture. Audio tapes only capture the verbal utterances and necessarily miss any non-verbal communication and visual signals which occur during the interview. That is why researchers are encouraged to make field notes to fill in the missing bits as far as possible. Video-recording manages to capture more of the totality of the interview. Yet, even here, the camera cannot capture all the action. The position of the camera, its breadth of focus etc. will still impose limitations on how far this method can store a complete record of events.

Second, the very presence of the recording equipment can have an impact on the interview situation. Informants will vary in the extent to which they are affected by the tape-recorder or camera. Some will be shy and nervous, others less so. It is generally the case that people become less conscious of the recording equipment the longer the interview lasts. None the less, *the process of recording has a bearing on the freedom with which people speak, and the visual appearance of the equipment serves to remind informants of the fact that they are being recorded.*

7 Interview skills

The good interviewer needs to be attentive. This may sound obvious, but it is all too easy to lose the thread of the discussion because the researcher needs to be monitoring a few other things while listening closely to what the informant has to say: writing the field notes, looking for relevant non-verbal communication, checking that the tape-recorder is working.

The good interviewer is sensitive to the feelings of the informant. This is not just a matter of social courtesy, though that is certainly a worthy aspect of it. It is also a skill which is necessary for getting the best out of an interview. Where the interviewer is able to empathize with the informant and to gauge the feelings of the informant, he or she will be in a better position to coax out the most relevant information.

The good interviewer is able to tolerate silences during the talk, and knows when to shut up and say nothing. Anxiety is the main danger. Fearing that the interview might be on the verge of breaking down, the researcher can feel the need to say something quickly to kick-start the discussion. Worrying about cramming in every possible gem of wisdom in the allotted time, the interviewer can be inclined to rush the informant on quickly to the next point. But, most of all, feeling uncomfortable when the conversation lapses into silence, the interviewer can be all too quick to say something when a more experienced interviewer would know that the silence can be used as a wonderful resource during interviews (see below).

The good interviewer is adept at using prompts. Although silences can be productive, the interviewer needs to exercise judgement on this. There are times during an interview when the researcher may feel that it is necessary to spur the informant to speak. Listed below are some examples of how this can be done. What the examples share is a degree of subtlety. It is not normally acceptable for research interviewers to *demand* that the informant answers the questions. Research interviews are not police interviews. The idea is to nudge the informant gently into revealing their knowledge or thoughts on a specific point.

The good interviewer is adept at using probes. There are occasions during interview when the researcher might want to delve deeper into a topic rather than let the discussion flow on to the next point. An informant might make a point in passing which the researcher thinks should be explored in more detail. Some explanation might be called for, or some justification for a comment. Some apparent inconsistency in the informant's line of reasoning might be detected, an inconsistency which needs unravelling. Examples of how this can be done are listed below. Again, they attempt to be subtle and avoid an aggressive stance.

The good interviewer is adept at using checks. One of the major advantages of interviews is that they offer the researcher the opportunity to check that he or she has understood the informant correctly. As an ongoing part of the normal talk during interviews, the researcher can present a summary of what he or she thinks the informant has said, which the informant can then confirm as an accurate understanding, or can correct it if it is felt to be a misunderstanding of what has been said. Such checks can be used at strategic points during the interview as a way of concluding discussion on one aspect of the topic.

With group interviews, the good researcher manages to let everyone have a say. It is vital to avoid the situation where a dominant personality hogs the discussion and bullies others in the group to agree with his (less often her) opinion.

Tactics for interviews: prompts, probes and checks

Remain silent	(prompt)
Repeat the question	(prompt)
Repeat the last few words spoken by the informant	(prompt)
Offer some examples	(prompt)
Ask for an example	(probe)
Ask for clarification	(probe)
Ask for more details	(probe)
Summarize their thoughts ('So, if I understand you correctly . . . What this means, then, is that . . .')	(check)

The good interviewer is non-judgemental. As the researcher enters the interview situation he or she should, as far as is possible, suspend personal values and *adopt a non-judgemental stance* in relation to the topics covered during the interview. This means not only biting your lip on occasion, but also taking care not to reveal disgust, surprise or pleasure through facial gestures. The good researcher must also *respect the rights of the interviewee.* This means accepting if a person simply does not wish to tell you something and knowing when to back off if the discussion is beginning to cause the interviewee particular embarrassment or stress. This is a point of personal sensitivity and research ethics.

8 Conducting the interview

In the intensity of a research interview it is not easy to attend to all the points that should be remembered and, in any case, interviews are 'live' events which require the interviewer to adjust plans as things progress. Nevertheless, there are some pretty basic formalities which need to be observed. There are also a number of skills the researcher should exercise and, despite the fluid nature of interviews, it is worth spelling out a list of things that go towards a good interview.

Introduction and formalities

At the beginning there should be the opportunity to say 'Hello', to do some introductions, to talk about the aims of the research and to say something about the origins of the researcher's own interest in the topic. During the initial phase, there should also be confirmation that you have permission to tape-record the discussion and reassurances about the confidentiality of comments made during the interview. The aim is to set the tone for the rest of the interview – normally a relaxed atmosphere in which the interviewee feels free to open up on the topic under consideration. *Trust* and *rapport* are the keywords.

During the pre-interview phase, the interviewer should do two other things:

▶ prepare the recording equipment;

▶ as far as possible, arrange the seating positions to best advantage.

Starting the interview

The first question takes on a particular significance for the interview. It should offer the interviewee the chance to settle down and relax. For this reason it is normally good practice to *kick off with an 'easy' question*: something on which the interviewee might be expected to have well formulated views and something that is quite near the forefront of their mind. Two tactics might help here.

▶ Ask respondents, in a general way, about themselves and their role as it relates to the overall area of the interview. This allows the researcher to collect valuable *background information about informants* while, at the same time, letting informants start off by covering familiar territory.

▶ Use some 'trigger' or 'stimulus' material, so that the discussion can relate to something concrete, rather than launch straight into abstract ideas.

Monitoring progress

During the interview, the researcher should keep a discreet eye on the time. The good researcher needs to wind things up within the allotted time and will have covered most of the key issues during that time. While doing this, the good interviewer also needs to attend to the following things during the progress of the interview itself.

▶ *Identify the main points being stated by the interviewee* and the priorities as expressed by the interviewee. With group interviewers, what consensus is emerging about the key points?

▶ Look for the underlying logic of what is being said by the informant. *The interviewer needs to 'read between the lines'* to decipher the rationale lying beneath the surface of what is being said. The interviewer should ask 'What are they really telling me here?' and, perhaps more significantly, 'What are they *not* mentioning?'

▶ *Look for inconsistencies* in the position being outlined by the respondent. If such inconsistencies exist, this does not invalidate the position. Most people have inconsistencies in their opinions and feelings on many topics. However, such inconsistencies will be worth probing as the interview progresses to see what they reveal.

▶ Pick up clues about whether the informant's answers involve an element of *boasting* or are answers intended to *please the interviewer*.

▶ *Be constantly on the look out for the kind of answer which is a fob-off.*

▶ *Get a feel for the context* in which the discussion is taking place. The priorities expressed by the interviewee might reflect events immediately prior to the interview, or things about to happen in the near future. They might be 'issues of the moment', which would not assume such importance were the interview to be conducted a few weeks later. The researcher needs to be sensitive to this possibility and find out from the interviewee if there are events which are influencing priorities in this way.

▶ Keep a suitable level of eye contact throughout the interview and *make a note of non-verbal communication* which might help a later interpretation of the interview talk.

Finishing the interview

Interviews can come to an end because the interviewee has run out of things to say and the interviewer cannot goad any more information from the person. This is not a good state of affairs unless the interview has no outside time limit. It is better for the interview to come to a close in some orderly fashion guided by the interviewer. Having kept an eye on the time, and having ensured that most of the required areas for discussion have been covered, the interviewer should draw events to a close making sure that:

▶ the interviewee is invited to raise any points that they think still need to be covered and have not been covered so far;

▶ normal courtesies are extended to the interviewee for having given up the time to participate in the interview.

Notes on the interview

Researchers should make notes on an interview as a complement to a tape-recording. During the interview itself, if it is possible, the researcher should write down as field notes any impressions he or she might have about the situation. The ambience, significant bits of non-verbal communication, the things the tape-recorder cannot capture: these are the things that need to be noted by the researcher and kept alongside the tape when it comes to using that tape for analysis. As soon as possible after the interview, notes should be written up covering the physical context of the interview and any other impressions the researcher might have about the interview and the situation.

9 Transcribing the interview

Audio tapes

There might be a temptation to regard transcribing audio tapes as a straight-forward process. In practice, researchers soon find that it is not. First of all, it is very time-consuming. For every hour of talk on a tape it will take several more to transcribe it. The actual time will depend on the clarity of the tape-recording itself, the availability of transcription equipment and the typing speed of the researcher. When you are planning interview research, it is important to bear this in mind. From the point of view of the project researcher, the process of *transcribing needs to be recognized as a substantial part of the method*

Transcription of the tapes is generally far more time-consuming than the actual collection of the data.

Checklist for evaluating an interview ✓

When evaluating an interview you should feel confident about answering 'yes' to the following questions:

❶ Were the necessary *formalities observed at the start* (introductions, confidentiality etc.)? ☐

❷ Were the *rights of the informant* respected (consent, sensitivity)? ☐

❸ Were *relevant details* about the informant collected? ☐

❹ Did I exercise a suitable level of *control* over the progress of the interview (time, agenda)? ☐

❺ Was a *non-judgemental stance* maintained towards the informant's answers? ☐

❻ Was the discussion monitored appropriately in terms of:
- ▶ informant's *key points*? ☐
- ▶ reading between the lines? ☐
- ▶ trying to identify any inconsistencies? ☐
- ▶ being aware of the 'fob-off' answer? ☐
- ▶ looking for boastful or exaggerated answers? ☐
- ▶ looking for the answer simply aimed to please the interviewer? ☐

❼ Were field notes taken about:
- ▶ the impact of the *context*? ☐
- ▶ relevant *non-verbal communication* (gestures etc.)? ☐

❽ Were *prompts, probes and checks* used to good effect where appropriate? ☐

❾ Were the appropriate *courtesies* given at the end (thanks, reassurances)? ☐

© M. Denscombe, *The Good Research Guide*. Open University Press.

of interviewing and not to be treated as some trivial chore to be tagged on once
the real business of interviewing has been completed.

The value of transcription

The process of transcription is certainly laborious. However, it is also a very valuable part of the research, because it brings the researcher 'close to the data'. The
process brings the talk to life again, and is a real asset when it comes to using
interviews for qualitative data. Added to this, the end-product of the process
provides the researcher with a form of data that is far easier to analyse than an
audio tape. It is easier to flick through pages of text to pick out the interesting
sections than it is to move back and forth through a tape-recording. When the
tape has been transcribed into a text file, there are a growing number of computer packages specifically designed to help the researcher to analyse the data.

 Link up with **Computer-aided analysis of qualitative data, p. 218**

Annotations

When transcribing a tape, the researcher should put informal notes and comments alongside the interviewee's words. These annotations can be based on
the memories that come flooding back during the process of transcribing.
They should also draw on field notes taken during the interview or notes made
soon afterwards about the interview. They should include observations about
the ambience of the interview and things like gestures, outside interferences,
uncomfortable silences or other feelings that give a richer meaning to the
words that were spoken. These annotations should be placed in a special
column on the page.

Line numbering and coding

Each line in the transcript is given a unique line number, so that parts of the
data can be identified and located precisely and quickly. The researcher codes
the material, and it is useful to leave a column on the sheet of paper to allow
for this. There can be more than one code placed against a piece of speech if
the words cover more than one area which the researcher has identified as 'of
interest' and which has been allocated a unique code to represent an issue, a
topic or a meaning.

Problems of transcription

The difficulty of transcribing a taped interview stems principally from three
things.

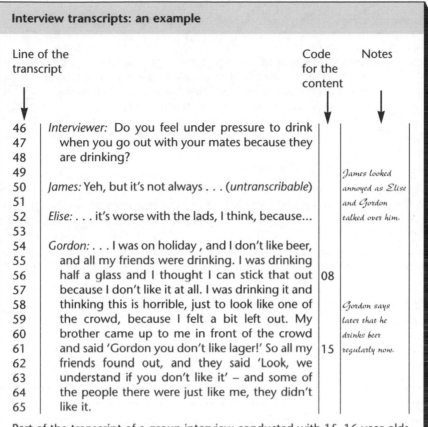

Interview transcripts: an example

Line of the transcript →   Code for the content →   Notes →

Line	Transcript	Code	Notes
46	*Interviewer:* Do you feel under pressure to drink		
47	when you go out with your mates because they		
48	are drinking?		
49			*James looked*
50	*James:* Yeh, but it's not always . . . (*untranscribable*)		*annoyed as Elise*
51			*and Gordon*
52	*Elise:* . . . it's worse with the lads, I think, because...		*talked over him.*
53			
54	*Gordon:* . . . I was on holiday , and I don't like beer,		
55	and all my friends were drinking. I was drinking		
56	half a glass and I thought I can stick that out	08	
57	because I don't like it at all. I was drinking it and		
58	thinking this is horrible, just to look like one of		*Gordon says*
59	the crowd, because I felt a bit left out. My		*later that he*
60	brother came up to me in front of the crowd		*drinks beer*
61	and said 'Gordon you don't like lager!' So all my	15	*regularly now.*
62	friends found out, and they said 'Look, we		
63	understand if you don't like it' – and some of		
64	the people there were just like me, they didn't		
65	like it.		

Part of the transcript of a group interview conducted with 15–16-year-olds about peer pressure and alcohol consumption. The names have been changed.

Notice how, typical of a group interview, more than one person is trying to talk at once. Elise cuts across James, and then gets interrupted in turn by Gordon, who manages to hold the spotlight for a moment or two. When more than one person is talking at a time it makes transcription difficult, because it is hard to capture on tape what is being said. It tends to become something of a cacophony.

The recorded talk is not always easy to hear

Especially with group interviews, but also with one-to-one versions, there can be occasions when more than one person speaks at the same time, where outside noises interfere or where poor audio quality itself makes transcribing the words very difficult. There is a fine dividing line here between the need to ditch these parts of the interview records and disregard them as worthwhile data, and the need to exercise some reasonable interpretation about what was actually said.

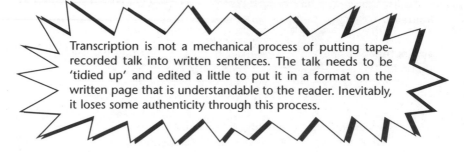

Transcription is not a mechanical process of putting tape-recorded talk into written sentences. The talk needs to be 'tidied up' and edited a little to put it in a format on the written page that is understandable to the reader. Inevitably, it loses some authenticity through this process.

People do not always speak in nice finite sentences

Normally, the researcher needs to add punctuation and a sentence structure to the talk, so that a reader can understand the sequence of words. The talk, in a sense, needs to be reconstructed so that it makes sense in a written form. This process takes time – and it also means that the crude data get cleaned up a little by the researcher so that they can be intelligible to a readership who were not present at the time of the recording.

Intonation, emphasis and accents used in speech are hard to depict on a transcript

There are established conventions which allow these to be added to a written transcript, but the project researcher is unlikely to be able to devote the neces-sary time to learning these conventions. The result is that interview transcripts in small-scale research are generally based on the words and the words alone, with little attempt to show intonation, emphasis and accents. This conse-quence is that, in practice, the data are stripped of some of their meaning in transcription.

10 How do you know if the informant is telling the truth?

This is a crucial question facing the researcher who uses interview data. When the interview is concerned with gathering information of a factual nature, the researcher can make some checks to see if the information is broadly corrobo-rated by other people and other sources. When the interview concerns matters such as the emotions, feelings and experiences of the interviewee, it is a lot more difficult to make such checks. Ultimately, there is no absolute way of veri-fying what someone tells you about their thoughts and feelings. Researchers are not 'mind readers'. But there are still some practical checks researchers can make to gauge the credibility of what they have been told. It should be stressed, though, that these are not watertight methods of detecting false statements given during interviews. They are practical ways of helping the researcher to avoid being a gullible dupe who accepts all that he or she is told at face value. They help the researcher to 'smell a rat'. By the same token, if the follow-ing checks are used, the researcher can have greater confidence in the interview data, knowing that some effort has been made to ensure the validity of the data.

Checking the transcript with the informant

Where possible, the researcher should go back to the interviewee with the transcript to check with that person that it is an accurate statement. Now, of course, checking for accuracy is not strictly what is going on here. Unless the interviewer also sends a copy of the tape, the interviewee has no way of knowing if what appears on the transcript is actually what was said. The point of the exercise is more to do with 'putting the record straight'. If the researcher is solely concerned with gathering facts from the interview, this is an opportunity to ensure that the facts are correct and that the interviewer has got the correct information. That is a nice safeguard. If, alternatively, the interview is concerned with a person's emotions, opinions and experiences, the exercise invites the interviewee to confirm that what was said at the time of the interview was what was really meant, and not said 'in the heat of the moment'. Either way, there is an initial check on the accuracy of the data.

Check the data with other sources

The researcher should make efforts to corroborate the interview data with other sources of information on the topic. *Triangulation* should be used. Documents and observations can provide some back-up for the content of the interview, or can cast some doubt on how seriously the interview data should be taken. Interview content can even be checked against other interviews to see if there is some level of consistency. The point is that interview data should not be taken at face value if it is at all possible to confirm or dispute the statements using alternative sources.

 Link up with **Triangulation, p. 83**

Check the plausibility of the data

Some people are interviewed specifically because they are in a position to know about the things that interest the researcher. The 'key players' are picked out precisely because they are specialists, experts, highly experienced – and their testimony carries with it a high degree of credibility. This is not necessarily the case with those chosen for interview on some other grounds. When assessing the credibility of information contained in an interview, the researcher needs to gauge how far an informant might be expected to be in possession of the facts and to know about the topic being discussed. The researcher should ask if it is reasonable to suppose that such a person would be in a position to comment authoritatively on the topic – or is there a chance that they are talking about something of which they have little knowledge?

Look for themes in the transcript(s)

Where possible, avoid basing findings on one interview – look for themes emerging from a number of interviews. Where themes emerge across a number of interviews, the researcher does not have to rely on any one transcript as the sole source of what is 'real' or 'correct'. A recurrent theme in interviews indicates that the idea/issue is something which is shared among a wider group, and therefore the researcher can refer to it with rather more confidence than any idea/issue which stems from the words of one individual.

11 The analysis of interview data

After having transcribed the audio-recording and made some checks on the validity of the data, the researcher is faced with the task of analysing the material. This means deciding what meaning can be attributed to the words and what implications the words have in relation to the topic that is being investigated. If the researcher prefers to use a quantitative approach to the analysis of the transcript, he or she will use *content analysis*.

If, on the other hand, the researcher prefers to use a qualitative approach, he or she can use the procedures outlined in Chapter 11.

Link up with **Content analysis, p. 167**

When analysing the data, the researcher should be aware of the role of the 'self' in the interview process. The researcher inevitably uses some amount of judgement and interpretive skills throughout the whole process of interviewing: in the conduct of the interview itself, in the transformation of the discussion into transcript data and in the analysis of the data. This is why *it is good research practice to acknowledge the impact of the researcher's own identity and values in the analysis of interview data.*

12 The use of interview extracts in research reports

Extracts from transcripts can be used to good effect in social research. For one thing, they can be interesting in their own right, giving the reader a flavour of the data and letting the reader 'hear' *the points as stated by the informants.* For another, they can be used as a *piece of evidence* supporting the argument that is being constructed in the report by the researcher. It is very unlikely, however, that an extract from an interview transcript can be presented as proof of a point. There are two reasons for this.

▶ *The significance of extracts from transcripts is always limited by the fact that they are, to some extent, presented out of context.* Extracts, as the very word itself suggests, are pieces of the data that are plucked from their context within the rest of the taped interview. This opens up the possibility that the quote could be taken 'out of context'. Everyone knows the danger of being quoted out of context. The meaning of the words is changed by the fact that they are not linked to what came before and what was said after. The shrewd researcher will try to explain to the reader the context within which the extract arose but, inevitably, there is limited opportunity to do this in research reports.

▶ *The process of selecting extracts involves a level of judgement and discretion on the part of the researcher.* The selection of which parts of the transcript to include is entirely at the discretion of the researcher, and this inevitably limits the significance which can be attached to any one extract. It is an editorial decision which reflects the needs of the particular research report. How does the reader know that it was a fair selection, representative of the overall picture?

As a result, in the vast majority of reports produced by project researchers extracts will serve as illustrations of a point and supporting evidence for an argument – nothing more and nothing less. It is important that the project researcher is aware of this when using extracts, and avoids the temptation to present quotes from interviewees as though they stand in their own right as unequivocal proof of the point being discussed.

Having made this point, there are some things the researcher can do to get the best out of the extracts that are selected.

▶ Use quotes and extracts verbatim. Despite the points above about the difficulty of transcribing tapes, the researcher should be as literal as possible when quoting people. Use the exact words.

▶ Change the names to ensure anonymity (unless you have their explicit permission to reveal the person's identity).

▶ Provide some details about the person you are quoting, without endangering their anonymity. The general best advice here is to provide sufficient detail to distinguish informants from one another and to provide the reader with some idea of relevant background factors associated with the person, but to protect the identity of the person you quote by restricting how much information is given (e.g. teacher A, female, school 4, geography, mid-career).

▶ Try to give some indication of the context in which the quotation arose. Within the confines of a research report, try to provide some indication of the context of the extract so that the meaning *as intended* comes through. As far as it is feasible, the researcher should address the inevitable problem of taking the extract 'out of context' by giving the reader some guidance on the background within which the statement arose.

13 Advantages of interviews

▶ *Depth of information*. Interviews are particularly good at producing data which deal with topics in depth and in detail. Subjects can be probed, issues pursued and lines of investigation followed over a relatively lengthy period.

▶ *Insights*. The researcher is likely to gain valuable insights based on the depth of the information gathered and the wisdom of 'key informants'.

▶ *Equipment*. Interviews require only simple equipment and build on conversation skills which researchers already have.

▶ *Informants' priorities*. Interviews are a good method for producing data based on informants' priorities, opinions and ideas. Informants have the opportunity to expand their ideas, explain their views and identify what *they* regard as the crucial factors.

▶ *Flexibility*. As a method for data collection, interviews are probably the most flexible. Adjustments to the lines of enquiry can be made during the interview itself. Interviewing allows for a developing line of enquiry.

▶ *Validity*. Direct contact at the point of the interview means that data can be checked for accuracy and relevance as they are collected.

▶ *High response rate*. Interviews are generally prearranged and scheduled for a convenient time and location. This ensures a relatively high response rate.

▶ *Therapeutic*. Interviews can be a rewarding experience for the informant. Compared with questionnaires, observation and experiments, there is a more personal element to the method, and people tend to enjoy the rather rare chance to talk about their ideas at length to a person whose purpose is to listen and note the ideas without being critical.

14 Disadvantages of interviews

▶ *Time-consuming*. Analysis of data can be difficult and time-consuming. Data preparation and analysis is 'end-loaded' compared with, for instance, questionnaires which are pre-coded and where data are ready for analysis once they have been collected. The transcribing and coding of interview data is a major task for the researcher which occurs after the data have been collected.

▶ *Data analysis*. The interview method tends to produce *non-standard responses*. Semi-structured and unstructured interviews produce data that are not pre-coded and have a relatively open format.

▶ *Reliability*. The impact of the interviewer and of the context means that consistency and objectivity are hard to achieve. The data collected are, to an extent, unique owing to the specific context and the specific individuals involved. This has an adverse effect on *reliability*.

▶ *Interviewer effect*. The data from interviews are based on what people say rather than what they do. The two may not tally. What people say they do, what they say they prefer and what they say they think cannot automatically be assumed to reflect the truth. In particular, interviewee statements can be affected by the identity of the researcher.

▶ *Inhibitions*. The tape-recorder (or video-recorder) can inhibit the informant. Although the impact of the recording device tends to wear off quite quickly, this is not always the case. The interview is an artificial situation (as, of course, are experiments) where people are speaking for the record and on the record, and this can be daunting for certain kinds of people.

▶ *Invasion of privacy*. Tactless interviewing can be an invasion of privacy and/or upsetting for the informant. While interviews can be enjoyable, the other side of the coin is that the personal element of being interviewed carries its own kinds of dangers as well.

▶ *Resources*. The *costs* of interviewer's time, of travel and of transcription can be relatively high if the informants are geographically widespread.

Checklist for the use of interview data ✓

When using interview data for your research you should feel confident about answering 'yes' to the following questions:

1 Have relevant details been given about the *context* of the interviews (location, prior events, ambience etc.)? ☐

2 Has consideration been given to the effect of the recording equipment on the *openness* with which informants replied? ☐

3 Was it possible to *transcribe* the interview talk without too many gaps and without too much 'tidying up' of the talk to make it intelligible? ☐

4 Has the transcription of the interview been checked for accuracy and meaning with the interviewee? ☐

5 Is the analysis based on 'themes' running through a number of interviews? ☐

6 Are the quotations used in the report of the research attributed to a category of person without revealing specific identities of the informants? ☐

7 Are the quotations that are used in the report of the research presented in the *context*:
  ▶ of the surrounding talk? ☐
  ▶ of the social situation of the interview itself? ☐

8 Has an account of the researcher's *self* been provided with a consideration of how it might have affected the:
  ▶ interaction during the interview? ☐
  ▶ interpretation of the data? ☐

► ▷ ▷ **8**

OBSERVATION

Observation offers the social researcher a distinct way of collecting data. It does not rely on what people *say* they do, or what they *say* they think. It is more direct than that. Instead, it draws on the direct evidence of the eye to witness events first hand. It is based on the premise that, for certain purposes, it is best to observe what actually happens.

There are essentially two kinds of observation research used in the social sciences. The first of these is *systematic* observation. Systematic observation has its origins in social psychology – in particular the study of interaction in settings such as school classrooms (Flanders 1970; Simon and Boyer 1970; Croll 1986). It is normally linked with the production of quantitative data and the use of statistical analysis. The second is *participant* observation. This is mainly associated with sociology and anthropology, and is used by researchers to infiltrate situations, sometimes as an undercover operation, to understand the culture and processes of the groups being investigated. It usually produces qualitative data.

These two methods might seem poles apart in terms of their origins and their use in current social research, but they share some vital characteristics.

► *Direct observation*. The obvious connection is that they both rely on direct observation. In this respect they stand together, in contrast to methods such as questionnaires and interviews, which base their data on what informants tell the researcher, and in contrast to documents where the researcher tends to be one step removed from the action.

► *Fieldwork*. The second common factor is their dedication to collecting data in real life situations – out there in the field. In their distinct ways, they both involve fieldwork. The dedication to fieldwork immediately identifies observation as an *empirical* method for data collection. As a method, it requires the researcher to go in search of information, first hand, rather than relying on secondary sources.

▶ *Natural settings*. Fieldwork observation – distinct from laboratory observations – occurs in situations which would have occurred whether or not
the research had taken place. The whole point is to observe things as they
normally happen, rather than as they happen under artificially created conditions such as laboratory experiments. There is a major concern to avoid
disrupting the *naturalness of the setting* when undertaking the research. In
this approach to social research, it becomes very important to minimize the
extent to which the presence of the researcher might alter the situation
being researched.

▶ *The issue of perception*. Systematic observation and participant observation
both recognize that the process of observing is far from straightforward.
Both are acutely sensitive to the possibility that researchers' perceptions of
situations might be influenced by personal factors and that the data collected could thus be unreliable. They tend to offer very different ways of
overcoming this, but both see it as a problem that needs to be addressed.

1 Perception and observation

Two researchers looking at the same event ought to have recorded precisely
the same things. Or should they? Using common sense, it might seem fairly
obvious that, as long as both researchers were present and able to get a good
vantage point to see all that was happening, the records of the events – the
data – should be identical. Yet in practice we know that this is unlikely to be
the case, very unlikely. In all probability, the two researchers will produce
different records of the thing they jointly witnessed.

Why should this be the case? Obviously, the competence of each individual
researcher is a factor which has to be taken into consideration. The powers of
observation, the powers of recall and the level of commitment of individual
researchers will vary, and this will have an effect on the observational data
that are produced.

The variation in records also reflects psychological factors connected to
memory and perception. Obviously, the research information on this area is
vast but, as far as the use of observation as a research method is concerned,
there are three things which are particularly important that emerge from the
work of psychologists on these topics.

First, they point to the frailties of human memory and the way that we
cannot possibly remember each and every detail of the events and situations
we observe. Basically, we forget most of what we see. But what we forget and
what we recall are not decided at random. There is a pattern to the way the
mind manages to recall certain things and forget others. There is *selective recall*.

Second, they point to the way the mind filters the information it receives
through the senses. It not only acts to reduce the amount of information, it
also operates certain 'filters' which let some kinds of information through to
be experienced as 'what happened', while simultaneously putting up barriers
to many others. There is *selective perception*.

Third, they point to experiments which show how these filters not only let in some information while excluding the rest, but also boost our sensitivity to certain signals depending on our emotional and physical state, and our past experiences. What we experience can be influenced to some extent by whether we are, for instance, very hungry, angry, anxious, frustrated, prejudiced etc. What we experience is shaped by our feelings at the moment and by the emotional baggage we carry around with us as a result of significant things that have happened to us during our lifetime. These things account for *accentuated perception*.

The selection and organization of stimuli, then, is far from random. In fact, there is a tendency to highlight some information and reject some other, depending on:

▶ *Familiarity*. We tend to see what we are *used* to seeing. If there is any ambiguity in what is being observed, we tend to interpret things according to frequent past experiences.

▶ *Past experiences*. Past experience 'teaches' us to filter out certain 'nasty' stimuli (avoidance learning) or exaggerate desirable things.

▶ *Current state*. Physical and emotional states can affect what is perceived by researchers. Physiological states such as hunger and thirst can influence the way we interpret what we 'see'. Emotions, anxieties and current priorities can likewise alter our perceptions.

Without delving too deeply into the psychology of perception, it is easy to appreciate that, as human beings, researchers do not simply observe and record the events they witness in some mechanical and straightforward fashion. Evidence in relation to memory and perception indicates that the mind acts as an intermediary between 'the world out there' and the way it is experienced by the individual. There is almost inevitably *an element of interpretation*.

2 Systematic observation and observation schedules

The psychology of memory and perception explains why the facts recorded by one researcher are very likely to differ from those recorded by another, and why different observers can produce different impressions of the situation. However, all this is rather worrying when it comes to the use of observation as a method for collecting data. It suggests that the data are liable to be inconsistent between researchers – too dependent upon the individual and the personal circumstances of each researcher. It implies that different observers will produce different data.

It is precisely this problem which is addressed by systematic observation and its use of an *observation schedule*. The whole purpose of the schedule is to minimize, possibly eliminate, the variations that will arise from data based on individual perceptions of events and situations. Its aim is to provide a framework for observation which *all* observers will use, and which will enable them to:

▶ be alert to the same activities and be looking out for the same things;

▶ record data systematically and thoroughly;

▶ produce data which are consistent between observers, with two or more researchers who witness the same event recording the same data.

To achieve these three aims, observation schedules contain a list of items that operate something like a checklist. The researcher who uses an observation schedule will monitor the items contained in the checklist and make a record of them as they occur. All observers will have their attention directed to the same things. The process of systematic observation then becomes a matter of measuring and recording how many times an event occurs, or how long some event continues. In this way, there will be a permanent record of the events which should be consistent between any researchers who use the schedule, because *what* is being observed is dictated by the items contained in the schedule. When researchers are properly trained and experienced, there should be what is called high 'inter-observer' reliability.

The value of findings from the use of an observation schedule will depend, however, on how appropriate the items contained in the schedule are for the situation. Precise measurements of something that is irrelevant will not advance the research at all. It is imperative, for this reason, that the items on the schedule are carefully selected. The findings will only be worth something if the items can be shown to be appropriate for the issues being investigated, and for the method of observation as well.

3 Creating an observation schedule

Literature review

Initially, the possible features of the situation which might be observed using a schedule can be identified on the basis of a literature review. Such a literature review will present certain things as worthy of inclusion, and should allow the researcher to prioritize those aspects of the situation to be observed. It would be nice to have a huge number of items in the schedule, but this is not practical. Researchers are limited by the speed and accuracy with which it is possible to observe and record events they witness. So the items for inclusion need to be restricted to just the *most* significant and *most* relevant, because it is simply not feasible to include everything. Previous research and previous theories provide the key to deciding which features of the situation warrant the focus of attention.

Types of events and behaviour to be recorded

Observers can measure what happens in a variety of ways. The choice will depend on the events themselves and, of course, the purpose to which the results will be put. Observations can be based on:

▶ *Frequency of events*. A count of the frequency with which the categories/items on the observation schedule occur.

▶ *Events at a given point in time*. At given intervals (for instance, 25 seconds) the observer logs what is happening at that instant. This might involve logging numerous things which happen simultaneously at that point.

▶ *Duration of events*. When instances occur they are timed, so that the researcher gets information on the total time for each category, and when the categories occurred during the overall time-block for the period of observation.

▶ *Sample of people*. Individuals can be observed for predetermined periods of time, after which the observer's attention is switched to another person in a rota designed to give representative data on all those involved in the situation.

Suitability for observation

When one is selecting the items for inclusion in the schedule there are seven conditions which need to be met. The things to be observed need to be:

▶ *Overt*. First and foremost, items should entail *overt behaviour* which is observable and measurable in a direct manner. Things like attitudes and thoughts need to be inferred by the researcher, and are not observable in a direct manner.

▶ *Obvious*. They should require a minimum of interpretation by the researcher. The researcher should have little need to decipher the action or fathom out whether an action fits one or another category.

▶ *Context independent*. Following from the point above, this means that the context of the situation should not have a significant impact on how the behaviour is to be interpreted.

▶ *Relevant*. They should be the most relevant indications of the thing to be investigated. It is important that the researcher chooses only valid indicators, things that are a good reflection of the things being studied.

▶ *Complete*. They should cover all possibilities. Care needs to be taken to ensure, as far as is possible, that the categories on the observation schedule cover the full range of possibilities and that there are not gaps which will become glaringly evident once the observation schedule is used in the field.

▶ *Precise*. There should be no ambiguity about the categories. They need to be defined precisely and there should be no overlap between them. There should be the most *relevant indicators* of the thing being investigated.

▶ *Easy to record*. They should occur with *sufficient regularity and sequence* for the observer to be able to log the occurrences accurately and fruitfully. If the category is something that is relatively rare, it will prove frustrating and wasteful of time to have a researcher – pen poised – waiting, waiting, waiting for something to happen. And if, like buses, the events then all come at once, the observer might well find it impossible to log all instances. There is a practical consideration here which affects the categories to be observed. (Choose one-at-a-time events, avoid simultaneously occurring events.)

Sampling and observation

When deciding what thing is to be observed, the researcher also needs to make a strategic decision concerning the kind of *sampling* to be used. Researchers using systematic observation generally organize their research around set *time-blocks of observation in the field*. For example, these might be one-hour chunks of time *in situ*. These time-blocks themselves need to be chosen so as to avoid any bias and to incorporate a representative sample of the thing in question. So, if the research were to be observations of interaction in school classrooms, the researcher would need to ensure that the research occurred across the full school week, the full school day and a cross-section of subjects. To confine observations to Friday afternoons, or to one subject such as history, would not provide an accurate picture across the board.

The same applies to the selection of *people* for inclusion in the study. To get a *representative* picture of the event or situation, the use of systematic observation can involve a deliberate selection of people to be observed, so that there is a cross-section of the whole research population. In the case of observation in a school classroom, for example, the researcher could identify in advance a sample according to the sex and ability of students, thus ensuring that the observations that take place are based on a representative sample.

Recording contextual factors

Precisely because the use of an observation schedule has the tendency to decontextualize the things it records, more advanced practice in this area has made a point of insisting that researchers collect information about relevant background matters whenever they use a schedule (Galton *et al.* 1980). Such background information helps to explain the events observed, and should be logged with the schedule results to help the observer understand the data he or she has collected.

Example of an observation schedule

For the purposes of illustration, consider an observation schedule intended for use in *art classes in a secondary school*. The art classes are the 'situation' for which the observation schedule needs to be designed. Its 'purpose' is to measure the amount of lesson time wasted by students queuing to clean their paint brushes in the sink.

Example of an observation schedule – *continued*

Its aim might be to provide quantitative, objective data in support of the art teacher's bid for resources to have a second sink installed in the art classroom. The simple observation schedule to be used in this context could take the following format.

Location: School A
Date: 28 April
Time: 11 a.m. to 12 noon

Identity of student	Student starts queuing	Student arrives at sink	Queuing time
Student Ann	11.15	11.15	0
Student Tom	11.15	11.18	3
Student David	11.15	11.20	5
Student Diane	11.16	11.23	7
Student Tony	11.17	11.24	7
Student Eileen	11.19	11.26	7
Student			
Student			
Student			

In this example, a decision has been made to record the duration of the event: queuing time. It would have been possible to record the number of occasions that students in the class queued, or to have noted at intervals of say 30 seconds over a one-hour period how many students were queuing at that moment. These would have provided slightly different kinds of results. If we were concerned with how queuing interrupted the concentration of students on a task it would have been more appropriate to record the frequency. Had the aim been to look at bottlenecks in the queuing, time sampling would have allowed the ebb and flow of students to the sink to be shown quite clearly. When the aim is to support the claim that students' time is wasted in queues for the sink, it is appropriate to record the total time spent in the queue.

The item in this example is suitably straightforward to observe. We would presume that standing in line is an obvious and observable form of behaviour and that, despite some occasions when students might not be solely concerned with getting their paint brushes clean when they join the queue (they might be socializing or wasting time deliberately), standing in line offers a fairly valid indicator of the thing that is of interest to the researcher: time wasted queuing.

4 Retaining the naturalness of the setting

With systematic observation, the issue of retaining the naturalness of the setting hinges on the prospect of the researcher fading into the background and becoming, to all intents and purposes, invisible. At first this might seem an implausible thing. Armed with a clipboard and pen, and looking like a 'time and motion' researcher, it would seem unlikely that such systematic observation could avoid disrupting the events it seeks to measure. However, those who engage in this style of research report that it is indeed possible to 'merge into the wallpaper' and have no discernible impact. They stress that to minimize the likelihood of disruption researchers should pay attention to three things:

▶ *Positioning*. Unobtrusive positioning is vital. But the researcher still needs to be able to view the whole arena of action.

▶ *Avoiding interaction*. The advice here is to be 'socially invisible', not engaging with the participants in the setting if at all possible.

▶ *Time on site.* The experience of systematic observers assures them that the longer they are 'on site', the more their presence is taken for granted and the less they have any significant effect on proceedings.

Link up with **Observer effect, p. 47**

5 Advantages of systematic observation

▶ *Direct data collection*. It directly *records what people do*, as distinct from that they say they do.

▶ *Systematic and rigorous*. The use of an observation schedule provides an answer to the problems associated with the selective perception of observers, and it appears to produce *objective* observations. The schedule effectively eliminates any bias from the current emotions or personal background of the observer.

▶ *Efficient*. It provides a means for collecting substantial amounts of data in a relatively *short timespan*.

▶ *Pre-coded data*. It produces *quantitative data* which are pre-coded and ready for analysis.

▶ *Reliability*. When properly established, it should achieve high levels of inter-observer reliability in the sense that two or more observers using a schedule should record very similar data.

Checklist for the use of observation schedules ✓

When using observation schedules you should feel confident about answering 'yes' to the following questions:

1 Has the observation schedule been *piloted*? ☐

2 Have efforts been made to minimize any disturbance to the *naturalness* of the setting caused by the presence of the observer? ☐

3 Do the planned periods for observation provide a *representative* sample (time, place, context)? ☐

4 Are the events/behaviour to be observed:
(a) sufficiently clear-cut and unambiguous to allow *reliable coding*? ☐
(b) the most *relevant indicators* for the purposes of the research? ☐

5 Is the schedule *complete* (incorporating all likely categories of events/behaviour)? ☐

6 Do the events/behaviour occur regularly enough to provide *sufficient data*? ☐

7 Does the schedule avoid multiple *simultaneous occurrences* of the event/behaviour which might prevent accurate coding? ☐

8 Is the *kind of sampling* (event/point/time) the most appropriate? ☐

9 Is there provision for the collection of *contextual information* to accompany the schedule data? ☐

© M. Denscombe, *The Good Research Guide.* Open University Press.

6 Disadvantages of systematic observation

▶ *Behaviour, not intentions.* Its focus on overt behaviour describes what happens, but not *why* it happens. It does not deal with the intentions that motivated the behaviour.

▶ *Oversimplifies.* It assumes that overt behaviours can be measured in terms of categories that are fairly straightforward and unproblematic. This is premised on the idea that the observer and the observed share an understanding of the overt behaviour, and that the behaviour has no double meaning, hidden meaning or confusion associated with it. As such, systematic observation has the *in-built potential to oversimplify*; to ignore or distort the subtleties of the situation.

▶ *Contextual information.* Observation schedules, by themselves, *tend to miss contextual information* which has a bearing on the behaviours recorded. It is not a holistic approach.

▶ *Naturalness of the setting.* Despite the confidence arising from experience, there remains a question mark about the observer's ability to fade into the background. Can a researcher with a clipboard and observation schedule really avoid disrupting the naturalness of the setting?

7 Participant observation

A classic definition of participant observation spells out the crucial characteristics of this approach, and the things which distinguish it from systematic observation.

> By participant observation we mean the method in which the observer participates in the daily life of the people under study, either openly in the role of researcher or covertly in some disguised role, observing things that happen, listening to what is said, and questioning people, over some length of time.
>
> (Becker and Geer 1957: 28)

As Becker and Geer indicate, the participant observer can operate in a completely covert fashion – like an undercover agent whose success depends on remaining undetected, whose purpose remains top secret. If no one knows about the research except the researcher, the logic is that no one will act in anything but a normal way. Preserving the *naturalness of the setting* is the key priority for participant observation. The principal concern is to minimize disruption so as to be able to see things as they normally occur – unaffected by any awareness that research is happening.

Another priority is to gain information about cultures or events which would remain hidden from view if the researcher were to adopt other methods. Such information could remain hidden for two reasons. Those involved in the culture or event could deliberately hide or disguise certain 'truths' on occasions when they are 'under the microscope'. In this case, covert participant observation reveals such events by doing the research secretly. Nothing will get hidden. The 'participant observer' will be able to see every-thing – the real happenings, warts and all. Alternatively, aspects of the culture/events could remain hidden because researchers using other methods would remain unaware of them. In this case, participant observation discloses things through the researcher's *experience* of participating in the culture or event. Only by experiencing things from the insider's point of view does the researcher become aware of the crucial factors explaining the culture or event. With participant observation the aim is to get *insights* into cultures and events – insights only coming to one who experiences things as *an insider*.

The insider experience puts participant observation in a particularly strong position to deal with the *meaning of actions* from the participants' point of view.

The nature of participant observation also allows the researcher to place greater *emphasis on depth* rather than breadth of data. In principle, participant observation can produce data which are better able than is the case with other methods to reflect the detail, the subtleties, the complexity and the inter-connectedness of the social world it investigates. In the spirit of anthropology, cultures and events are subject in the first instance to *detailed study*. Attention is given to intricate details of the social world being studied, and on the routine as well as the special and the extraordinary. Emphasis is placed on *holistic* understanding, in which the individual things being studied are exam-ined in terms of their relationships with other parts, and with the whole event or culture. And, in similar vein, things are examined in relation to their *context*. In those respects, participant observation scores highly in terms of the *validity* of the data.

Link up with **Ethnography, p. 68**

However, the participant observer role need not involve this total im-mersion. There are versions of participant observation in which the partici-pation element is rather different. Participation, in this sense, means 'being there' and 'in the middle of the action'. One possibility here is that the researcher's role as an observer is still kept secret. Particularly when contem-plating fieldwork in more salacious settings, this strategy can be very valuable (Humphreys 1970). O'Connell Davidson (1995), studying the working prac-tices of a prostitute, acted occasionally as a receptionist for Madame Desirée, thus allowing her to be part of the normal scene but also allowing a judicious distance from the heart of the action.

Another possibility involves hanging out with a group rather than becom-ing a member of that group. And this can allow the researcher to be open about his or her purpose – to get consent for the research – in a way that is denied to the total version of participant observation. Of course, the down-side of this is that the presence of the researcher can serve to disrupt the nat-uralness of the setting.

There are numerous variations which have been used that tinker with the extent of total participation and the extent of open observation, but the essential notion of participant observation revolves around the three possibilities:

▶ *Total participation*, where the researcher's role is kept secret. The researcher assumes the role of someone who normally participates in the setting. Consent cannot be gained for the research, which poses ethical problems.

▶ *Participation in the normal setting*, where the researcher's role may be known to certain 'gatekeepers', but may be hidden from most of those in the setting. The role adopted in this type of participant observation is chosen deliberately to permit observation without affecting the naturalness of the setting, but it also allows the researcher to keep a distance from the key group under study. This distance might be warranted on the grounds of propriety, or the researcher lacks the personal credentials to take on the role in question.

▶ *Participation as observer*, where the researcher's identity as a researcher is openly recognized – thus having the advantages of gaining informed consent from those involved – and takes the form of 'shadowing' a person or group through normal life, witnessing first hand and in intimate detail the culture/events of interest.

8 What to observe, what to record

Starting fieldwork

The researcher should not enter the field with pre-established hypotheses to be tested. The researcher is *there to learn about the situation*. The longer the researcher is able to spend 'on site' the better, because the longer he or she is part of the action the more can be learnt about the situation. Good participant observation demands that the researcher devotes *considerable time* to the fieldwork. This is not a hit and run research method. Time on site is needed to gain trust, to establish rapport and foster insights, insights that are the trade mark of participant observation as a research method.

Then there is the question of what to observe during the time on site. The researcher should start out being fairly non-selective in terms of what he or she observes. Before anything else, the participant observer should aim to *get an 'overall feel' for the situation*, and to do this he or she should engage in what can be termed 'holistic observation'.

Of course, getting a general feel for the setting, while it is valuable as a background scene-setting device, is really a prelude to more *focused observations*. As things emerge which appear to have particular significance or interest, observation will shift from the broad canvas of activity in the setting towards specific areas. Things which emerge as important, strange or unusual invite closer scrutiny.

Following from focused observations, the researcher might be able to undertake *special observations* which concentrate on aspects of the setting in which there appear to be things which are unexpected or contradictory. Attention can be focused upon things that, according to the observer's common sense, ought not to happen.

Finally, observations can try to *identify issues and problems* which participants themselves regard as crucial. The point is to observe instances which indicate how members of the setting see things – *their* views, beliefs and experiences.

Making field notes

The fieldwork researcher needs to translate the observations into some permanent record at the very earliest opportunity. This might be 'field notes' in the form of written records or tape-recorded memos. Whatever the form, the researcher doing fieldwork needs to develop a strategy for writing up field notes as soon as possible after the observation.

The need to do so stems from two things. First, the human memory is not only selective, but also frail. It is so easy to forget things, particularly the minor incidents and passing thoughts, if field notes are delayed for a matter of days, let alone weeks. *Field notes are urgent business.* The researcher needs to build into the research some provision to make the field notes on a regular and prompt basis. The second factor involved here is the general need to take field notes outside the arena of action. To take field notes while engaging in the action as a participant, to state the obvious, would be (a) to disrupt the naturalness of the setting and (b) to disclose the researcher's role as observer. As a general rule, then, participant observers need to establish occasions during fieldwork, or very soon afterwards, when they can make field notes in private and unknown to those being observed. The simplest strategy is to write up the field notes as soon as you get home – assuming that home is separate from the field being studied.

Ethics

Participant observation can pose particular ethical problems for the researcher. If 'total' participation is used, then those being studied will not be aware of the research or their role in it. They can hardly give 'informed consent'. The justification for such covert research cannot depend on consent, but draws instead on two other arguments. First, if it can be demonstrated that none of those who were studied suffered as a result of being observed, the researcher can argue that certain ethical standards were maintained. Second, and linked, if the researcher can show that the identities of those involved were never disclosed, again there is a reasonable case for saying that the participant observation was conducted in an ethical manner.

Whichever variant of participant observation is used, there is the possibility that confidential material might 'fall into the hands' of the researcher. Now, while this is true of most research methods, its prospects are exacerbated with the use of participant observation, owing to the closeness and intimacy of the researcher's role *vis-à-vis* those being researched. Confidential material might be disclosed inadvertently by someone who does not know the research interest of the participant. Or, possibly even more problematic, things might get revealed as a result of the trust and rapport developed between the researcher and those being observed. This could be true for any of the variants of participant observation. The ethical problem is whether to use such material and how to use it. And here the guidelines are quite clear: (a) any use of the material should ensure that no one suffers as a result, and (b) any use of the material should avoid disclosing the identities of those involved. Any departure from these guidelines would need very special consideration and justification.

9 Self, identity and participant observation

Equipment for research: the 'self'

One of the attractions of participant observation is that it hinges on the researcher's 'self', and does not call on much by the way of technical back-up in the form of gadgets or software. Nor does it tend to produce data that call for statistical analysis. *The key instrument of participant observation methods is the researcher as a person.*

This suggests that there is little in the way of 'entry costs' to act as a deterrent. Equipment costs are very low. There might appear to be no need for training (though this, of course, would be a fallacy). The researcher, it might seem, can jump right into the fieldwork and get on with it. However, as we see in the next sections, this dependence on the 'self' is not altogether a straightforward advantage.

Access to settings

There is the need to gain access. For participant observation this has a special twist. It is not necessarily to do with getting approval from relevant authorities or getting a 'gatekeeper' to help open doors to the necessary contacts and settings. As well as these, when engaging in the total version of participant observation there is a special, peculiar issue affecting access. If the researcher is to adopt a role in the setting then he or she needs to have the *necessary credentials* – both personal and qualifications.

To operate 'under cover' in a setting it is obvious that the researcher should not stand out like a sore thumb. Depending on the situation, this can effectively exclude many researchers from many roles. The age factor will bar most (all?) researchers from using participant observation to investigate student cultures in schools. Observing the setting as a teacher is a more likely prospect. Sex will offer other barriers. Male researchers will be hard pushed to use total participant observation for the study of, for example, cocktail waitresses. Observing as a barman in the setting is a more likely prospect. Black researchers will find it exceptionally difficult to infiltrate the Ku Klux Klan. The biological factors place severe constraints on access to situations. Skills and qualifications provide another barrier. To participate in the sense of adopting a role it is necessary to have the necessary skills and qualifications associated with that group. As Polsky (1967) points out, his study of pool hall hustling was only possible as a participant observer because – through a 'misspent youth' – he was already something of an accomplished pool player himself. The would-be researcher, however, might be reluctant or unable to achieve such a skill specifically for the purpose of a piece of research. Following the logic here, there are many, many roles which the researcher will be unable to adopt – from brain surgeon to tree surgeon – because of a lack of credentials.

Selecting a topic

In view of the constraints on access and the potential hazards of doing field-work as a full participant, there are two things which emerge that have a direct bearing on the selection of a topic.

▶ To a large extent, researchers who do participant observation have their topic selected for them on the basis of their pre-existing personal attributes. The 'choice' is rarely much of a free choice. The researcher's self – age, sex, ethnicity, qualifications, skills, social background and lifestyle – tends to direct the possibilities and provide *major constraints on the roles that can be adopted.*

▶ While it is arguably the most revealing and sensitive of research methods in the social sciences, it is also very demanding. *It is not a soft option.* The level of commitment needed for full participant observation can be far more than that demanded by other methods – commitment in terms of researcher's time and the degree to which the act of research invades the routine life of the researcher.

It is not surprising, then, that many of the fascinating studies emerge as 'one-offs' in which researchers have explored an area of social life for which they are uniquely qualified to participate through their own past experience. It is far more unusual to find examples where researchers have been deliberately employed to infiltrate a group (e.g. Festinger *et al.* 1956) or where researchers have consciously adopted a role which is alien to them and which involves danger and discomfort (e.g. Griffin 1962).

Another consequence of the restrictions to full participation is the decision of many social researchers to opt for the version of participant observation which is not 'total participation'. Participation in the setting and participation as observer offer approaches which side-step some of the dangers of total participation and offer a more palatable experience for the researcher on many occasions (e.g. Humphreys 1970; Whyte 1981; O'Connell Davidson 1995).

Going native

If the researcher has the necessary credentials and personal resources to gain access as a participant observer, he or she is then faced with the need to operate at two levels while in the setting. The success of participant observation relies on the researcher's ability, at one and the same time, to be a member of the group being studied *and* to retain a certain detachment which allows for the research observation aspect of the role. It is vital, in this respect, that the researcher does not lose sight of the original purpose for being there, does not get engulfed by the circumstances or swallowed up. The success of participant observation depends on being able to walk a tightrope between the involvement and passion associated with full participation and the cool detachment associated with research observation. If the researcher's self gets lost, this is rather like an anthropologist forgetting all about his or her research and settling down to live out his or her days as a member of the 'tribe' that he or she had originally set out to study: *'going native'*.

> Going native is an objectionable term, deservedly, for an objectionable phenomenon. It means over-identifying with the respondents, and losing the researcher's twin perspective of her own culture and, more importantly, of her 'research' and outlook.
>
> (Delamont 1992: 34)

Dangers of fieldwork

Doing participant observation can be dangerous. First, there is *physical danger*. As Lee (1995) points out, being physically injured while doing fieldwork is fairly unlikely but, depending on the circumstances, cannot be ignored as a possibility. It is a potential built into some forms of fieldwork. Danger lurks for anthropologists who travel in remote regions with inhospitable climates and treacherous terrains. In the early years of the century, evidently, there were instances where anthropologists were actually killed by the people they were studying (Howell 1990). Danger lurks for political scientists who operate in unstable societies where the rule of law is tenuous and civilians can get caught up in factional disputes. Danger lurks for sociologists and ethnographers when they make contact with groups whose activities are on the margins of, or even outside, the law. As they tap into the underworlds of drugs, prostitution, football hooligans, bikers, religious sects and the like, they take a risk.

Imagine, for the sake of illustration, that a researcher sees the need to investigate the culture surrounding the use of hard drugs by young people. The use of a participant observation approach would seem well suited to such a study. After all, the 'reality' of how, when and why hard drugs are used is hardly likely to emerge by using questionnaires or experiments. Interviews might be useful, but there is a *prima facie* case for participant observation as the method best suited to this particular issue. Provided that a researcher can overcome the first hurdle – to 'look the part' – the fieldwork then involves a range of dangers. There is actual physical danger. This is not just a reference to the prospect of getting mugged or assaulted, or of retribution if the cover is blown at some stage. There is also the danger posed by the lifestyle itself and the impact on health of a changed diet and changed accommodation. Changing lifestyle carries its own hazards. Of course, if the researcher were to become dependent on the use of hard drugs, the health consequences could be far more dramatic.

The fieldwork could involve a second danger: *legal prosecution*. Being 'part of the scene' when hard drugs are around immediately puts the researcher at risk of prosecution. There are no special immunities afforded to social researchers.

The researcher who chooses to engage in such fieldwork might also jeopardize his or her social well-being. The 'other' life he or she is called upon to live for the purposes of the research can have an adverse effect on domestic life, on relationships with others and on commitments to do with work and leisure which make up the 'normal' life of the researcher. *The researcher, in effect, needs to sustain two lifestyles*, and these may not be compatible. Being away from home, being out late and doing fieldwork at 'unsocial' hours can tax the patience of the nearest and dearest. (Let alone what the researcher does while in the field!)

> Researchers often work in settings made dangerous by violent conflict, or in situations where interpersonal violence and risk are commonplace. Indeed, in many cases it is the violence itself, or the social conditions and circumstances that produce it, that actively compel attention from the social scientist.
>
> (Lee 1995: 1)

Finally, there is the psychological danger resulting from the dual existence demanded of fieldwork such as this. The lifestyle, at its worst, can have something of a traumatic effect on the researcher, or can have a lasting or permanent effect on the researcher's personality.

10 Advantages of participant observation

▶ *Basic equipment.* Participant observation uses the researcher's 'self' as the main instrument of research, and therefore requires little by way of technical/statistical support.

▶ *Non-interference.* It stands a better chance of retaining the *naturalness* of the setting than other social research methods.

▶ *Insights*. It provides a good platform for gaining rich insights into social processes and is suited to dealing with complex realities.

▶ *Ecological validity*. The data produced by participant observation has the potential to be particularly context sensitive and ecologically valid.

▶ *Holistic*. Participant observation studies offer holistic explanations incorporating the relationships between various factors.

▶ *Subjects' points of view*. As a method of social research, participant observation is good for getting at *actors' meanings* as they see them.

11 Disadvantages of participant observation

▶ *Access*. There are *limited options* open to the researcher about which roles to adopt or settings to participate in.

▶ *Commitment*. Participant observation can be a very demanding method in terms of personal commitment and personal resources.

▶ *Danger*. Participant observation can be potentially *hazardous* for the researcher; physically, legally, socially and psychologically risky.

▶ *Reliability*. Dependence on the 'self' of the researcher and on the use of field notes as data leads to a lack of verifiable data. *Reliability is open to doubt*. Because participant observation relies so crucially on the researcher's 'self' as the instrument of research, it becomes exceedingly difficult to repeat a study to check for reliability. The dependence on field notes for data, constructed (soon) after fieldwork and based on the researcher's recollections of events, does little to encourage those who would want to apply conventional criteria for reliability to this method.

▶ *Representativeness of the data*. There are problems of generalizing from the research. The focal role of the researcher's 'self' and the emphasis on detailed research of the particular setting opens participant observation to the criticism that it is difficult to generalize from the findings. In one sense, this might hold water as a valid criticism. After all, the situations for research using participant observation are not selected on the grounds of being representative. As we have seen, they tend to be chosen on the basis of a mixture of availability and convenience. However, it might be argued that it is inappropriate to apply standard criteria of reliability and generalizability to this method.

▶ *Deception*. When researchers opt to conduct full participation, keeping their true identity and purpose secret from others in the setting, there are *ethical problems* arising from the absence of consent on the part of those being observed, and of deception by the researcher.

Checklist for participant observation

When undertaking participant observation you should feel confident about answering 'yes' to the following questions:

1 Is it clear which *type of participant observation* was used (total participation, participation in normal setting, participation as observer)? ☐

2 Is there evidence that the participant observation did not disturb the *naturalness* of the setting? ☐

3 Has consideration been given to the *ethics* of the fieldwork (secrecy, consent, confidentiality)? ☐

4 Has the influence of the researcher's *self-identity* been examined in terms of:
(a) the choice of fieldwork situation? ☐
(b) *access* to the setting? ☐
(c) the perception of events and cultures? ☐

5 Was sufficient *time* spent in the field:
(a) to allow trust and rapport to develop? ☐
(b) to allow detailed observations and an *in-depth* understanding of the situation (detail, context, interconnections)? ☐

6 Does the participant observation allow *insights* to events and meanings that would not be possible using other methods? ☐

7 Were *field notes* made at the time or soon after participating in the field? ☐

© M. Denscombe, *The Good Research Guide*. Open University Press.

9

DOCUMENTS

All investigations that lay claim to being 'research' should start off with a
literature review.

A literature review serves certain essential functions for research. It:

▶ shows that the researcher is aware of the available *existing work* already
undertaken in the area;

▶ identifies what the researcher takes to be the key *issues*, the crucial *questions*
and the obvious *gaps* in the current state of knowledge;

▶ provides *signposts* for the reader about 'where the research is coming from'
– it allows the reader to see which theories and principles have been influential in shaping the approach adopted in the proposed research.

The literature review, then, tries to establish the existing state of knowledge
in the area of proposed research and, drawing on this, to set out research questions which will help to advance our understanding of the topic. Its purpose
is to avoid repeating research that has been conducted already and to provide
a foundation on which to build new research. A word of clarification is warranted here, however. The idea that research 'builds upon' earlier work does
not necessarily imply that it extends, follows or approves of the earlier work.
It may be highly critical of the earlier work and even seek to discredit it. In
this case, the researcher still needs to review the literature to argue the weaknesses of the work and the benefits of an alternative approach. What is
unacceptable in terms of good research is to offer no such location of the proposed research within the existing knowledge in the area.

Quite apart from the literature review, there is another way in which documentary sources can be used for research. Rather than act as an introduction
to the research they can take on a central role as the actual thing that is to
be investigated. In this sense, documents can be treated as a source of *data in*

their own right – in effect an alternative to questionnaires, interviews or observation.

In the social sciences, library-based research, desk research, black letter research and archive research are all types of research in which the data comes from documents of one kind or another. They are typical of research in areas such as philosophy, social theory, law and history which rely heavily, if not exclusively, on documents as their key sources.

From the researcher's point of view, documentary research has two facets: one an essential part of any investigation and the other a specific method of investigation which offers itself as an alternative to questionnaires, interviews or observation as a means for collecting data. It can occur:

▶ to provide background information which is used as a platform for a research project;

▶ as a source of data in its own right.

1 Types of documentary data

The documentary sources identified below are *written* sources. There are alternative types of documents for research, which take the form of visual sources (pictures, artefacts etc.) and even sounds (music). These also constitute some form of 'document' which has a value for research but, because they are used relatively rarely within the social sciences, the comments are restricted to written forms of documents.

Books and journals

From the academic researcher's point of view, books and journals should be the first port of call. In principle, they contain the accumulated wisdom on which the research project should build, and also the latest cutting-edge ideas which can shape the direction of the research. Libraries provide a means for accessing the publications and, for most purposes, the costs to the researcher should not prove to be a deterrent.

Books and journals, as with any other source of data used for research purposes, need to be assessed in terms of the quality of the ideas and information they contain. It would be naive in the extreme to accept everything at face value or, for that matter, to treat all documentary sources as being equally valid. The researcher needs to evaluate the various sources and discriminate between them in terms of the amount of credibility that is afforded to them and the reliance that is placed upon them.

Academic journals and commercial publishers generally have their material refereed by experts in the field before the work is published, so the researcher has some assurance about the quality of the ideas he or she reads. However, this offers no absolute guarantee. And how does the reader find out which journals are refereed and which publishers are reputable? Some rules of thumb might help here. For journals:

► How long has the journal existed? Generally, a journal which has existed for a long time will be OK. Less confidence can be held about new journals. However, this does not mean old equals good, new equals bad: that would be far too simplistic.

► Does the title involve a national title (e.g. *British Medical Journal*, *American Journal of Sociology*)? Again, there is nothing cast iron about this, but it offers some clue as to the standing of the journal.

► Is the journal published by, or on behalf of, a professional association or some authority?

► Does the journal contain a list of its editorial board and editorial advisers, and do these people strike you as 'of high standing' in the field?

► Is there a clear statement that articles are refereed?

Books and their publishers are even more difficult to evaluate in terms of their 'reputation'. Some things which might help here are:

► Have you heard of the publisher before? If so, this might be reassuring.

► Is the publisher a university press (e.g. Cambridge University Press)? If so, again this offers some confidence about the academic quality of the work being published.

► Is the book in a second or subsequent edition? If so, there has been sufficient demand for the book to warrant new editions, and this would suggest that it has something worthwhile to say. The same applies to a lesser extent where a book has been reprinted several times. Look for the details, usually contained at the start of the book between the title and contents pages.

► If it is a library book, how frequently has it been out on loan recently? The chances are that a book that is frequently on loan has been recommended, and that is why it is in demand.

Web site pages and the Internet

Restricting attention to the written forms of documents does not exclude documents obtained from the *Internet*. In a sense, the medium through which the document is obtained is not the issue. We can read newspapers in their original paper form, or we can read them on microfiche or via a CD-ROM. Equally, we can obtain documents through Web site pages or email, and this does not, of itself, have a bearing on the use of the output as a document for research. However, there is one particular issue which arises in connection with the use of the Internet as a source of documents for research: there are few restrictions on what is placed on the Internet. Internet documents, therefore, needed to be subjected to the researcher's own quality audit along the lines of those recommended in relation to books and journals – but with even more vigour and rigour.

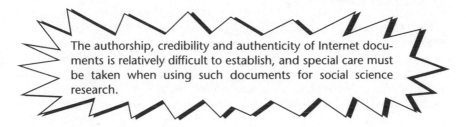

The authorship, credibility and authenticity of Internet documents is relatively difficult to establish, and special care must be taken when using such documents for social science research.

Newspapers and magazines

The 'press' provides a potentially valuable source of information for research purposes. One reason for this is that newspapers and magazines can supply *good, up-to-date information*. In this case, the value of the newspaper or magazine for the research will stem from one or a combination of:

▶ The *expertise* of the journalists;
▶ The *specialism* of the publication;
▶ The *insider information* which the correspondents can uncover.

So, for example, in the UK, business researchers might use the *Economist* or the *Financial Times* for these reasons. Of course, the discerning researcher will also realize that there are plenty of newspapers and magazines whose contents should not be relied upon to reflect anything approaching an objective account of real events!

Records

The bureaucratization of industrial society has created a wealth of documentation in relation to administration, policy, management, finance and commerce. These provide an abundant source of data for social researchers in whatever field they operate.

The purpose of most such documentation is to enhance accountability. The records which are kept of meetings (minutes), the records kept of transactions, the records kept of finances etc. are kept in principle so that people and institutions can be held accountable for their actions. This means that the records need to have two qualities, both of which happen to be of particular value for research.

▶ First, they need to contain *a pretty systematic picture of things that have happened*. These might be decisions of a committee or transfers of money between accounts. Whatever the records, though, the principle behind them is that they provide a detailed and accurate picture of what took place. They have got to make events sufficiently transparent for the readers to comprehend what took place and why.
▶ Second, they should be *publicly available*. The records only serve the function of accountability to the extent that they are made available to relevant people to scrutinize.

⚠ **Caution**

Records, whether publicly available or on restricted access, purport to depict things that have happened in a full and accurate manner. However, there is ample evidence that such records tend to be partial – in both senses of the word. They will tend to be selective in terms of what they report, emphasizing some things and ignoring others, and thus recording only part of the overall event. They will also tend to reflect a particular interpretation of what happened, recording events from a particular angle. We should remember that when such records are produced as part of public accountability, there will be a tendency to be cautious about what is recorded. Things might have been said 'off the record' or following 'Don't minute this but . . .'. The records, in other words, may be subtly edited to exclude things which might render people vulnerable to criticism when the record is published. *The researcher, therefore, needs to be cautious about accepting such records at face value.* Publicly available records reflect upon matters in a way that is publicly acceptable at a given time and in a given social sphere. They tend to offer a version of reality massaged to meet public expectations.

Letters and memos

Private correspondence between people can be used for research purposes. This can take the form of memos sent between people at work or even personal letters exchanged between people. The more private the correspondence, of course, the more difficult it is for the researcher to gain access to the documents. These are really at the other end of the spectrum from the publicly available reports, and pose far more of a challenge for the researcher when it comes to getting hold of such documents and, especially, when it comes to getting permission to use them as research data.

Letters and memos also differ from reports in terms of the extent to which there is any formal obligation on the writer to give a full and accurate portrayal of events. Because they are written to specific people, rather than for a broader public, their contents are likely to rely far more on assumptions about what the other person already knows or what that person feels. They are more likely to 'fill in the bits' rather than paint the whole picture. They can be expected to be from a personal point of view rather than be impartial. When contemplating the use of letters or memos as data for research, then, you need to recognize that they are not very reliable as accounts which depict objective reality, but they are extremely valuable as a source which reveals the writer's own perceptions and views of events.

Diaries

As a source of information, researchers can use diaries which are kept by informants specifically for the purposes of the research. In this sense, such diaries differ from the kind of diaries often associated with research: diaries kept by researchers to help them recall events. As a *source* of documentary data, diaries are written by people whose thoughts and behaviour the researcher wishes to study. It is *informants' diaries*, not researchers' diaries, which are the source of research data.

We should be clear, too, that for research purposes such diaries are important in terms of recording things that have already happened. We are not talking about the kind of diaries which act as a planner, noting commitments in the future that need to be scheduled. For research purposes, the diary is normally a *retrospective account* of things that have happened.

There are three crucial elements to this kind of diary – three elements which, incidentally, are shared with the literary diary and the statesman's diary.

▶ *Factual data*: a log of things that happened, decisions made and people involved.

▶ *Significant incidents*: the identification of things seen as particularly important and a description of the diary-writer's priorities.

▶ *Personal interpretation*: a personal reflection and interpretation of happenings, plus an account of the personal feelings and emotions surrounding the events described.

Each of these three things has the potential to provide a rich source of data for the researcher. However, the accounts they provide should not be used by the researcher as a statement of objective fact. That would be very naive. As a retrospective account, diaries must always be seen as a *version* of things as seen by the writer, filtered through the writer's past experiences, own identity, own aspirations and own personality.

There are some interesting ethical issues associated with this type of documentary data. Operating ethically, any researcher might be expected to offer assurances that the information supplied in the diaries will be treated in confidence. However, there is also a delicate issue of who 'owns' the diary. In the case of interview material it is always assumed that the researcher owns the tape and will hold it for future reference. In the case of the diary, however, ownership of the document might be less clear-cut. The best advice here is that matters concerning the ownership of the diaries, dates for collection and long-term location of the diaries is discussed and formally agreed at the outset of the research project. Uncertainty over ownership of the diaries seems a recipe for disaster later in the research project.

Government publications and official statistics

At first glance, government publications and official statistics would seem to be an attractive proposition for the social researcher. They would appear to provide a documentary source of information which is:

▶ *Authoritative*. Since the data have been produced by the state, employing large resources and expert professionals, they tend to have *credibility*.

▶ *Objective.* Since the data have been produced by officials, they might be regarded as *impartial.*

▶ *Factual.* In the case of the statistics, they take the form of numbers that are amenable to computer storage/analysis, and constitute 'hard facts' around which there can be *no ambiguity.*

It is not surprising, then, that in the Western world government publications and official statistics have come to provide a key source of documentary information for social scientists. However, the extent to which such documents can live up to the image of being authoritative, objective and factual depends very much on the data they contain. Certain types of official statistics will, to all intents and purposes, provide an objective picture of reality. Unfortunately, the same cannot be said for certain other types of official statistics. When politicians debate the accuracy of unemployment figures or the significance of particular national economic figures, there is clearly room for some doubt and controversy about the objectivity, the accuracy, the completeness and the relevance of some official statistics. This should alert us to the point that official statistics cannot always to be taken as 'objective facts'.

To say this is not to reject the use of all official statistics as a source of data for social research. Far from it. But what it *does* mean is that before treating a set of official statistics as accurate and objective, the researcher should consider the following factors.

▶ *The extent to which the event or thing being measured is clear-cut and straight-forward.* Basically, the more clear-cut the event, the more confidence we can have in the data. The official statistics on things like births, deaths, marriages and divorce are likely to be virtually complete. Whether or not someone is born or dies, whether a marriage or divorce occurs, does not require much in the way of interpretation by the registrars involved. The events themselves happen or don't happen, with little scope for 'creative accounting' or biased interpretation. All right, a very small number of births and deaths might go unrecorded and slip through the net of the tight official procedures for collecting such data. But the numbers will be sufficiently low not to present any serious challenge to the idea that these official statistics are a full and accurate record. Things like unemployment, homelessness and ill-health, though, are far less clear-cut. There are a number of ways of defining these things, and this opens up the possibility of disputes about whether the statistics depict real levels of unemployment etc., or whether they offer a picture biased by the nature of the definition that has been used.

▶ *Whether there are vested interests in the statistics that are produced.* When those who produce the statistics stand to gain or lose on the basis of what the figures reveal, the astute researcher should treat them with some caution. Trade figures, hospital waiting lists, sales figures: all have consequences for people who want or need the statistics to reveal a particular trend. And official statistics are not immune to the point. Governments can have a vested interest in a variety of statistics, from trade to inflation, from unemployment to health.

▶ *The extent to which the statistics are the outcome of a series of decisions and judgements made by people.* The more the statistics rely on decisions and choices by those who produce them, the more the eventual official statistics become open to being challenged. The more the statistics are the end-product of a series of choices made by people – choices that involve judgement and discretion – the more the official statistics can be regarded as a 'social construction' rather than a detached, impartial picture of the real world.

Crime statistics provide a good illustration of the *construction* of official statistics. Crime statistics are based on those crimes that people decide to report to the police. A large proportion of crime, however, never gets reported. Petty crimes may go unreported. Theft is frequently not reported, particularly when people see no chance of recovering their property and when the property is not insured. (If a claim is to be made through insurance, a 'crime number' is needed from the police, and this motivates people to report the crime.) Many crimes are not discovered and so obviously do not get reported (e.g. embezzlement). There are the 'crimes with no victims', where, unless someone is caught by the police, no record of the offence will ever appear (e.g. recreational drug use). In the case of some crimes, there may be an unwillingness of the victim to complain because of the accruing stigma (e.g. rape) or fear of retribution.

Even when a crime is reported to the police, there is a level of discretion open to them about how they interpret things and whether to formalize the matter. A lot of 'crime' is sorted out informally, without ever entering the system as a recorded crime. Even when it is in the system, the nature of the offence is open to some degree of interpretation. From the police officer receiving the report onwards, there is some scope for leeway and interpretation about (a) whether to prosecute, (b) what offence gets noted, (c) whether a caution is given, (d) whether the matter proceeds to court and (e) whether the prosecution is successful or not.

At each stage people are taking decisions, using discretion and making judgements. Overall, these can have a marked impact on the end-product: the official statistics. It means that there will be a huge difference (in the case of crime) between the real level of crime in society and the figures that get published by the government as 'the crime rate'. *It is estimated that recorded crime may be as little as one-fifth of 'actual' crime.*

2 Access to documentary sources

Probably the greatest attraction of using documentary sources is their accessibility. To get hold of the material the researcher needs only to visit the library or use the World Wide Web via a home computer. Vast amounts of information are conveniently available without much cost, without much delay, without prior appointment, without the need for authorization and without any likelihood of ethical problems. Documents, in other words, pose considerably fewer problems than people as a source of data for social researchers.

There are times, however, when the use of documents does not completely side-step the kind of problems that face researchers using other sources. While access to documents *in the public domain* is certainly straightforward, researchers can sometimes need to use materials whose availability is deliberately restricted. When this is the case, access becomes a crucial part of the research method – more than something that can be taken for granted. When documents are *on restricted access* researchers need to enter negotiations with those who hold the data in order to persuade them to allow the researcher the privilege of access to the material. Documents such as police files and medical records, and certain kinds of company reports and memos, might rightly be considered sensitive and confidential by those who 'own' them, and they are only likely to grant access when they are convinced that the researcher will honour the confidentiality of the material and use it in a way that will not harm the interests of anyone concerned.

In the case of documents considered to be *secret*, of course, the holders will seek to deny any access to outsiders. Companies may have secret strategic plans regarded as too sensitive for even a *bona fide* researcher. The government wishes to keep many documents secret 'in the national interest'. Records of illegal activities, whether a drug smuggler's diary or a second set of books for VAT returns, are extremely unlikely to be opened to the researcher. Access will not be willingly given. To get access to such secret documents requires the approach of investigative journalism or participant observation with a degree of deception and covert infiltration being used.

Types of document

Type of document	Examples	Access via	Typical use
Public domain	Books, journals, official statistics, some company records	Libraries, Internet, Office for National Statistics	Academic research and consultancy
Restricted access	Medical records, police files, internal memos, personal papers/diaries, some tax accounts	Negotiations gate-keepers, sponsors	Consultancy and academic research
Secret	Cabinet minutes, illegal trade, second set of books for VAT or Inland Revenue, corporate plans	Insider knowledge, participation, deception	Investigative journalism, fraud detection, undercover work

3 Evaluating documentary sources

The good researcher should always ask, 'Have I evaluated the documents rather than accepted them at face value?' Some guidance has already been given in relation to journals, books, the Internet, newspapers etc. At a general level, though, good documentary research can use four basic criteria to evaluate documents. Following Platt (1981) and Scott (1990), these can be summarized as follows.

Authenticity

Is it the genuine article? Is it the real thing? Can we be satisfied that the document is what it purports to be – not a fake or a forgery?

Credibility

Is it accurate? Is it free from bias and errors? This will depend on factors like:

► What *purpose* was the document written for?

► *Who produced the document*? What was the status of the author and did he or she have a particular belief or persuasion that would colour the version of things?

► if it reports on events, *was it a first hand report* directly witnessed by the author? How long after the event was the document written?

► *When was the document produced*? In what social context and climate?

Representativeness

Is the document typical of its type? Does it represent a typical instance of the thing it portrays? Is the document complete? Has it been edited? Is the extract treated 'in context'?

Meaning

Is the meaning of the words clear and unambiguous? Are there hidden meanings? Does the document contain argot and subtle codes? Are there meanings which involve 'what's left unsaid' or 'reading between the lines'?

4 Content analysis

Content analysis is a method which helps the researcher to analyse the content of documents. Basically, it is a method that can be used with any 'text', whether it be in the form of writing, sounds or pictures, as a way of quantifying the contents of that text. Political scientists might use it to study the transcripts of speeches, educationists might study the content of children's books, historians might use it to study statesmen's correspondence.

Whatever its specific application, content analysis generally follows a logical and relatively straightforward procedure.

▶ *Choose an appropriate sample of texts*. The criterion for the choice of such a sample should be quite explicit.

▶ *Break the text down into smaller component units.*The unit for analysis can be each and every word. Alternatively, the analysis can use complete sentences as the unit, whole paragraphs or things like headlines. It can also be based on visual images or the content of pictures.

▶ *Develop relevant categories for analysing the data.* The researcher needs to have a clear idea of the kinds of categories, issues and ideas that he or she is concerned with and how these might appear in the text. This might take the form of 'key words' associated with the theme. So, for example, a search for sex bias in children's stories might look for instances of boys' names and girls' names – the names being treated as indicative of the nature of the content. The researcher might also wish to code the text in terms of the kinds of names, rather than just how many times such names occur.

▶ *Code the units in line with the categories*. Meticulous attention to the text is needed to code all the relevant words, sentences etc. These codes are either written on the text and subsequently referred to, or entered via a computer program specially designed for the purpose.

Link up with **Computer-aided analysis of qualitative data, p. 218**

▶ *Count the frequency with which these units occur*. The first part of analysis is normally a tally of the times when various units occur.

▶ *Analyse the text in terms of the frequency of the units and their relationship with other units that occur in the text*. Once the units have been coded, a more sophisticated analysis is possible which links the units and attempts to explain when and why they occur in the way they do.

Content analysis has the potential to disclose many 'hidden' aspects of what is being communicated through the written text. The idea is that, quite independent of what the writer had consciously intended, the text carries some clues about a deeper rooted and possibly unintentional message that is actually being communicated. You do not have to base the analysis on what the author *thought* he or she was saying when the text contains more tangible evidence about its message (Gerbner *et al.* 1969).

Content analysis	
. . . reveals	. . . by measuring
1 What the text establishes as *relevant*	What is contained (e.g. particular words, ideas)
2 The *priorities* portrayed through the text	How frequently it occurs; in what order it occurs
3 The *values* conveyed in the text	Positive and negative views on things
4 How ideas are *related*	Proximity of ideas within the text, logical association

The main strength of content analysis is that it provides a means for quantifying the contents of a text, and it does so by using a method that is clear and, in principle, repeatable by other researchers. Its main limitation is that it has an in-built tendency to dislocate the units and their meaning from the context in which they were made, and even the intentions of the writer. And it is difficult for content analysis to deal with the meaning of the text in terms of its *implied* meanings, how the meaning draws on what has just been said, what follows or even what is left unsaid. In many ways, it is a rather crude instrument for dealing with the subtle and intricate ways in which a text conveys meaning.

In practice, therefore, *content analysis is at its best when dealing with aspects of communication which tend to be more straightforward, obvious and simple*. The more the text relies on subtle and intricate meanings conveyed by the writer or inferred by the reader, the less valuable content analysis becomes in revealing the meaning of the text.

5 Advantages of documentary research

▶ *Access to data*. Vast amounts of information are held in documents. Depending on the nature of the documents, most researchers will find access to the sources relatively easy and inexpensive.

▶ *Cost-effective*. Documentary research provides a cost-effective method of getting data, particularly large-scale data such as those provided by official statistics.

▶ *Permanence of data*. Documents generally provide a source of data which is permanent and available in a form that can be checked by others. The data are open to public scrutiny.

6 Disadvantages of documentary research

▶ *Credibility of the source*. Researchers need to evaluate the authority of the source and the procedures used to produce the original data in order to gauge the credibility of the documents.

▶ *Secondary data*. When researchers use documents as a source of data, they generally rely on something which has been produced for other purposes and not for the specific aims of the investigation.

▶ *Social constructions*. Documents can owe more to the interpretations of those who produce them than to an objective picture of reality.

Checklist for the use of books and other documents ✓

When using books or other documents in social research you should feel confident about answering 'yes' to the following questions:

1 Am I satisfied that the *documents are genuine* in terms of what they purport to be (not drafts, forgeries, misleading second versions etc.)? ☐

2 Have I considered the *credibility of the documents* in terms of:
- ▶ The *type* of document (published book, journal article, official statistics)? ☐
- ▶ The *author*(s) of the document (status, role, in a position to know)? ☐
- ▶ The *sponsorship* of the document (organization, funding, pressure group)? ☐
- ▶ The *accessibility* of the information they use (public domain, restricted, secret)? ☐

3 Am I satisfied that I have taken account of *possible bias in the documents* arising from:
- ▶ The *purpose* of the document (description, theory, persuasion)? ☐
- ▶ How *representative* the document is (typical, extreme)? ☐
- ▶ The editing and *selection of extracts* used by the author(s)? ☐
- ▶ The *interpretation* of facts, theories or statistics given by the author(s)? ☐
- ▶ The *sensitivity* of the information contained? ☐

© M. Denscombe, *The Good Research Guide*. Open University Press.

Part III

ANALYSIS

The terms 'qualitative research' and 'quantitative research' are widely used and understood within the realms of social research as signposts to the kind of assumptions being used by the researchers and the nature of the research being undertaken. As we probe deeper into the distinction between 'qualitative research' and 'quantitative research', however, it becomes apparent that, in the real world of social research, things do not fall neatly into the two categories. There are three reasons for this.

1 *In practice, the approaches are not mutually exclusive.* Social researchers rarely, if ever, rely on one approach to the exclusion of the other. Good research tends to use parts of both approaches, and the difference lies in *the degree* to which the research is based in one camp or the other.

2 *In theory, the distinction is too simplistic.* The assumptions associated with the two approaches are frequently shared, frequently overlap and basically do not fall either side of a clear dividing line.

3 Strictly speaking, the distinction between 'qualitative' and 'quantitative' *relates to the treatment of data*, rather than the research methods as such. As Strauss (1987: 2) argues, 'the genuinely useful distinction is in how data are treated analytically.' This is dealt with in Chapters 10 and 11.

We must recognize, then, that a distinction between qualitative and quantitative research is far from 'watertight'.

Bearing this in mind, what is conveyed through the use of labels such as 'qualitative research' and 'quantitative research'? The terms 'qualitative' and 'quantitative' have come to denote contrasting positions in relation to a number of dimensions of social research. Each term implies a commitment to a particular set of assumptions about the nature of the social world being investigated and the appropriate way to investigate it, a position which is in opposition to that linked with the other term. As these polar opposites are listed, though, it is important to bear in mind that the distinctions are based on something of an oversimplification and a caricature, not a depiction of the real world of social research, with people in two entirely separate camps.

Words or numbers

Qualitative research tends to be associated with words as the unit of analysis.

Quantitative research tends to be associated with numbers as the unit of analysis.

The most elementary distinction between the two approaches lies in the use of words or numbers as the basic unit for analysis. On the one hand, there is 'quantitative research', whose aim is to measure phenomena so that they can be transformed into numbers. Once the phenomena have been quantified, they lend themselves to analysis through statistical procedures – procedures which are very powerful but utterly dependent on receiving numerical data as the input. The obsession of quantitative approaches, then, is with generating data that are numerical, with transforming what is observed, reported or recorded into quantifiable units. On the other hand, qualitative research relies on transforming information from observations, reports and recordings into data in the form of the written word, not numbers. The sources of information, it should be noted, need not differ between qualitative and quantitative approaches. What *is* different is the way the information is transformed into qualitative *data* (words) or quantitative *data* (numbers). In the case of qualitative data, taped interviews get transformed into transcripts, observations get recorded in field notes, pictures get described in words.

> More than anything else the feature which sets qualitative research apart from quantitative research is the focus on words rather than numbers as the unit for analysis.

Description or analysis

Qualitative research tends to be associated with description.

Quantitative research tends to be associated with analysis.

Again, it is the potential of numbers to be analysed using statistical procedures which places quantitative data in a strong position when it comes to analysis. The numbers are particularly well suited to the kind of comparisons and correlations demanded by any analysis of results.

Qualitative research is better suited to description. Whether dealing with meanings or with patterns of behaviour, qualitative researchers tend to rely on a detailed and intricate description of events or people. Such 'thick description' (Geertz 1973), as it is known, is necessary in order to convey the complexity of the situation and to provide the reader with sufficient detail to judge for himself or herself whether the researcher's interpretation of the phenomenon is justifiable and relevant for other circumstances.

Small-scale or large-scale

Qualitative research tends to be associated with small-scale studies.

Quantitative research tends to be associated with large-scale studies.

Statistics tend to operate more safely with larger numbers. It is not surprising, then, that quantitative research tends to favour larger-scale research with larger numbers and greater quantities. The sheer amounts involved, once they have been transformed into numerical data, do not slow down the analysis to any discernible degree. A statistical procedure can be undertaken by a computer on a sample of 2,000 pretty much as quickly as it can on a sample of 20. The results, though, will be more reliable when conducted on 2,000 than on 20. The larger the numbers involved, the more the results are likely to be generalizable and reliable statistically speaking. Size matters.

The same might be said for qualitative research, but, in this case, the adage is more likely to be 'small is beautiful'. There is nothing inherently opposed to large-scale qualitative research, but there *is* a strong tendency for qualitative research to be relatively focused in terms of the scope of the study and to involve relatively few people or situations. Much of this reflects the preference for depth of study and the associated 'thick description' which only becomes possible in relation to limited numbers. It equally reflects the fact that words do not lend themselves to the kind of analysis that can utilize the power of computers, at least nowhere near as much as numbers do. So, for the qualitative researcher, there *is* a vast difference in the time it takes to analyse results from larger amounts of data compared with smaller amounts. Together, these factors account for the association of qualitative research with small-scale studies.

Holistic or specific focus

Qualitative research tends to be associated with holistic perspective.

Quantitative research tends to be associated with a specific focus.

The approach of quantitative research is to focus on specific factors and to study them in relation to specific other factors. To do this, it is necessary to isolate variables – to separate them from their natural location intertwined with a host of others – in order to study their working and their effect. Qualitative research, on the other hand, rather than isolating variables and focusing on specific factors, generally exhibits a preference for seeing things 'in context' and for stressing how things are related and interdependent. In line with Lincoln and Guba's 'naturalistic' approach, qualitative research tends to operate on the assumption that social 'realities are wholes that cannot be understood in isolation from their contexts, nor can they be fragmented for separate study of their parts' (Lincoln and Guba 1985: 39).

Researcher involvement or detachment

Qualitative research tends to be associated with researcher involvement.

Quantitative research tends to be associated with researcher detachment.

The whole point of quantitative research is to produce numerical data that are 'objective' in the sense that they exist independently of the researcher and are not the result of undue influence on the part of the researcher himself or herself. Ideally, the numerical data are seen as the product of research instruments which have been tested for validity and reliability to ensure that the data accurately reflect the event itself, not the researcher's preferences. Qualitative research, by contrast, tends to place great emphasis on the role of the researcher in the construction of the data. There is typically little use of standardized research instruments in qualitative research. Rather, it is recognized that the researcher is the crucial 'measurement device', and that the researcher's self (his or her social background, values, identity and beliefs) will have a significant bearing on the nature of the data collected and the interpretations of that data.

Emergent or predetermined research design

Qualitative research tends to be associated with an emergent research design.

Quantitative research tends to be associated with a predetermined research design.

One of the key features of quantitative research is the precision with which research designs are established at the outset of the study. Hypotheses establish exactly the nature of the research question(s), and there is a definite sample or experimental procedure to be undertaken. In marked contrast to this, qualitative research is frequently premised on the idea that the theory and the methods will emerge during the course of the research, and will not be specified at the beginning. Theories can be developed and tested as part of an ongoing process (what Glaser and Strauss (1967) call 'grounded theory'). And the sample to be investigated will depend on following up leads so that the researcher can know neither how many or which people or events will be investigated until the end of the research. As Maykut and Morehouse (1994) point out, the emphasis is on 'discovery', not 'proof'.

10

QUANTITATIVE DATA

The use of quantitative data in social research has its attractions. For one thing, it carries with it an aura of scientific respectability. Because it uses numbers and can present findings in the form of graphs and tables, it conveys a sense of solid, objective research.

In the past, there has been a limit on the extent to which newcomers might want to indulge in the numbers game. To play the game, the researcher needed to devote time, effort and considerable skill to the process of subjecting data to statistical analysis and to producing appropriate graphs and tables to represent the results. The advent of the personal computer and powerful statistical software packages has altered all this. Social researchers, as we enter the twenty-first century, have at their disposal the means to do the kind of number-crunching that used to be reserved for the seasoned statistical expert. All the more reason, one might suppose, to use quantitative data.

The availability of such software, however, is a mixed blessing. Relative novices can undertake fairly complex statistical tests – but there is the very real danger that they could be the wrong tests! The computer will undertake the analysis, but it is the researcher who needs to choose which test to apply. Fortunately, though, the use of quantitative data in social research need not entail the researcher in the use of sophisticated statistical analysis. In the case of much project research – small-scale research with quite limited resources –

Provided the researcher has a vision of the pros and cons, and appreciates the limitations to what can be concluded on the basis of the data collected, *good quantitative research need not require advanced statistical knowledge.*

the use of quantitative data need not go beyond the use of what are called 'descriptive' statistics.

This chapter on the analysis of quantitative data is deliberately restricted to the *elementary aspects* of analysis and presentation of quantitative data. For the project researcher this will generally be sufficient. Properly organized, simple statistics can be used to very good effect in such research. They can provide a clear foundation for discussion and critique – a solid foundation from which to progress the argument.

1 Types of quantitative data

Social researchers who want to use quantitative data need to be clear about the type of data they are using. This makes a major difference to what can be done with the data, statistically speaking, and the kind of conclusions that can be drawn from the analysis. There are certain statistical techniques that work with some kinds of data that will not work with others.

Nominal data

Nominal data come from counting things and placing them into a category. They are the lowest level of quantitative data, in the sense that they allow little by way of statistical manipulation compared with the other types. Typically, there is a head count of members of a particular category, such as male/female or White/South Asian/Afro-Caribbean. These categories are based simply on names; there is no underlying order to the names.

Ordinal data

Like nominal data, ordinal data based on counts of things assigned to specific categories, but, in this case, the categories stand in some clear, ordered, ranked relationship. The categories are 'in order' . This means that the data in each category can be compared with data in the other categories as being higher or lower than, more or less than etc., those in the other categories.

The most obvious example of ordinal data comes from the use of questionnaires in which respondents are asked to respond on a five-point scale such as:

Strongly agree	Agree	Neutral	Disagree	Strongly disagree
1	2	3	4	5

The responses coded as 2 (agree) can legitimately be seen as more positive than those coded as 3, 4 or 5 (neutral, disagree, strongly disagree), but less positive than those coded 1 (strongly agree). This scale is known as the Likert scale.

It is worth stressing that *rank order is all that can be inferred*. With ordinal data we do not know the *cause* of the order, or by how much they differ.

Interval data

Interval data are like ordinal data, but the categories are ranked on a scale. This means that the 'distance' between the categories is a known factor and can be pulled into the analysis. The researcher can not only deal with the data in terms of 'more than' or 'less than', but also say how much more or how much less. The ranking of the categories is *proportionate*, and this allows for direct contrast and comparison.

Calendar years provide a suitable example of such data. Data collected for the years AD 1960, 1970, 1980, 1990 and 2000 not only differ in terms of being earlier or later than one another, they are also earlier or later by a known time-span interval. This allows the researcher to use addition and subtraction (but not multiplication or division) to contrast the difference between various periods: the difference between 1960 and 1970 can be directly compared with the difference between 1970 and 1980, and so on.

Ratio data

Ratio data are like interval data, except that the categories exist on a scale which has a 'true zero' or an absolute reference point. When the categories concern things like incomes, distances and weights, they give rise to ratio data because the scales have a zero point. Calendar years, in the previous example, do not exist on such a scale, because the year 0 does not denote the beginning of all time and history. The important thing about the scale having a true zero is that the researcher can compare and contrast the data for each category in terms of ratios, using multiplication and division, rather than being restricted to the use of addition and subtraction as is the case with interval data. Ratio data are the highest level of data in terms of how amenable they are to mathematical manipulation.

Discrete data

Certain data are based on phenomena which naturally come in whole units. Numbers of children per family, in reality, have to be whole numbers. We might aggregate the numbers to arrive at an average figure of 1.9 or whatever, but we do not suppose that there exists anywhere 0.9 of a child belonging to a family. In this example, our measurement of children per family can be exact for each and every household, with no need for approximations or results accurate to the nearest fraction. The *discrete data* come in chunks: 1, 2, 3, 4 and so on.

Continuous data

Contrasted with this there are certain kinds of data which, for practical purposes, are inevitably measured 'to the nearest unit' simply because they do not come in neat, discrete chunks. Such things are measured to the nearest small unit because, as a variable, they are *continuous*. People's height, age and weight are obvious examples here. In principle, there is no end to the precision with which we might try to measure these items. We could measure height in millimetres, weight in grams, age in seconds. For practical purposes, however, such precision would be counter-productive, because it would throw up vast arrays of data which would not lend themselves to analysis. When variables are continuous, the researcher, in effect, needs to categorize the data. The unit of data is not exact height, exact weight, exact age; rather, it is 'height falling within a range of 2 cm', 'weight to the nearest 0.5 kilograms', or 'age at last birthday'.

The significance of continuous data lies with the implicit categories which are formed by the researcher to cope with difficulties of measuring points/units on a sliding scale. The researcher needs to be absolutely clear about the boundaries to such categories and exactly where the mid-point of the category resides. The accuracy of statistics based on continuous data depends on knowing the boundaries and mid-point to the categories of the data.

2 Preparing quantitative data for analysis

Coding the data

The raw data with which the social researcher works sometimes occur 'naturally' in the form of numbers. This is convenient. However, on many occasions the researcher starts off with material in the form of words or pictures and needs to transform the material from this format into the only format suitable for quantitative analysis: numbers. This involves a process of 'coding' the data. Coding, in essence, entails the attribution of a number to a piece of data, or group of data, with the express aim of allowing such data to be analysed in quantitative terms. Such coding is usually done at an early stage in the research process and, in fact, the general advice as far as quantitative analysis is concerned is to do the coding prior to the collection of the data.

Link up with **Questionnaires, p. 87**

If this sounds a bit abstract, it might be useful to illustrate the process briefly in relation to the use of questionnaires. Suppose that the researcher is interested in people's occupations, and intends to conduct a survey of 1,000 people. The questionnaire might contain a question asking the respondent to state his or her occupation. This would result in a mass of data, all in the form of words, covering a huge range of possibilities. In this format the data are difficult to handle and very difficult to analyse. Imagine the researcher's problem when faced with a list of 1,000 separate jobs. To make the task of analysis possible, the researcher needs to identify a smaller number of *categories* of jobs, and then to assign each job listed to one of the categories. Each category will have a numerical code, and so the process of analysis involves coding each of the words by giving it a numerical value which accords with the category of job to which it fits.

Where the researcher knows in advance that he or she wants to generate quantitative data, it makes good sense to sort out the categories and their respective numbers and build these into the design of the research. Things like a person's occupation can be categorized in advance using existing official classifications. Instead of people being asked to state what their job is, they can be asked to identify which category of occupations best fits their own. The result of doing it this way is that, if there are, say, ten categories of occupation used, the researcher will obtain results in the form of numbers in each of the ten categories, rather than the list of 1,000 words. The data, in this format, are ready for analysis.

Grouping the data

The first stage in the analysis of quantitative data is to organize the raw data in a way that makes them more easily understood. As Figure 1 shows, it is rather difficult to make sense of raw data when the number of items goes above ten.

Days absent from work through illness during the previous year, 30 employees					
1	12	0	9	4	7
5	3	6	15	10	8
4	36	3	13	3	3
3	6	3	6	0	0
10	5	8	0	10	2

(Source: Human Resource Dept, Healthy Life Insurance Co.)

Figure 1 Raw data example

Initially, it is some help to construct an *array of the raw data*, i.e. to arrange the data in order. As Figure 2 shows, this immediately helps in terms of getting some grasp of what the data hold.

Days absent from work through illness during the previous year, 30 employees					
0	2	3	5	8	10
0	3	3	6	8	12
0	3	4	6	9	13
0	3	4	6	10	15
1	3	5	7	10	36

(Source: Human Resource Dept, Healthy Life Insurance Co.)

Figure 2 Array of raw data example

A further stage in organizing the data is to make a *tally of the frequencies* (see Figure 3). This gives a clearer picture of which frequencies were the most common and is far better in terms of being able to 'read' the data. It immediately suggests certain things about the data and invites questions about why certain frequencies are more common than others. Is this sheer fluke, or is there some underlying cause?

Days absent from work through illness during the previous year, 30 employees					
Days	Frequency	Days	Frequency	Days	Frequency
0	4	5	2	10	3
1	1	6	3	12	1
2	1	7	1	13	1
3	6	8	2	15	1
4	2	9	1	36	1

(Source: Human Resource Dept, Healthy Life Insurance Co.)

Figure 3 Tally of frequencies example

Where there are a large number of frequencies, the researcher can organize the data by grouping the frequencies (see Figure 4). Such *grouped frequency distributions* are a very valuable and commonly used strategy for the organization of raw data.

Days absent from work through illness during the previous year, 30 employees	
Group	Frequency
0–2 days	6
3–5 days	10
6–8 days	6
9–11 days	4
12–14 days	2
15+ days	2

(Source: Human Resource Dept, Healthy Life Insurance Co.)

Figure 4 Grouped frequency distribution example

 Caution

It is worth bearing in mind that as soon as the researcher creates groups, he or she is imposing on the data in a pretty strong way. The data in the format of a grouped frequency distribution may be easier to understand, but they have moved away from a natural or raw state and begin to bear the hallmarks of the creative shaping of data by the researcher.

3 The presentation of data

With descriptive data, the process of transforming a mass of raw data into tables and charts is vital as part of *making sense of the data*. And it is, indeed, a process of *making* sense. The transformation is done by researchers on the data. It is a process of artfully moulding, extracting and refining the raw data, so that the meaning and significance can be grasped.

Computer software provides a major help on this score. Statistical packages allow the researcher to code and recode data, to group and regroup data and to undertake statistical analyses. And there are packages which help with the presentation of tables and charts based on the data. However, the problem is that the project researcher can actually become overwhelmed by the help on offer through such packages. The power of such software can produce a rather daunting range of possibilities for analysing and presenting the data.

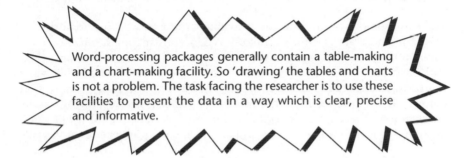

Word-processing packages generally contain a table-making and a chart-making facility. So 'drawing' the tables and charts is not a problem. The task facing the researcher is to use these facilities to present the data in a way which is clear, precise and informative.

What follows is not an attempt to cover this vast range of possibilities. This would take a separate book. There are, though, certain 'basics' that can help the project researcher to keep an eye on the target and not get side-tracked by the plethora of statistical analyses which are available at the press of a button, or the bewildering variety of templates for presenting results through tables and charts.

Essentials for the presentation of tables and charts

The point of producing a table or chart is to convey information in a succinct manner and use visual impact to best effect. Its success or otherwise hinges on how well it achieves these things. The skill of producing good tables and charts rests on the ability to:

▶ *present enough information* without 'drowning' the reader with information overload;

▶ help the reader to interpret the table or chart through *visual clues and appropriate presentation*;

▶ use an *appropriate type of table or chart* for the purpose at hand.

There are certain bits of information which must always be included. If these are absent, then the table or chart ceases to have much value as far as the reader is concerned (see Figure 7 as an illustration). The table or chart must always have

► a *title*, effectively indicating what the data is about;

► *information about the units being represented* in the columns of the table or on the axes of the chart (sometimes this is placed by the axes, sometimes by the bars or lines, sometimes in a *legend*);

► the *source* of the data, if they were originally produced elsewhere.

Added to this, in most cases – though not all:

► the horizontal axis is the '*x* axis' and is used for the independent variable;

► the vertical axis is the '*y* axis' and is used for the dependent variable.

There are some exceptions to the rule about the *x* axis being the horizontal axis, and these are mentioned below. When constructing a chart or table, though, it is important for the researcher to have a clear view about which variable is seen to be the 'cause' and which is the 'effect'. The variable which is treated as the 'cause' is the independent variable (normally on the horizontal axis) and the variable which is being affected is the dependent variable (normally on the vertical axis). Dates (for example, 1970, 1980, 1990, 2000) are usually on the horizontal axis and are treated as an independent variable.

As far as tables and charts are concerned, *simplicity is a virtue.*

If the researcher pays attention to these points, the remaining dangers to the success of the table or chart generally come from trying to be too ambitious and putting in too much detail. Simplicity is a virtue that is hard to overstress in relation to the production of tables and charts. If too much data are supplied in a table, it becomes almost impossible for the reader to decipher the meaning of the data. If too many frequencies are presented in a chart, it becomes difficult to grasp the key points. Too many patterns, too many words, too many figures, and the impact of the table or chart is lost. Having said this, of course, there need to be sufficient data in the table or chart to make it worthwhile and 'say something' of interest, and essential details need to be incorporated for the sake of precision. This means that *the researcher is often obliged to compromise between the amount of information that can be conveyed and the visual impact of the table or chart.*

Tables

A main virtue of tables is their flexibility. They can be used with just about all types of numerical data. Computer software offers a variety of templates for tables, which aid the presentation of data in a visually attractive fashion.

The degree of complexity of the table depends on two things: the audience being addressed and the restrictions imposed by the format of the document in which the table appears. For the purposes of most project researchers it is likely that tables will remain fairly simple in structure. If the table *does* need to involve a considerable number of rows, the researcher should be prepared to insert horizontal and vertical 'breaks' or blank lines to ease reading and to avoid the eye slipping to the wrong line of data (see Figure 5).

Days absent from work through illness during 1997, 30 employees							
Days	Frequency		Days	Frequency		Days	Frequency
0	4		5	2		10	3
1	1		6	3		12	1
2	1		7	1		13	1
3	6		8	2		15	1
4	2		9	1		36	1

(Source: Human Resource Dept, Healthy Life Insurance Co.)

Figure 5 Table example

One particularly common use of tables is to present a comparison of sets of nominal data. Such tables are known as *contingency tables* (see Figure 6). They allow a visual comparison of the data and also act as the basis for statistical tests of association, such as the *chi-squared test*.

Days absent from work through illness during the previous year, 30 employees		
	Sex	
Days	Male	Female
lost	(n=14)	(n=16)
0–5 days	21	18
6 or more	74	82

(Source: Human Resource Dept, Healthy Life Insurance Co.)

Figure 6 Contingency table example

Bar charts

Bar charts are an effective way of presenting frequencies, and they are very common in reports of small-scale research. *They can be used with nominal data and with discrete data.* The principle behind them is that the bars should be of equal width, with the height of the bars representing the frequency or the amount for each separate category. Conventionally, there is a gap between each bar. Their strength is that they are visually striking and simple to read – provided, that is, that not too many categories are used. The fewer the categories (bars) the more striking the impact. Beyond ten categories bar charts tend to become too crowded and confusing to read. Figure 7 shows a simple bar chart.

There are many variations on the standard bar chart. The *pictogram* embellishes the basic idea by using symbols or images instead of the standard bar. It does not tell you anything more, but it catches the eye more readily.

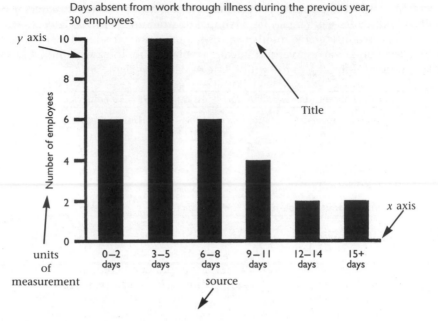

(Source: Human Resource Dept, Healthy Life Insurance Co.)

Figure 7 Simple bar chart example

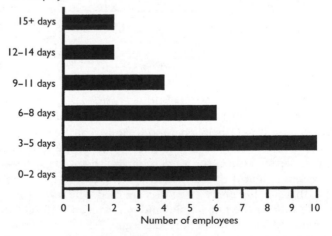

(Source: Human Resource Dept, Healthy Life Insurance Co.)

Figure 8 Horizontal bar chart example

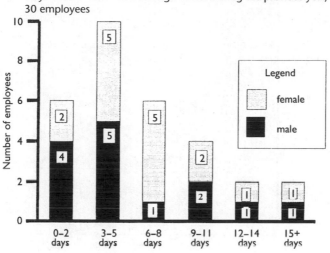

Days absent from work through illness during the previous year, 30 employees

(Source: Human Resource Dept, Healthy Life Insurance Co.)

Figure 9 Stacked bar chart example

Bar charts are sometimes turned on their sides to make it easier to label the categories (see Figure 8). In such *horizontal bar charts*, the vertical axis becomes the *x* axis – as an exception to the convention.

Sometimes each bar incorporates the component elements of the total for a category. This is known as a *stacked bar chart* (see Figure 9). Interestingly, stacked bar charts can be used as an alternative to pie charts (see below) because they show clearly the relative proportions of the factors that make up the total. They have an advantage, too. A number of stacked bars can be incorporated into the same chart, allowing a more direct visual contrast than could be achieved by placing a similar number of pie charts together.

Histogram

A histogram, like a bar chart, is a valuable aid to presenting data on frequencies or amounts. Like a bar chart, the bars are normally of equal width and where they *are* of equal width, the height of the bar is used to depict variations in the frequencies or amounts. However, what distinguishes a histogram from a bar chart is that the *histogram is used for continuous data*, whereas a bar chart is used for discrete data or nominal data. In contrast to the bar chart,

▶ there are no gaps between the bars;

▶ the data 'flow' along the *x* axis, rather than being distinct and separate items.

Days absent from work in the previous year by age* of employees

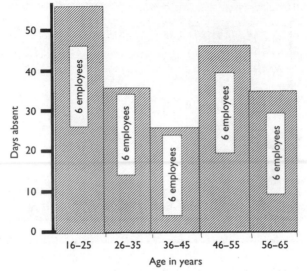

(* age at last birthday)
(Source: Human Resource Dept, Healthy Life Insurance Co.)

Figure 10 Histogram example

Scatter plot

A scatter plot is used to display the *extent of a relationship* between two variables (see Figure 11). The data are represented by unconnected points on a

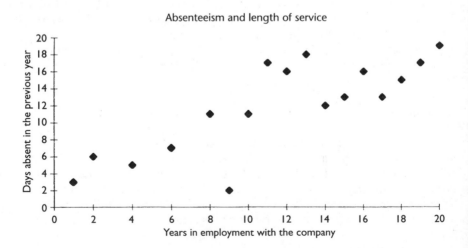

(Source: Human Resource Dept, Healthy Life Insurance Co.)

Figure 11 Scatter plot example

grid, and the clustering or spread of such points is the basis for detecting a close co-variation between two variables, or a not so close co-variation. The more closely the points come together, the closer the relationship between the variables on the x axis and the y axis. The more spread out the points are, the less closely the variables are connected. The extent of the relationship is made nicely visible; indeed the scatter plot is particularly good at showing patterns and deviations. There is a drawback, however. It does need a reasonable amount of data to reveal such a pattern.

Line graph

A line graph is used for depicting development or progression in a sequence of data (see Figure 12). It is good for showing *trends in data*. The most common use of the line graph is with dates. A time sequence is plotted left to right on the x axis. The line varies in height according to the frequency or the amount of the units. Line graphs work better with large data sets and big variations. A bar chart can be used to do the same thing, and sometimes bars and lines are combined within the same chart.

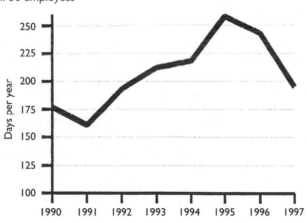

Total days absent from work through illness per year (1990–1997), all 30 employees

(Source: Human Resource Dept, Healthy Life Insurance Co.)

Figure 12 Line graph example

Pie charts

Pie charts, as their name suggests, present data as segments of the whole pie (see Figure 13). Pie charts are visually powerful. They convey simply and

Proportion of employees absent from work through illness during the previous year,
by total days absent, 30 employees

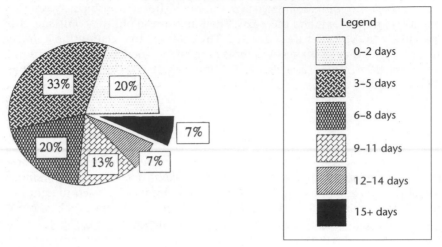

(Source: Human Resource Dept, Healthy Life Insurance Co.)

Figure 13 Pie chart example

straightforwardly the *proportions* of each category which go to make up the total. In most cases, the segments are presented in terms of percentages.

To enhance their impact, pie charts that wish to draw attention to one particular component have that segment extracted from the rest of the pie. On other occasions, all segments are pulled away from the core in what is known as an *exploded pie chart*.

Weighed against their visual strength, pie charts can only be used with one data set. Their impact is also dependent on not having too many segments. As a rule of thumb, a pie chart should have no more than seven segments and not have a segment which accounts for less than 2 per cent of the total.

As a form of chart they tend to take up quite a lot of space on a page. The labels need to be kept horizontal, and this spreads the chart out across the page. As good practice, incidentally, the proportions should be shown as a figure, where possible *within the segments*.

⚠ Caution

The presentation of quantitative data in graphs and charts can be used to mislead and give the wrong impression. Playing around with the scales on the *x* axis and the *y* axis can artificially exaggerate or underplay the appearance of differences in the data. Care needs to be taken to avoid distorting the data in this way.

Checklist for the presentation of quantitative data ✓

When presenting quantitative data you should feel confident about answering 'yes' to the following questions:

1. Is the choice of table or chart *appropriate for the specific purpose* of the data? ☐

2. Does the table or chart contain *enough information* to 'say something' significant? ☐

3. Does the table or chart avoid *'information overload'*? ☐

4. Is the table or chart *clear* and thoughtfully designed? ☐

5. Is there a *title* effectively indicating what the information is about? ☐

6. Have the *columns* and *rows* (tables) or the *axes* (charts) *been labelled*? ☐

7. Has information been supplied on the *units* being represented in the columns of the table or on the axes of the chart? ☐

8. Has the *source* of the data been indicated if they are taken from elsewhere? ☐

9. Is the *independent variable* on the *horizontal axis* (*x* axis) (unless a horizontal bar chart or a pie chart)? ☐

10. Has a *legend* been incorporated where appropriate? ☐

11. Does the contrast in *shading* adequately distinguish the separate bars/segments? ☐

© M. Denscombe, *The Good Research Guide*. Open University Press.

Tables and charts: which ones to choose

The researcher needs to make certain strategic decisions in relation to the choice of which way to represent the quantitative data. It is not a matter of some charts being better than others as much as some charts being better suited to specific purposes than others. Early on, researchers need to decide whether the chart they have in mind is concerned with presenting information:

▶ On amounts or *frequencies*   (in which case *tables, bar charts* or *histograms* are appropriate)

▶ Showing the *extent of a relationship*   (in which case *scatter plots* or *contingency tables* are appropriate)

▶ Covering a *span of time*   (in which case *line graphs* are appropriate)

▶ About *proportions* of a total   (in which case *pie charts* or *stacked bar charts* are appropriate)

---

4 Basic statistics

Evidence based on frequencies and amounts forms the bedrock of quantitative data and, as we have seen, well constructed tables and charts are a valuable asset for organizing and presenting such evidence. However, in a sense the data they contain need to be taken at face value. The tables and charts, of course, are designed to bring out the key points of the data, and the researcher can back them up with a statement drawing attention to possible implications of the data. Beyond that, though, the data are more or less left to speak for themselves.

Social researchers will often want to move beyond this point in search of something a little more 'scientific' that will help them interpret the information and allow them to draw more generalized conclusions on the basis of the evidence. This is where statistics come in. By subjecting the data to statistical analysis, social researchers can move beyond individual interpretations of the data towards some more *universal criteria* for assessing key facets of the data. Specifically, when (a) *describing the frequencies* and their distribution, or (b) *looking for connections* between variables or categories in the data, researchers are able to draw upon scientifically based tests to help their interpretation and to bolster their belief in the data.

The use of statistics can give researchers additional credibility in terms of the interpretations they make and the confidence they have in their findings.

5 Descriptive statistics: describing the frequencies and their distribution

When describing the distribution of a set of data there are two basic questions that might be asked.

▶ What is the mid-point or the average?

▶ How wide is the spread, and how even is the spread?

Whether or not the researcher chooses to use statistics, it seems that these are very reasonable and common-sense things to consider. They are elementary. The use of statistics, though, adds something to the way these are considered by providing some universal benchmarks for dealing with each and some precision to the way in which researchers deal with the questions.

What is the mid-point or average?

Statisticians will point out that there are *three types of average*, which are collectively known as 'measures of central tendency'. These are the *mean*, the *median* and the *mode*. When describing data, then, social researchers need to be aware of the difference between the three and decide which is most appropriate for their specific purposes.

The mean (the arithmetic average)

The mean is what most people have in mind when, in common parlance, they think about 'the average'. It is a measure of central tendency in the sense that it describes what would result if there were a totally *equal distribution of values* – if the total amount or frequencies were spread evenly.

1	4	7	11	12	17	17	47

To calculate the mean of the values above:

1 Add together the total of all the values for a variable or category (= 116).

2 Divide this total by the number of cases (÷ 8).
    Mean = 14.5

For social researchers, the mean has certain strengths and certain limitations when it comes to describing the data.

▶ *The mean can be used only with real (cardinal) numbers.* This gives it precision and opens it up to further mathematical processing. Weighed against this strength, calculations of the mean are not appropriate for some kinds of social data. Clearly it makes no sense to think of this kind of average when the researcher is dealing in nominal data; how can you average two sexes, four ethnic groups or ten occupations? The mean only works with real numbers.

▶ *The mean is affected by extreme values ('outliers').* Because the mean includes *all* values it is prone to being affected by the odd one or two values that might be vastly different from the rest. Extreme or unusual values get included in the overall mean, and can shift the figure for the mean towards any such 'outliers'. Two things will minimize the impact of such outliers. First, a *large data set* will shroud the influence of the odd one or two outliers. An outlier will have less of a distorting impact on a large sample than it will on a small sample, because the extent of its deviation from the rest will get subdivided more and more as the size of the sample gets bigger. Second, and linked to this, calculations of the mean are safest when there are relatively few outliers, and the outliers that do exist have a tendency to balance up and cancel each other out.

▶ *Use of the mean may lead to strange descriptions.* When we conclude, for example, that the average size of households in Britain has fallen from 2.91 persons in 1979 to 2.4 persons in 1995, we clearly do not mean this as a *literal* description of the situation. What does 0.4 of a person look like? It is a *statistical* description.

The median (the middle point)

The idea of 'average' can sometimes carry with it the idea of 'middle of the range', and this is the sense in which the median operates. The median is the mid-point of a range.

   Calculation of the median is really very straightforward. Values in the data are placed in either ascending or descending rank order and the point which lies in the middle of the range is the median. With even numbers of values, it is the mid-point of the two central values. So, in the following set of data, the *median is 11.5*, half-way between the two middle values.

1	4	7	11	12	17	17	47

There are some crucial advantages and limitations connected with the use of the median as a measure of central tendency.

▶ *It can be used with ordinal data* as well as interval and ratio data. This opens up the scope of uses to many areas which are not suitable for the arithmetic mean.

▶ Because it is an ordinal operation, *the median is not affected by extreme values*, the 'outliers'. Looking at the values above, it should be clear that the value of 47, an obvious outlier, does not affect the calculation of the median. It would, though, affect the calculation of the mean. As far as the median is concerned, that value could lie anywhere between 18 and infinity because its sole significance is that it exists as a value in the range which is greater than 17. Now this, of course, can cut both ways. While the median is unaffected by outliers, it is equally insensitive to the implications of any such extreme values. It effectively eliminates such data from the picture.

▶ *The median works well with a low number of values.* In fact, in contrast to the mean, it is better suited to low numbers of values.

▶ We have the advantage of knowing that *exactly half the values are above the median* and half the values are below the median. It offers a quick and easy-to-grasp measure of the central point of the data.

▶ The main disadvantage of the median is that it does not allow for further mathematical processing.

The mode (the most common)

As the name suggests, when social researchers use the mode as a measure of central tendency they have in mind the most fashionable or popular figure. But this does not imply that they are looking for the best liked value in the data. It is the value which is *most common* that is the mode.

Identification of the modal value simply consists of seeing which value among a set occurs most frequently: this is the mode. In the set below, *the mode is 17.*

$$1 \quad 1 \quad 4 \quad 4 \quad 7 \quad 11 \quad 12 \quad 17 \quad 17 \quad 17 \quad 47$$

As with the mean and the median, there are certain strengths and weaknesses pertaining to the use of the mode, and these need to be considered.

▶ *The mode can be used with nominal data*, as well as ordinal, interval and ratio data. It has the widest possible scope for application, then, in relation to social data. As a measure of central tendency it makes sense, for example, to talk about the most commonly watched soap opera on TV, whereas we cannot sensibly talk about the mean or median soap opera.

▶ Like the median, it is *unaffected by outliers* or extreme values. It focuses only on the most common value and ignores all others.

▶ It shares with the median the limitation that the mode *does not allow any further mathematical processing to* be undertaken on it. It is a stand-alone end-product.

▶ One other limitation: there *might not be one most popular value*, or some values might share top spot, so that there might be two or more modes.

How wide is the spread of data? How even is the spread of data?

If researchers wish to describe a set of frequencies it will help if they can provide a measure of central tendency. The *profile* of the data, however, can only be described effectively when there is also some idea of the way the data are spread out from that central point – how they are dispersed.

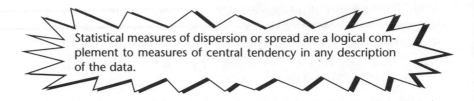

Statistical measures of dispersion or spread are a logical complement to measures of central tendency in any description
of the data.

The range

This is the most simple way of describing the spread of data. It is none the less
effective, and a valuable method of giving an instant image of the dispersion
of the data. The range of the data is calculated by subtracting the minimum
value from the maximum value. In the set of values below, *the range is 44*
(i.e. 47 minus 3).

3	4	7	11	12	17	17	47

Although a statement of the range has value as an instant picture of how wide
the data are spread, it does have a rather serious limitation as a statistic. It is
governed by the extreme values in any set and may consequently give a biased
picture of the spread of the values between the extremes. In the example
above, the range of 44 is obviously determined by the outlier value of 47. Visually, it is evident that seven of the eight values lie within a range of just 14.
So, although reference to the range of values is quick and easy, it needs to be
used cautiously and with a special lookout for any extreme values and the way
these might give a misleading impression of the spread.

Fractiles

Fractiles are based on the idea of dividing the range of the data into fractions,
so that comparisons can be made about the spread of the values across the
range. The starting point for this is the median. The median, as we have seen,
is the mid-point of the range. It is the half-way point, always with 50 per cent
of the cases to one side and 50 per cent of cases to the other. Fractiles develop
on this.

	Q1		Median		Q3	

Quartiles, for instance, subdivide the range into four equal parts. Each quartile contains exactly one-quarter of the cases contained in the whole range.
Deciles operate on the same principle but, as the name suggests, they divide
the range into tenths. Percentiles divide the range into hundredths.

There are two uses of this for social researchers. First, researchers can use
quartiles as a way of eliminating extreme highs and lows from the data they
wish to examine. By focusing on those cases which fall between the first

quartile (Q1) and the third quartile (Q3), researchers know that they are dealing with exactly half of all the cases and, more than that, they are dealing with the half that are 'in the middle'. This middle part of the range is known as the 'inter-quartile range'. With incomes, for instance, use of the inter-quartile range overcomes the possibility of some very high incomes distorting the overall picture, since these would occur in the top quartile. Likewise, by not using the bottom quartile the researchers would eliminate very low incomes from their analysis. So, *one use of fractiles is the selection of cases to analyse.*

A second use is for comparison. Researchers know that a given proportion of their cases occur within a specific fractile of the range. This is true by definition. But this allows them to compare data from one fractile with data from another. The most prominent use of this is in comparisons of income and wealth. The top decile (the 10 per cent of all earners who earn more than the other 90 per cent of earners) can have their pay compared with the 10 per cent of all earners who earn the least. The comparison can be in terms of how much is earned. Here the researchers can calculate the mean earnings of the top decile and compare this with the mean earnings of the bottom decile. Or the proportion of all income going to those in the top decile can be compared with the proportion going to those in the lowest decile. Used in this way, *fractiles are a valuable tool for the social scientist in describing the spread in a frequency distribution.*

Standard deviation

An alternative method of dealing with the spread of data comes in the form of the *standard deviation* (symbolized as σ). Instead of treating the spread in terms of the overall range of the values, the standard deviation measures the spread of data relative to the arithmetic mean of the data. It is not an absolute measure of the difference between the highest value and the lowest value, as is the case with the use of ranges. More subtly, *the standard deviation uses all the values (not just top and bottom) to calculate how far in general the values tend to be spread out around the mean.*

There are variations in the formulae used for calculating the standard deviation, and there are certain complications that set in when it is used with grouped frequencies. However, these should not detain us, because computer software will generally take care of the mathematics involved.

The basic point is this: the greater the dispersion, the larger the standard deviation.

There are a number of factors associated with the use of the standard deviation as a measure of dispersion.

▶ The standard deviation lends itself to further mathematical analysis in a way that a straightforward description of the spread does not.

▶ Following from this, the standard deviation assumes huge importance in social research, because it is the basis of so many other statistical procedures.

▶ Because it takes the arithmetic mean as the basis of its calculations, only those kinds of data that lend themselves to this measure of central tendency can be used. That is, the standard deviation can be used only with cardinal numbers (interval and ratio data). It is meaningless to use it with nominal or even, strictly speaking, with ordinal data.

6 Tests for association and difference: looking for connections

One of the main things we might wish to do once we have collected our quantitative data is to check whether there is any *association*, or link, between two or more sets of data. Does one category of data match another, or does one category vary along with another? Alternatively, we might wish to check whether there is any *difference* between two sets of data where we might have expected there to be a similarity. Either way, we want to move beyond describing and presenting the data (descriptive statistics) to a position where we are *looking for connections*.

Looking for connections, at one level, can be a very straightforward process. In essence, it need only involve looking at the data in the tables or the charts to see what links are evident. However, appearances can be deceptive. They may not tell the whole truth. They may not tell the truth at all! Looking at the data for connections may be a good starting point but, from the point of view of good research, it remains just that – a starting point. Suppose there is an *apparent* connection between two variables. Should this lead the researcher to conclude that the association is real and prompt him or her to conduct further research on the basis that a link had been discovered between the two variables? The answer has to be 'No, at least not yet.'

For research purposes, the mere appearance of a connection is not enough. Good researchers want to know:

▶ whether the findings were a fluke;

▶ how strong the connection is between the two variables;

▶ whether one causes the other, or whether the two are mutually interdependent.

These seem reasonable questions to ask of the data. Although we may be able to 'see' a link in a table or chart, we really need something more positive to support what appears on the surface to be a link between the variables. We need some reassurance that the findings were not a one-off fluke. We need something to give us confidence that what we have found is a genuine association of the two. And this is where *statistical tests of significance* prove to be of enormous benefit. Such statistical tests provide an estimate of the probability that any association we find between two or more variables is the product of sheer chance rather than a genuine connection between such variables – connections that will be found on other occasions. They provide a benchmark for researchers, indicating whether to proceed on the assumption that the apparent connection is real or whether to treat the data as unreliable evidence on the point.

Statistical tests of significance start from the assumption that, despite what might appear in the data, there is no real association between the variables. The frame of mind is that of the sceptic. 'Go on. Convince me that the apparent relationship should be taken seriously. Convince me it is not a fluke, a one-off chance happening!' In the trade this takes the form of what is called the *null hypothesis*. Using the null hypothesis, researchers do not set out to prove the existence of an apparent relationship between variables. Instead, they start from the premise that there is no such relationship – a position that, as scientists, they will hold unless they can be convinced that what was found did not arise by chance.

Statistical tests of significance arrive at a figure that is an estimate of the likelihood that any perceived association is due to chance. The figure is a *probability*, based on statistical theory and procedures, that what *appears* to be contained in the data is actually the outcome of chance. It appears at the end of the computation of statistics in the form '$p < 0.12$' or whatever figure pertains.

If the probability is estimated to be greater than 1 in 20 that the results are a one-off, the sceptically minded researcher will consider that the null hypothesis stands. The researcher will not be convinced that any connection in the data is to be taken seriously. If, on the other hand, it is estimated that there is a probability of less than 1 in 20 that the results arose by chance, the apparent connection is deemed to be *statistically significant*. Within the conventions of statistics, it is held that where the probability is less than 1 in 20 any association in the data may be treated as likely to be genuine and real.

Researchers look for a probability of less than 1 in 20 ($p < 0.05$) that the results arose by chance.

Statistical tests for association and difference

There is little virtue in the context of this book in trying to outline the mechanics of conducting the statistical tests referred to below. Partly, this is because many project researchers will blanch at the sight of the relevant formulae and decide to focus on collecting qualitative data instead. Partly, it is because there are many other sources which offer detailed guidance on statistics for the social scientist. Mostly, though, it is because computer software that will do the necessary calculations is now readily available to the vast majority of social researchers. This means that researchers are released from the burden of long-winded procedures and can pay proper attention to the suitability of the statistics they are using for the specific purposes at hand.

It should also be noted that reference is made only to the basic, standard statistics – the type that might interest the project researcher. The advice at this point: *seek independent expert advice on the choice of statistical analysis.*

⚠ **Caution**

Statistical significance does not necessarily imply social significance. The researcher needs to be wary of mixing the two senses of 'significance'.

Statistical significance only relates to the amount of confidence we have that the findings we obtained were not the product of pure chance. It does *not* automatically imply that the findings are 'important'. That is something to be shown elsewhere by other means.

How do I find out if two variables are associated to a significant level?

Probably the most flexible and certainly the most commonly used statistical test for this is the *chi-square test*. The chi-square test works with nominal data as well as ordinal, interval and ratio data – which does much to explain its popularity. The columns and rows can use nominal data based on things like sex, ethnicity and occupation, factors which feature prominently in data collected by social researchers. See Figure 14.

Days absent from work through illness during the previous years, by sex of employee

| | | | Sex | | |
			Male	Female	Total
Days lost	0–5 days	Count	8	7	15
		Expected count	7.0	8.0	15.0
	6 or more days	Count	6	9	15
		Expected count	7.0	8.0	15.0
Total		Count	14	16	30
		Expected count	14.0	16.0	30.0

	Value	d.f.	(2-sided)
Pearson chi-square	0.536*	1	0.464

* 0 cells (0.0%) have expected count less than 5. The minimum expected count is 7.00.

Figure 14 Chi-square and contingency table examples

It works on the supposition that if there were no relationship between the variables then the units would be distributed in the cells of the contingency table in equal proportion. This means that if there were three times as many women as men in a sample, we would start from the assumption that women would account for 75 per cent of the amounts or frequencies we are measuring – for instance, absences from work. If there is no connection between sex and absenteeism from work, we might expect the larger proportion of women in the sample to account for a larger proportion of absences – in the strict ratio of 3:1. This 'expected' distribution (based on the null hypothesis) is, in other words, a theoretical distribution based on a starting premise that the two variables concerned do not affect each other. In reality, it is extremely unlikely that the research findings will match this theoretical distribution. Almost certainly there will be a difference between what might be expected and what is actually found in practice. And this difference, the difference between what was 'observed' and what was 'expected', is the key to the chi-squared test. The chi-squared test uses the extent of difference (in the cells of a contingency table) between what was observed and what might have been expected in order to calculate whether we can have confidence that the observed relationship was actually due tò something other than pure chance – whether it was real or a fluke.

The main restriction on the use of the chi-square test is that there needs to be a sufficiently large data set and/or a sufficiently even distribution among the various categories in order to get a minimum of five in each cell. Where cells in the contingency table have fewer than five in them it threatens the accuracy of the statistic. There are ways around this should it become a problem. There is a statistical fix which can be used (e.g. Yates correction factor), and most computer programs will put this into operation automatically. Alternatively, the categories can be combined and reduced in number to ensure that each cell has enough data in it.

There is a danger with the use of the chi-square test that the results are heavily affected by the categories which are used. Where categories are combined (for example, to ensure a minimum of five in each cell) or where categories are based on *grouped* frequencies, the researcher needs to be very aware that.

▶ the 'boundaries' for the categories are creations of the researcher;

▶ use of different combinations or boundaries will affect the chi-square statistic.

The flexibility in terms of categories in the columns and rows, then, turns out to be both a strength and a potential weakness of the test.

How do I see if two groups or categories are different to a significant level?

Project researchers often wish to compare two sets of data to see if there is a significant difference between them. For example, a teacher might wish to compare two sets of test scores obtained from students: one set obtained at the start of the school year, the other set obtained from the same students on the same test at the end of the school year. Alternatively, she might wish to compare the results obtained from students in one class with those from another. In small-scale research the need to compare two such groups or categories in these ways is very common.

The most appropriate statistical test for this purpose is the *t-test*. The *t*-test provides the researcher with a statistical test of significance. It uses the means of the two sets of data and their standard deviations to arrive at a figure which tells the researcher the specific likelihood that any differences between the two sets of data are due to chance.

Researchers using the *t*-test take the null hypothesis as their starting point. They presume that there is no real difference until they can be persuaded otherwise by a statistical test which tells them that there is a very strong likelihood that any variation found between the two sets of data were the result of something other than pure chance. As with the chi-shared test, researchers normally treat differences as 'real' (not a fluke) when they find that there is a probability of less than one in twenty, usually expressed as '$p. < 0.05$', that any difference between the two sets of data were due to chance.

The *t*-test

We have two sets of marks obtained from two classes who have both taken the same test at about the same time. Is there a significant difference between the scores obtained by students in class A and the scores obtained by those in class B? The *independent groups t-test* can be used to answer this.

class A (%)	class B (%)
70	55
60	45
45	70
80	75
55	50
65	55
65	40
50	60
80	75
55	50
65	55
65	40
50	60
25	70
80	55
45	
75	
70	
55	
50	

The *t*-test has two notable strengths which are of particular benefit for small-scale research. The *t*-test works well with small sample sizes (less than 30) – an obvious advantage with small-scale research – and the groups do not have to be exactly the same size. A data set of 20 items can be compared with data set of 15, for example.

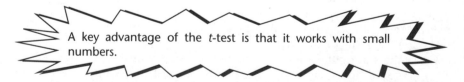

A key advantage of the *t*-test is that it works with small numbers.

There are other statistical tests which compare the results from two sets of data that will work with ordinal data rather than interval or ratio data. For example, the Mann–Whitney U test is a well known test that works by using the rank-ordering of cases in each group. This is why it can work with ordinal data such as examination *grades* (A, B+, B etc.) if actual percentage scores are not available. The Mann–Whitney U test works by producing one overall ranking which is made from both groups being investigated. The positions of members of each group on this combined ranking are then used as the basis for calculating whether there is a statistically significant difference between the two groups.

How do I see if three or more groups or categories are significantly related?

This question is likely to be moving beyond the scope of interest for project researchers. It suggests a fairly large data set with more than two variables potentially connected and worthy of statistical test. It calls for a basic *factor analysis*, such as one-way *ANOVA* (analysis of variance). This test analyses the variation within and between groups or categories of data using a comparison of means.

How do I assess the strength of a relationship between two variables?

This question is not concerned with the *likelihood* of any apparent connection between two variables being real; it is concerned with how *closely* two variables are connected. The relevant statistics here are *correlations*.

Correlations between two variables can be visualized using a *scatter plot*. These need ratio, interval or ordinal data, and cannot be used with nominal data. They also require reasonably large data sets to work best. See Figure 15.

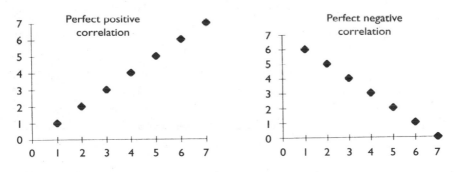

Figure 15 Correlations and scatter plot examples

The two most commonly used correlation statistics are Spearman's rank correlation coefficient (which works with ordinal data) and Pearson's product moment correlation coefficient (which works with interval and ratio data). These statistical tests are used to arrive at a *correlation coefficient* based on the data. The correlation coefficients range as follows:

+1	0	−1
perfect positive correlation (one goes up, other goes up)	no relationship	perfect negative correlation (one goes up, other goes down)

In reality, correlations are unlikely to be perfect. Researchers generally regard any correlation coefficient between 0.3 and 0.7 (plus or minus) as demonstrating some reasonable correlation between two variables. 0.3 is reasonably weak, 0.7 is reasonably strong.

It is important to appreciate that correlation is different from cause. The connection between two variables that might be demonstrated using a correlation test says nothing about which variable is the dependent and which is the independent one. It says nothing about which is the cause and which is the effect. It only establishes that there is a connection, with a specified closeness of fit between the variables.

Researchers wishing to investigate connections in terms of cause and effect need to use *regression analysis*.

7 Types of quantitative data and appropriate descriptive statistics

Type of data	Central tendency	Dispersion	Statistical test
Nominal	Mode	Frequency distribution	Chi-square
Ordinal	Median	Range	Mann–Whitney U test
Interval	Mean	Standard deviation	t-test Analysis of variance

Adapted from Worthington and Holloway (1997: 76).

8 Advantages of quantitative analysis

▶ *Scientific*. Quantitative data lend themselves to various forms of statistical techniques based on the principles of mathematics and probability. Such statistics provide the analyses with an aura of scientific respectability. The analyses *appear* to be based on objective laws rather than the values of the researcher.

▶ *Confidence*. Statistical tests of significance give researchers additional credibility in terms of the interpretations they make and the confidence they have in their findings.

▶ *Measurement*. The analysis of quantitative data provides a solid foundation for description and analysis. Interpretations and findings are based on measured quantities rather than impressions, and these are, at least in principle, quantities that can be checked by others for authenticity.

▶ *Analysis*. Large volumes of quantitative data can be analysed relatively quickly, provided adequate preparation and planning has occurred in advance. Once the procedures are 'up and running', researchers can interrogate their results relatively quickly.

▶ *Presentation*. Tables and charts provide a succinct and effective way of organizing quantitative data and communicating the findings to others. Widely available computer software aids the design of tables and charts, and takes most of the hard labour out of statistical analysis.

9 Disadvantages of quantitative analysis

▶ *Quality of data*. The quantitative data are only as good as the methods used to collect them and the questions that are asked. As with computers, it is a matter of 'garbage in, garbage out'.

▶ *Technicist*. There is a danger of researchers becoming obsessed with the techniques of analysis at the expense of the broader issues underlying the research. Particularly with the power of computers at researchers' fingertips, attention can sway from the real purpose of the research towards an overbearing concern with the technical aspects of analysis.

▶ *Data overload*. Large volumes of data can be a strength of quantitative analysis but, without care, it can start to overload the researcher. Too many cases, too many variables, too many factors to consider – the analysis can be driven towards too much complexity. The researcher can get swamped.

▶ *False promise*. Decisions made during the analysis of quantitative data can have far-reaching effects on the kinds of findings that emerge. In fact, the analysis of quantitative data, in some respects, is no more neutral or objective than the analysis of qualitative data. For example, the manipulation of categories and the boundaries of grouped frequencies can be used to achieve a data fix, to show significance where other combinations of the data do not. *Quantitative analysis is not as scientifically objective as it might seem on the surface.*

Checklist for the use of basic statistics

When using basic statistics in the research you should feel confident about answering 'yes' to the following questions:

1 Am I clear about *which type(s)* of data I am using (nominal, ordinal, interval, ratio)? ☐

2 Has due consideration been given to how the *type of data* affects their use with statistical procedures? ☐

3 If the analysis is *describing frequencies*, has any statistical test used with the data been confirmed as appropriate? ☐

4 If the analysis is *looking for connections*, has any statistical test used with the data been confirmed as appropriate? ☐

5 Have research questions been couched in the form of a *null hypothesis?* ☐

6 Are there *sufficient numbers* involved to warrant statistical analysis? ☐

7 Have any statistical tests of significance achieved a satisfactorily low probability ($p < 0.05$) to justify conclusions based on the data? ☐

11

QUALITATIVE DATA

Qualitative research is an umbrella term that covers a variety of styles of social research, drawing on a variety of disciplines such as sociology, social anthropology and social psychology. Tesch (1990) lists 26 distinct kinds of social research which can fall under the term 'qualitative' and, no doubt, as time goes by the list could be extended. But, as she goes on to indicate, there are some common elements to these approaches which begin to give some sense to the term 'qualitative research'.

▶ *A concern with meanings and the way people understand things.* Human activity is seen as a product of symbols and meanings that are used by members of the social group to make sense of things. Such symbols and meanings need to be analysed as a 'text' – to be interpreted rather like a literary critic interprets a book.

▶ *A concern with patterns of behaviour.* Here the focus is on regularities in the activities of a social group, such as in rituals, traditions and relationships, and the way these are expressed as patterns of behaviour, cultural norms and types of language used.

In their own right, however, these two strands of interest are not enough to give qualitative research its distinctive character. These interests have also been the concern of approaches which would never align themselves with the word 'qualitative'. Strictly speaking, it is neither the topics it investigates nor even the nature of its data, which is truly at the heart of qualitative research. What actually separates qualitative research and gives it its distinct identity is the fact that it has its own special approach to the collection and analysis of data, which, as this chapter shows, marks it out as quite different from its quantitative counterpart.

1 The *self* and qualitative analysis

Qualitative data, whether words or images, are the product of a process of interpretation. The data only become data when they are used as such. The data do not exist 'out there' waiting to be discovered, as would be the case if a positivistic approach were adopted, but are *produced* by the way they are interpreted and used by researchers.

This is particularly important to recognize, because the nature of qualitative data – in the main, 'words' – lends itself to the temptation to present them as though they were pure and untouched by the act of research itself. It might be tempting, for example, to present a quote extracted from an interview transcript as though it needs no commentary and can be taken at face value. However, this is not a practice that would be supported by the vast majority of 'qualitative' researchers. And the reason they would not support it stems from the general premise underlying the analysis of qualitative data: that *the researcher's self plays a significant role in the production and interpretation of qualitative data*. The researcher's identity, values and beliefs cannot be entirely eliminated from the process – again in stark contrast to the ambitions of a positivistic approach to social research. Among practitioners of qualitative research there is a general acceptance that the researcher's self is *inevitably* an integral part of the analysis, and should be acknowledged as such.

Uses of qualitative data

Qualitative research can be part of an *information gathering* exercise and useful in its own right. Or, qualitative research can be used as the basis for *generating theories*. In neither case, however, are its descriptions ever 'pure' – they are always the outcome of an interpretation by the researchers.

There are two ways in which qualitative researchers can deal with this involvement of the self. On the one hand, they can deal with it by saying:

> the researcher's identity, values and beliefs play a role in the production and analysis of qualitative data and therefore researchers should be on their guard to distance themselves from their normal, everyday beliefs and to suspend judgements on social issues for the duration of their research.

At this end of the scale, researchers know that their self is intertwined with their research activity, but proceed on the basis that they can exercise sufficient control over their normal attitudes to allow them to operate in a detached manner, so that their investigation is not clouded by personal prejudices. In this case, the researcher needs to suspend personal beliefs for the purposes of the production and analysis of the data.

On the other hand, they can take the position that:

the researcher's identity, values and beliefs play a role in the production and analysis of qualitative data and therefore researchers should come clean about the way their research agenda has been shaped by personal experiences and social backgrounds.

At the extreme, this approach can take the form of celebrating the extent to which the self is intertwined with the research process. There are those who argue that their self gives them a privileged insight into social issues, so that the researcher's self should not be regarded as a limitation to the research but as a crucial resource. Some feminist researchers and some researchers in the field of 'race' make the case that their identity, values and beliefs actually *enable* the research and should be exploited to the full to get at areas that will remain barred to researchers with a different self. So some feminists argue that only a woman can truly grasp the significance of factors concerned with the subordination of women in society. Some black researchers would make a similar point in relation to 'race' inequality.

Between these two positions lie a variety of shades of opinion about the degree to which the researcher's self can and should be acknowledged as affecting the production and analysis of qualitative data.

2 Preparing qualitative data for analysis

Qualitative data can be obtained using a variety of research methods (see previous chapters) and can come in a variety of formats: fieldwork notes, interview transcripts, texts etc. Whatever the format, they need to be *organized* before they can lend themselves to a process of analysis, and the organization of qualitative data in preparation for analysis requires the following practical steps.

▶ As far as possible, get *all materials in similar format* (for example, all on A4 size pages, or all on record cards of the same size). This helps with storage and when sifting through the materials.

▶ Where possible, the raw data should be collated in a way that allows researchers' notes and comments to be added alongside. So, for example, when taped interviews are transcribed, there should be a *wide margin to the right-hand side of the page left blank*, so that the researcher can add notes next to the relevant words. Experienced researchers think ahead on this score. Field notes, for instance, will be kept in a notebook which is specially prepared to have a blank column on the right of each page for later comments.

▶ Each piece of 'raw data' material should be identified with a unique *serial number or code for reference purposes*. The format of the reference code is not important, as long as it enables each separate item to be identified exactly in terms of where it should be located. The importance of this is twofold. First, when analysing the data it is vital that the researcher is able to return to points in the data which are of particular interest. Without an adequate reference system, it will be virtually impossible for the researcher to navigate back and forth through the data, or to record which bits of data are significant. Second, on a very practical note, when you are sifting through mounds of papers or record cards, it is all too easy to muddle the order or lose the place where the piece of raw data was originally located. A sound reference code is needed to relocate such material.

Link up with **Computer-aided analysis of qualitative data, p. 218**

This *reference coding of the raw data* applies whatever the kind of materials. At its simplest, it means tagging an audio tape with details of when and where it was recorded. With field notes and transcripts, however, it is necessary to put a unique reference to each part of the material. This can mean a unique reference code for each page, or even for each paragraph. Note that this offers an early opportunity to retain the confidentiality and anonymity of data if required. So, for example, rather than code the tenth page of the transcript of an interview with Ms Hallam at Dovedale High School as [Hallam:Dovedale:p.10], the teacher and school could be identified via a separate coding list. Ms Hallam might be allocated T07 (the seventh teacher interviewed, perhaps), Dovedale High School might be allocated the code 13 (as school number 13), so that the actual code to appear on the raw data sheets would be [T07:13:p.10]. Such codes are, incidentally, a great saving of effort when this needs to be applied sequentially to every piece of data.

▶ *Make a back-up copy of all original materials*, and use the back-up copies for any analysis. Because qualitative data tend to be irreplaceable, it is good practice to make a duplicate of any tapes and to photocopy any documents, such as field notes or transcripts. This can prove to be something of a chore. It is time-consuming and can be expensive. But any loss or damage to the material is catastrophic for the research.

To save effort, it is best to duplicate the raw data as soon as they have been reference coded. This saves the need to do the reference coding on both the original and the back-up. The original should be stored safely – preferably in a location quite separate from the back-up copies, which now become the 'working copies' that the researcher uses for analysis.

3 Procedures for analysing qualitative data

Coding and categorizing the data

This process is quite distinct from putting a *reference* code on the various pieces of data so that parts can be identified and stored in an organized manner. Coding the data, in this sense, involves:

▶ Breaking the data down into units for analysis.
▶ Categorizing the units.

It is *analytic* coding. The raw data might take the form of interview transcripts, field notes, documents or video tapes. Whatever the form, the first thing the researcher needs to do is decide on the *units* that will be used for the analysis. This process is sometimes known as 'unitizing' the data. With documents the units might be specific *words*. In newspapers or interview transcripts, for example, the units might consist of a specific word appearing or being used. More commonly, qualitative researchers will be on the lookout for the occurrence in the data of particular *ideas* or *events*.

This begs the question, '*which* words, ideas or events should be looked for in the data, and which categories should they be put into?' Here, the answer from most qualitative researchers would be that, *at the beginning*, the choice is not crucial. The researcher can use existing theories, respondent categories or personal/professional hunches to guide how this is done in the first place. The reason it is not regarded as crucial at the initial phase of analysis is that the units and the categories are subject to a continual process of refinement during the research, so if the initial units and categories are 'incorrect', later versions will be refined and improved.

The initial stage of coding has been termed 'open coding'. 'The aim of open coding is to discover, name and categorize phenomena; also to develop categories in terms of their properties and dimensions' (Strauss and Corbin 1990: 181).

Reflections on the early coding and categories

The researcher needs to go through the field notes, transcripts or texts, adding comments and reflections in the margins alongside the raw data. As the analysis progresses, new things might emerge as relevant, or new interpretations might be given to the same extract of data. As *new insights* come to the researcher, they should be recorded on the (back-up copy of the) data.

Most experts in this approach to research also advocate the keeping of *memos to self* at all stages of the research. Such memos, like the comments in the margins on the raw data, serve two purposes. First, they act as a reminder about new thinking by the researcher on facets of the investigation. Second, they act as a log of the developing line of thinking, and this helps enormously with the *audit trail* (see below).

Identification of themes and relationships

A vital part of the reflections undertaken by the qualitative researcher will be the attempt to identify 'patterns and processes, commonalities and differences' (Miles and Huberman 1994: 9). When revisiting the field notes, transcripts or text, the researcher should be on the lookout for *themes* or *interconnections* that recur between the units and categories that are emerging.

It is worth emphasizing that this is a part of the analysis of qualitative data which is repeated time and again in order to refine the explanation to which the researcher is working.

Return to the field to check out emerging explanations

As various explanations and themes emerge from the early consideration of the data, the researcher should go back to the field with these explanations and themes to check their validity against 'reality'.

Develop a set of generalizations

Through the process of reflection on the materials and checking these out in the field, the researcher should aim to refine a set of generalizations that explain the themes and relationships identified in the data.

Use the new generalizations to improve any relevant existing theories

The researcher should compare the new generalized statements with existing theories or explanations and develop these in line with the findings from field-work.

4 Justifying the methods and conclusions

As with any kind of research, the methods and conclusions need to be justifiable. Such justification cannot be an assertion or an act of faith, but must rely on demonstrating to the reader the nature of the decisions taken during the research and the grounds on which the decisions can be seen as 'reasonable'. Equally, the issues of objectivity, reliability and validity are as relevant to qualitative research as to any other approach (Kirk and Miller 1986; Silverman 1993; Miles and Huberman 1994).

Objectivity

> The basic issue here can be framed as one of relative neutrality and reasonable freedom from unacknowledged researcher biases – at the minimum explicitness about the inevitable biases that exist.
>
> (Miles and Huberman 1994: 278)

As we have seen, the role of the self in qualitative research is important, and there is a growing acceptance among those involved in qualitative data analysis that some *biographical details about the researcher warrant inclusion as part of the analysis*, thus allowing the writer to explore the ways in which he or she feels personal experiences and values might influence matters. The reader of the research, by the same token, is given valuable information on which to base a judgement about how reasonable the writer's claims are with regard to the detachment or involvement of self-identity, values and beliefs. *The analysis of qualitative data calls for a reflexive account by the researcher concerning the researcher's self and its impact on the research.*

Reliability

In the classic meaning of reliability, the criterion of reliability is whether the research instruments are neutral in their effect, and would measure the same result when used on other occasions (applied to the same 'object'). But with qualitative research the researcher's self, as we have argued, is an integral part of the research instrument. The issue of reliability, then, is transformed into the question:

> If *someone else* did the research would he or she have got the same results and arrived at the same conclusions?

In an absolute sense there is probably no way of knowing this for certain. Yet there are ways of dealing with this issue in qualitative research. Principally, these involve providing an explicit account of:

▶ the aims of the research and its basic premises (purpose, theory);

▶ how the research was undertaken;

▶ most importantly in this context, *the reasoning behind key decisions made* (e.g. in relation to sampling).

Only if such information is supplied is it possible to reach conclusions about how far another researcher would have come up with the same findings. This is why it is good practice to keep a fairly detailed record of the process of the research decisions – what is sometimes termed an *audit trail*.

An audit trail (Lincoln and Guba 1985) should be constructed and mapped out for the reader – allowing him or her to follow the path and key decisions taken by the researcher from conception of the research through to the findings and conclusions derived from the research. But, as Lincoln and Guba stress, 'An inquiry audit cannot be conducted without a residue of records stemming from the inquiry, just as a fiscal audit cannot be conducted without a residue of records from the business transactions involved' (Lincoln and Guba 1985: 319).

Validity

There are many ways in which checks on the validity of the findings can be undertaken, but they boil down to the following items.

▶ Do the conclusions do justice to the complexity of the phenomenon being investigated and avoid 'oversimplifications', while also offering internal consistency?

▶ Has the researcher's self been recognized as an *influence* in the research but not a cause of biased and one-sided reporting? This is a difficult tightrope to walk, but vital in the context of such research.

▶ Have the instances selected for investigation been chosen on explicit and reasonable grounds as far as the aims of the research are concerned?

▶ Have alternative possible explanations been explored? The researcher needs to demonstrate that he or she has not simply plumped for the first explanation that fits, rather than seeing if rival theories work or whether there are hidden problems with the proposed explanation.

▶ Have the findings been 'triangulated' with alternative sources as a way of bolstering confidence in their validity?

▶ Have the research findings been fed back to informants to get their opinion on the explanation being proposed? The informants would normally be expected to identify with the research account and feel that it accords with their feelings and behaviours;

▶ How far do the findings and conclusion fit with existing knowledge on the area, and how far do they translate to other comparable situations? (external validity).

5 Grounded theory

Glaser and Strauss's *The Discovery of Grounded Theory* (1967) is frequently cited by researchers in relation to their analysis of qualitative data, and rightly so. The book built upon a long tradition of qualitative research in the USA to provide a referent point for qualitative researchers in the decades to follow.

Because the work features so prominently in the area of qualitative data analysis, some brief outline of its basic premises is warranted here. These premises have become established as accepted practice across a broad spectrum of qualitative approaches, beyond the particular scope of 'grounded theory' for which they were intended.

Premise 1: Glaser and Strauss's approach to the analysis of qualitative data is broadly speaking a 'pragmatic' one

They stressed in their work, and in subsequent writings, that research work is undertaken in very different settings by researchers who bring very different personal and professional qualities to bear. It is not feasible, therefore, to impose a set of methodological rules to be followed on all occasions. More than this, the imposition of a set of methodological rules would even prove detrimental to the quality of research: 'a standardization of methods (swallowed whole, taken seriously) would only constrain and even stifle social researchers' best efforts' (Strauss 1987: 7). As Glaser and Strauss see it, their approach offers 'guidelines and rules of thumb, not rules'.

Premise 2: The analysis of qualitative data should be geared towards generating new concepts and theories

As Strauss has made the point, 'theory at various levels of generality is indispensable for deeper knowledge of social phenomena' (Strauss 1987: 6). On one level, this might seem obvious. However, the premise is significant in the sense that it clearly separates the approach of Glaser and Strauss from 'descriptive' studies in which qualitative data are presented 'as found' as a portrait of the people and events concerned. The key word here is *analysis*. The 'grounded theory' approach is directly concerned with the ways in which social researchers organize their qualitative research materials, with how they code the material and with how they make sense of the material. It does not accept the notion that qualitative research materials can be left to 'speak for themselves'.

Premise 3: Theories should be 'grounded' in empirical reality

Glaser and Strauss argued that theories need to be based on empirical research, and that such theories should emerge and develop as part of the process of research.

> Generating a theory from data means that most hypotheses and concepts not only come from the data, but are systematically worked out in relation to the data during the course of the research.
>
> (Glaser and Strauss 1967: 6)

In their eyes, it is not good enough to do empirical work and then 'tag on theory'. Nor is it good enough to produce a theory without thoroughly testing it against the reality it purports to depict. Good qualitative social research, according to the principles of grounded theory, involves a constant *checking* of the analysis (theories, concepts) against the findings and a constant *refinement* of the theories and concepts during the process of research.

Premise 4: Qualitative social researchers should start out with an 'open mind'

In marked contrast to the researcher who sets out to *test* a theory, the researcher who follows the principles of grounded theory needs to approach the topic without a rigid set of ideas that shape what he or she focuses upon during the investigation. Rather than basing an investigation upon whether certain theories do or do not work, *the researcher embarks on a voyage of discovery*.

This should not be seen to imply that a good social researcher starts out with a 'blank' mind.

> To be sure, one goes out and studies an area with a particular . . . perspective, and with a focus, a general question or a problem in mind. But the researcher can (and we believe should) also study an area without any preconceived theory that dictates, prior to the research, 'relevancies' in concepts and hypotheses.
>
> (Glaser and Strauss 1967: 33)

So, an open mind is not a blank mind on a subject. It is informed about an area, but open to discovering new factors of relevance to an explanation of that area, rather than restricting the scope and vision of the research to whether a hypothesis based on existing theories had got it right (or not).

Premise 5: The selection of people, instances, etc. to be included reflects the developing nature of the research and cannot be predicted at the start

The units to be included follow a trail of discovery – like a detective follows a 'lead'. Each new phase of the investigation reflects what has been discovered so far, with new angles of investigation and new avenues of enquiry to be explored. Interviews with some informants might suggest that it would be useful to talk with other particular informants in order to shed light on a specific area, and it would have been impossible to predict such a pathway of investigation before having spoken to the first informants. The relevance of the second set of informants and the value of their information could not have been foreseen before the investigation had begun. Each new part of the investigation generates new areas of interest and new paths to follow. So, in the spirit of 'grounded theory' it is neither feasible nor desirable for the researcher to identify prior to the start exactly who or what will be included in the sample.

Link up with **Sampling and qualitative research, p. 25**

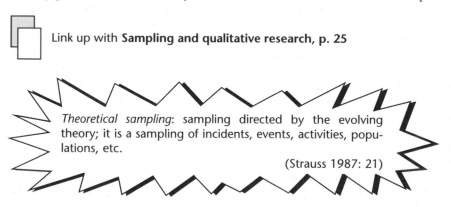

Theoretical sampling: sampling directed by the evolving theory; it is a sampling of incidents, events, activities, populations, etc.

(Strauss 1987: 21)

The researcher following the principles of grounded theory will not want, or be able, to specify at the outset exactly how *large* the sample will be. The process of research will involve the continued selection of units until the research arrives at the point of '*theoretical saturation*'. It is only when the new data seem to confirm the analysis rather than add anything new that the sampling ceases and the sample size is 'enough'.

Theoretical saturation: when additional analysis no longer contributes to discovering anything new about a category.

(Strauss 1987: 21)

This, of course, runs right against the grain as far as conventional social research practice is concerned. Normally, the social researcher would be expected to have a very clear vision of the intended sample, chosen on the basis of criteria linked to the ideas and theories being tested by the research.

The significance of grounded theory for qualitative social research goes beyond its use by disciples who would rigorously follow the word of the leaders. Layder (1993) has emphasized the point that it is a 'flexible interpretation' of their ideas across a range of research approaches that accounts for the significant impact of grounded theory on social research. Grounded theory 'must be viewed flexibly, as an approach which is potentially open to the influence of other approaches to research and theory' (Layder 1993: 69) and which, reciprocally, influences them.

The fact is that the term 'grounded theory' is often used in a rather loose way – a way that Glaser and Strauss themselves would not appreciate – to refer to approaches that accept some of the basic premises but do not adopt the methodological rigour espoused by the originators of the term. In its loose sense, grounded theory broadly indicates an approach which:

▶ uses *empirical* field research as its starting point;

▶ bases its analysis around the *fieldwork observations*;

▶ produces *explanations which are relevant* for those who are the subjects of research and recognizable to them;

▶ is geared to *modest localized explanations* based on the immediate evidence, rather than efforts to produce or prove grand theories;

▶ adopts an *emergent design*, where the samples and the focus of research develop during the course of the research rather than being preordained at the outset.

Social researchers should be aware when using the term 'grounded theory' of just how far they are justified in citing Glaser and Strauss as the key source for their approach, and how far their approach actually accords with the looser, flexible interpretation of the term. All too frequently, Glaser and Strauss are cited in the context of research methods that bear few of the hallmarks of the strict conception of 'grounded theory'.

 Caution

Grounded theory can prove a very attractive proposition for the project researcher. If it is taken at a very basic level it can seem to offer a sound rationalization for approaching research: (a) without too clear an idea of the topic of research; (b) without a clear sample in mind; and (c) with a general 'jump in at the deep end', 'try it and see', 'find out as we go' approach. There is a very real danger that Glaser and Strauss's work can be cited as justification for sloppy research – and this is certainly not in tune with the spirit of Glaser and Strauss's ideas. Indeed, their ideas are geared towards *increased* rigour in the analysis of qualitative data.

6 Computer-aided analysis of qualitative data

There are a growing number of computer software packages being developed which are specifically dedicated to the analysis of qualitative data. Perhaps the most well-known of these are *The Ethnograph* and *Nud.ist* (which stands for Non-numerical Unstructured Data. Indexing, Searching, Theorizing). Such packages operate off popular Windows and Macintosh machines and promise 'unparalleled support of the traditional processes of qualitative analysis'.

Word-processing packages also have potential for the analysis of qualitative data. The text management facilities with integral coding fields ensure that many, if not most, project researchers will have some computer software available to help with their analysis.

The main advantages of using such software to aid the analysis of qualitative data stem from the *superb abilities of computers to manage the data*. Computers offer a major advance in terms of:

▶ *Storage of data*. Interview transcripts, field notes and documents can be kept in text files. Copies are quick.

▶ *Coding of data*. The data can be easily coded – in the sense of both *indexing* the data (serial codes) and *categorizing* chunks of the data as a preliminary part of the analysis.

▶ *Retrieval of data*. The search facilities of the software make it easy to locate data once it has been coded and to pluck it out for further scrutiny.

Constant advances in computer technology and software design promise to make this *chunking and coding*, as Tesch (1990) puts it, even easier in the future. Developments such as hypertext will enhance the researcher's ability to store and manipulate qualitative data. Indeed, the capabilities of the hardware and software in respect of chunking and coding will exceed the needs of the vast majority of social researchers. In the words of Lyn and Tom Richards, designers of Nud.ist:

> Computerization removes barriers to scale and complexity of analyses. There are virtually no clerical limits to how *much* stuff you get now, and few to how complex it is.
>
> (Richards and Richards 1993: 40)

There are some spin-offs from the computer-aided management of data which offer further benefits for the analysis of qualitative data. As Fielding and Lee (1993: 3) argue:

▶ it makes it easier to find deviant cases or to extract small but significant pieces of information buried within a large mass of material;

▶ the mechanics of field research should become less likely to get in the way of analytic processes;

▶ following Tesch (1990), 'the computer encourages researchers to "play" with the data, a process which fosters analytic insight.'

The extent to which computer packages can aid the *analysis* of qualitative data, distinct from the storage/retrieval capability, is a matter of controversy. Some software packages lay claim to going beyond helping researchers with the management of the data to helping to undertake the analysis itself. Miles and Huberman refer to these as 'theory builder' programs.

> They usually include code-and-retrieve capabilities, but also allow you to make connections between codes (categories of information); to develop higher-order classifications and categories; to formulate propositions or assertions, implying a conceptual structure that fits the data; and/or to test such propositions to determine whether they apply.
>
> (Miles and Huberman 1994: 312)

The controversial issue is whether the formal logic used by the computer is suitable for the analysis of qualitative data. For those who follow a strict version of grounded theory, in which the text is to be taken at face value and theory emerges inductively from the data, the computer's logical analysis really can *do* the analysis – in part, if not in whole. The *Kwalitan* program developed by Fred Wester and Vincent Peters offers a good example here. It aims at data reduction and integration which leads to grounded theory.

However, Tesch (among others) warns of the dangers of overestimating the extent to which computer programs can actually *do* the analysis.

> In all qualitative analyses the process consists of two simultaneous activities. The *conceptual* operations involved can be carried out only in conjunction with or after the accomplishment of certain *mechanical* tasks in the management of the data . . . This, of course, is where the computer becomes useful . . .
>
> The thinking, judging, deciding, interpreting, etc. are still done by the researcher. The computer does not make conceptual decisions, such as which words or themes are important to focus on, or which analytic step to take next.
>
> (Tesch 1993: 25–6)

There is a justifiable fear, then, that slavishly following the conventions and procedures built into the software programs will kill off the intuitive art of analysis in qualitative research. It leaves little scope for interpretive leaps and inspirational flashes of enlightenment. It reduces analysis to a mechanical chore.

The use of computers for the analysis of qualitative data gives rise to a second concern not altogether unlinked to the first. It is likely to exacerbate the tendency to focus on the literal or superficial content of the text and further decontextualize the chunks of data that are analysed. Computer programs cannot analyse the temporal sequence in the data. They cannot understand the implied meanings which depend on events in the background. To be fair, the computer programs in this respect are only extending and exaggerating a potential hazard facing any procedure which seeks to analyse the data through a systematic chunking and coding. The point is that dedicated software packages do this more quickly and more extensively, and hence are potentially more dangerous.

There is a third kind of danger associated with the use of computer packages as an aid to the analysis of qualitative data: *data overload* and the tendency to distance the researcher from the data. The point is that the increasing power of the computer offers the researcher the enticing prospect of using ever more complex codes and connections. It can cope with vastly more complex procedures – and vastly more data. Yet this can actually turn out to be counterproductive as far as research is concerned. This is a point noted even by the designer of *The Ethnograph* – what John Seidel regards as 'an infatuation with the volume of data one can deal with, leading to a sacrifice of resolution for scope [and] distancing of the researcher from the data' (Seidel 1993: 107).

A fourth deterrent to the use of computers is the start-up time and costs involved. These might pay off for the large-scale projects, but not for the small-scale.

> Depending on the amount of data you have and the depth of analysis you
> want, it might make sense to use *The Ethnograph*, or a word processor and
> outlining software, or revert to highlighting pens and Post-it notes. The
> overhead in setting up and using packages is not always worth it.
>
> (Fielding 1993: 3)

From an expert, and one who supports the value of computers in the analysis of qualitative data, this statement spells out the main reason why there is not too much attention given at this point to computer-aided analysis. *Most small-scale research projects will find the set-up costs (time and money) of using computer software packages will outweigh any potential benefits.*

7 Advantages of qualitative analysis

▶ *The data and the analysis are 'grounded'.* A particular strength associated with qualitative research is that the descriptions and theories such research generates are 'grounded in reality'. This is not to suggest that they depict reality in some simplistic sense, as though social reality were 'out there' waiting to be 'discovered'. But it does suggest that the data and the analysis have their roots in the conditions of social existence. There is little scope for 'armchair theorizing' or 'ideas plucked out of thin air'.

▶ *There is a richness and detail to the data.* The in-depth study of relatively focused areas, the tendency towards small-scale research and the generation of 'thick descriptions' mean that qualitative research scores well in terms of the way it deals with complex social situations. It is better able to deal with the intricacies of a situation and do justice to the subtleties of social life.

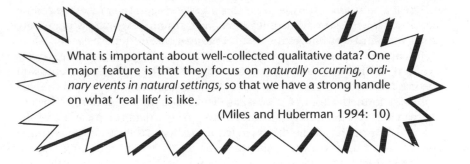

What is important about well-collected qualitative data? One major feature is that they focus on *naturally occurring, ordinary events in natural settings,* so that we have a strong handle on what 'real life' is like.

(Miles and Huberman 1994: 10)

▶ *There is tolerance of ambiguity and contradictions.* To the extent that social existence involves uncertainty, accounts of that existence ought to be able to tolerate ambiguities and contradictions, and qualitative research is better able to do this than quantitative research (Maykut and Morehouse 1994: 34). This is not a reflection of a weak analysis. It is a reflection of the social reality being investigated.

▶ *There is the prospect of alternative explanations.* Qualitative analysis, because it draws on the interpretive skills of the researcher, opens up the possibility of more than one explanation being valid. Rather than a presumption that there must be, in theory at least, one correct explanation, it allows for the possibility that different researchers might reach different conclusions, despite using broadly the same methods.

8 Disadvantages of qualitative analysis

▶ *The data may be less representative.* The flip-side of qualitative research's attention to thick description and the grounded approach is that it becomes more difficult to establish how far the findings from the detailed, in-depth study of a small number of instances may be generalized to other similar instances. Provided sufficient detail is given about the circumstances of the research, however, it *is* still possible to gauge how far the findings relate to other instances, but such generalizability is still more open to doubt than it is with well conducted quantitative research.

▶ *Interpretation is bound up with the 'self' of the researcher.* Qualitative research recognizes more openly than does quantitative research that the researcher's own identity, background and beliefs have a role in the creation of data and the analysis of data. The research is 'self-aware'. This means that the findings are necessarily more cautious and tentative, because it operates on the basic assumption that the findings are a creation of the researcher rather than a discovery of fact. Although it may be argued that quantitative research is guilty of trying to gloss over the point – which equally well applies – the greater exposure of the intrusion of the 'self' in qualitative research inevitably means more cautious approaches to the findings.

▶ *There is a possibility of decontextualizing the meaning.* In the process of coding and categorizing the field notes, texts or transcripts there is a possibility that the words (or images for that matter) get taken literally *out of context*. The context is an integral part of the qualitative data, and the context refers to both events surrounding the production of the data, and events and words that precede and follow the actual extracted pieces of data that are used to form the units for analysis. There is a very real danger for the researcher that in coding and categorizing of the data the meaning of the data is lost or transformed by wrenching it from its location (a) within a sequence of data (e.g. interview talk), or (b) within surrounding circumstances which have a bearing on the meaning of the unit as it was originally conceived at the time of data collection.

▶ *There is the danger of oversimplifying the explanation.* In the quest to identify themes in the data and to develop generalizations the researcher can feel pressured to underplay, possibly disregard, data that 'doesn't fit'. Inconsistencies, ambiguities, alternative explanations can be frustrating in the way they inhibit a nice clear generalization – but they are an inherent feature of social life. Social phenomena are complex, and the analysis of qualitative data needs to acknowledge this and avoid attempts to oversimplify matters.

Checklist for the analysis of qualitative data ✓

When analysing qualitative data you should feel confident about answering 'yes' to the following questions:

1. Has the research identified themes and relationships in the units of data? ☐

2. Have the emerging categories and explanations been checked out by returning to the field? ☐

3. Have sufficient details been incorporated to allow an 'audit' of key decisions in the process of the research? ☐

4. Does the analysis avoid decontextualizing the meaning of the data? ☐

5. Does the explanation avoid oversimplifying issues? ☐

6. Have the findings been checked for external reliability with other comparable studies? ☐

7. Has the topic been approached with an 'open mind'? ☐

8. Have alternative explanations been considered? ☐

9. Does the research report include some account of the researcher's *self* and its possible impact? ☐

12

WRITING UP

Only when there is a formal record of the research does it become open to public scrutiny and amenable to evaluation by others, things normally expected of anything which purports to be research. There may be some unusual exceptions to this – perhaps with 'action research' or research concerned with 'empowerment' – but as a general rule the research procedures and findings need to be recorded in writing if they are to be of any value.

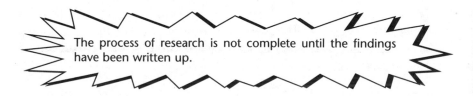

The process of research is not complete until the findings have been written up.

Having accepted this point, the project researcher might be tempted to regard such writing up as something to be tagged on at the end of the research. It might be seen as a bit of a chore – a mechanical process to be done once the real research has been completed, like writing up chemistry experiments once they have been conducted in the laboratory. Having observed and measured and made meticulous notes, the researcher produces a factual description of the events. This, however, would be a dangerous attitude to take, because:

▶ It would fail to appreciate the ways in which writing up is creative. It is not a matter of literal reportage; it is a matter of producing an *account* of the research.

▶ It would fail to acknowledge the influence of *different audiences* on the way in which the research is written up.

▶ It would fail to recognize the importance of 'writing up' as an aspect of research which is skilful in its own right. Writing up is something of a craft. It needs to adopt an appropriate *style of writing* and take account of *certain conventions* to do with the layout of the reports, their structure and style of writing.

Writing up involves a blend of interpretation, craft and convention aimed at producing a formal record of the research which can be evaluated by others. At one and the same time it is a creative enterprise and an activity constrained by convention.

1 Producing accounts of the research

Without getting side-tracked into the philosophical issues behind this, the project researcher would do well to recognize that, when one is writing about the research, what is being produced is unlikely to be a literal depiction of events. Indeed, it is almost impossible to envisage a literal account of the research process, because:

▶ There are always limitations to the space available to provide the account of what happened, which means the researcher needs to provide an *edited version* of the totality. Decisions need to be made about what details are included and which are considered less important and can be missed out of the account.

▶ The editorial decisions taken by the researcher are likely to be shaped by the researcher's need to present the methods in their best possible light. Quite rationally, the researcher will wish to put a positive spin on events and to bring out the best in the process. Without resorting to deceit or untruths, the account of research will almost certainly entail some upbeat *positive filtering*. The point, after all, is to justify the procedures as 'good' research.

▶ Although research notes will be used to anchor the description of what happened during the course of the research, the writing up of the research is inevitably *a retrospective vision*. Situations and data are likely to have a different meaning when viewed from the end of the research process from that at the time they occurred. They will be *interpreted with the wisdom of hindsight.*

▶ The impact of social norms and personal values on the way we interpret events pretty well guarantees that, to a greater or lesser extent, any account of research should be regarded as a *version of the truth* rather than a literal depiction of what happened. Within the social sciences, the idea of a purely objective position is controversial, and a researcher would be naive to presume that his or her account can stand, without careful consideration, as an 'objective' description of what really occurred.

The end product, therefore, no matter how scrupulous it attempts to be, must always be recognized for what it is – an *account* of the research.

2 Different audiences for writing up research

Differing audiences have differing expectations when it comes to reading the research, and the researcher needs to decide how to pitch the account of the research to meet the expectations of that group whose views are considered most important when it comes to evaluating the report. The easy illustration of this comes in the form of research reports produced for an academic qualification as part of an examined course – an undergraduate project, a masters dissertation, a doctoral thesis. The researcher should need little reminding that the work will be assessed by supervisors and examiners who will be focusing on detail, rigour, precision, coherence and originality as top priorities. A different audience might bring different expectations. In the case of commissioned research, the audience is likely to be more concerned with receiving a report which is succinct, easy to digest and strong on practical outcomes. In principle, the research could be just the same; the way it is written up, though, will reflect the needs of the differing audiences.

Link up with **The structure of research reports, p. 231**

3 Vital information to be included when writing up research

Although reports of research respond to the needs of a target audience and rely on an element of interpretation by the researcher, this does not make them idiosyncratic. Far from being one-offs that reflect just the specific audience and the specific researcher, there are some aspects of writing up research which are, if not universal, at least widely accepted. There are some common themes and shared concerns that underlie formal reports of research across the spectrum of approaches within the social sciences. There is some general consensus that when writing up research the aim is to:

1 Explain the purpose of the research.

2 Describe how the research was done.

3 Present the findings from the research.

4 Discuss and analyse the findings.

5 Reach conclusions.

4 Conventions for writing up research

There are conventions which cover the writing up of research. These conventions deal with things like *referencing* (the way in which references are made to sources used by the researcher and the way that these are listed in the References section towards the end of the report on the research), the *layout* of the document, the *order* in which material should be presented and the kinds of *essential information* the researcher needs to provide. There are guidelines on such conventions. For the production of dissertations there is, for example, the British Standards specification no. 4821. For the production of academic articles and for referencing techniques, the researcher could turn to the *Publication Manual of the American Psychological Association*. There are also books devoted to guidance for authors on the technical conventions associated with writing up research – for example, K. L. Turabian's *Manual for Writers of Term Papers, Theses and Dissertations* (University of Chicago Press, 5th edn, 1987). There is plenty of advice – but there is also a catch. *There is no single set of rules and guidelines for writing up research which covers all situations and provides a universally accepted convention.*

⚠ Caution

If the conventions for writing up research are ignored, the research is unlikely to gain much respect or credibility.

The advice here is that such general guidelines, valuable and authoritative though they are, should be reserved for use when the researcher is faced with any lack of direct guidance from the publisher or assessor of the work. When you are writing up the research, it is more important to be guided by the specifications given by, for instance, the university to whom a dissertation is being submitted. University regulations will contain details covering style and presentation. Academic journals usually include guidance to authors which spell out the journal's own policy as far as the presentation of work is concerned – particularly referencing style. In the case of commissioned or sponsored research, such details about the expectations of those who will evaluate the research is likely to be less specific, and this could well provide a suitable occasion on which to seek guidance from one of the more general sources.

Constructing a research report

The researcher needs to tailor the research report to meet:

► the expectations of the specific audience for whom the work is being written;
► the conventions which operate at a general level with respect to the production of reports on research in the social sciences.

These will affect:

► the style of presentation;
► the detail and length of the account;
► the amount of technical detail included;
► the terminology used.

5 The Harvard referencing system

There are certain conventions for referring to the ideas, arguments and supporting evidence gleaned from others. There are two that are generally recognized: the numerical system and the Harvard system. The numerical system involves placing a number in the text at each point where the author wishes to refer to a specific source. The full references are then given at the end of the book or individual chapters, and these can be incorporated into endnotes. It is the other system, the Harvard system, however, which is more commonplace these days and, for that reason, further details will concentrate on this convention.

In the Harvard system, the sources of ideas, arguments and supporting evidence are indicated by citing the name of the author and the date of publication of the relevant work. This is done at the appropriate point in the text. Full details of the author's name and the publication are subsequently given at the end of the report, so that the reader can identify the exact source and, if necessary, refer to it directly. As used in this book, the Harvard system involves referring to authors in the text in the following ways.

▶ Smithers (1998) argues that postmodernism has a dubious future.

▶ It has been argued that postmodernism has a dubious future (Smithers 1998).

▶ The point has been made that 'it is not easy to see what contribution postmodernism will make in the twenty-first century' (Smithers 1998: 131).

In the *References section* towards the end of the research report, the full details of 'Smithers 1998' are given, as they are for all the authors' works cited in the report. For Smithers, it might look like this:

Smithers, J. (1998) The meaning of postmodernism for research methodology, *British Journal of Sociological Research*, 15: 249–66.

As far as the References section is concerned, there are seven key components of the Harvard system:

▶ *Author's name and initial(s)*. Alphabetical order on authors' surnames. Surname followed by forename or initial. If the book is an edited volume, then (ed.) or (eds) should follow the name.

▶ *Date of publication*. To identify when the work was written and to distinguish different works published by the same author(s).

▶ *Title*. The title of a book is put in italics, and uses capital letters for the first letter of the main words. Papers and articles have titles in the lower case.

▶ *Journal name* (if applicable). This is put in italics and details are given of the number, volume and page numbers of the specified article. If the source is a contribution to an edited volume then details are given about the book in which it appears (i.e. editor's name, title of edited volume).

▶ *Publisher.* Vital for locating more-obscure sources. This is included for books but not for journals.

▶ *Place of publication.* Helpful in the location of obscure sources.

▶ *Edition.* If the work appears in a second, third etc. edition, this needs to be specified.

Real examples are to be found in the References section in this book, and can be used to illustrate the principles further.

6 Style and presentation when writing up

The rules of style for writing up research are really like the rules for writing which operate for the English language in general. Inexperienced writers should stick to the rules. Experienced writers might break the rules, but the assumption is that they know they are breaking the rules and are doing so consciously for a particular purpose, to achieve a specific effect. Project researchers, then, are best advised to stick to the rules.

Use the third person

Conventionally, researchers avoid the use of the first person when writing up research. It is not normal to write that 'I distributed 164 questionnaires . . . I received 46 per cent back . . . From the research I found that . . .'. Instead, the third person is used: 'Research involved the distribution of 164 question-naires . . . A response rate of 46 per cent was achieved . . . Findings from the research indicated that . . .'.

Use the past tense

For the most part, this convention poses little trouble because researchers are reflecting upon events that happened in the past. It might be the recent past, but nonetheless the writing up refers to things that were done and events that happened.

Achieve good standards of spelling and grammar

Perhaps obvious, this convention is still worth stressing. Word-processing packages can be used as spell-checkers and can help with the writing style. Scrutiny of the text by the researcher is still needed, however, to avoid those text errors which cannot be picked up by the spell-checker; where 'at' has been typed instead of 'an', for example.

Develop logical links from one section to the next

A good report is one that takes the reader on a journey of discovery. The pathways of this journey should be clear, and the reader should never be left in doubt about the direction of the discussion or the crucial points that are being argued. The logic of the discussion should build point on point towards a final conclusion.

 Link up with **The structure of research reports, p. 231**

Use headings and sub-headings to divide the text into clear sections

Judicious use of headings and sub-headings can separate the text into blocks in a way that makes the reader's task of understanding the overall report far easier. They act as signposts. As with signposts, too few and the reader gets lost, too many and the reader gets confused. As with signposts, their success depends on being clear and being in the right place.

Be consistent in the use of the referencing style

Whether the *Harvard* or the *numerical* style is used, there should be consistency throughout the report. Use one or the other, not both.

Use care with the page layout

The visual element of the presentation is important, and the researcher should give some consideration to things like the page layout and the use of graphs, tables and illustrations to enhance the appeal of the report.

Present tables and figures properly

Tables and figures should be presented in a consistent style that provides the reader with the necessary information to decipher the meaning of the data contained in them. There should be:

► a clear and precise title;

► the source of the table or figure (if it is not original material);

► the units of measurement being used (£, cm, tonnes etc.);

► x axis as the independent variable (where relevant).

 **Caution**

If project researchers choose to break these rules, they should be aware that they run the risk of having their report perceived as poorly written. If this is a risk that is deemed worth taking, they need to offer some explanation of why the rules have been broken to avoid any such impression. So, for example, if a researcher decides quite consciously to present an account of the research which uses the first person, there should be some acknowledgement that this is not conventional and some justification offered for its use.

7 The structure of research reports

Research reports tend to be structured according to certain conventions. The order in which they present material, and even the headings used, tend to conform to a familiar pattern – a pattern which is dictated largely by the need to present information in a logical order, with each new section building on information that has been provided earlier. The project researcher would do well to use such a structure for guidance when it comes to writing up.

The familiar structure for research reports, in some contexts, has become formalized into a template for dividing up the material and presenting it in a pre-ordained sequence. Following the lead of scientific journals, there are journals for social research which insist on the report conforming with the use of headings such as 'Abstract', 'Introduction', 'Methods', 'Findings', 'Discussion', 'Conclusions'. If researchers are writing for such journals they must adopt this rigid format. Elsewhere, researchers can exercise a little more freedom in their construction of the research report, being a bit flexible with the order and using headings that are somewhat different. Writing up research for a PhD, for instance, allows some leeway from this structure, as does writing up a commissioned piece of research whose audience is likely to have different priorities. But, even where researchers do not find themselves constrained by explicit, externally imposed formats, there remains the same underlying rationale to the writing up of research, and this should guide the researcher. The conventional structure can and should be adapted to meet the requirements of specific audiences and specific kinds of research, but it equally provides a robust template that all social researchers can use to guide their construction of a research report.

The conventional structure for reporting research divides the material into three parts: the preliminary part, the main text and the end matter. This is as true for a full length book as it is for a PhD, for a brief journal article and for a workplace project.

The preliminary part

Title

The title itself needs to indicate accurately the contents of the work. It also needs to be fairly brief. A good way of combining the two is to have a two-part title. The first part acts as the main title and gives a broad indication of the area of the work. The second part adds more detail. For example, 'Ethnicity and friendship: the contrast between sociometric research and fieldwork observation in primary school classrooms'.

Abstract

An abstract is a synopsis of a piece of research. Its purpose is to provide a brief summary which can be circulated widely to allow other people to see, at a glance, if the research is relevant to their needs and worth tracking down to read in full. An abstract is normally about 250–300 words in length, and is presented on a separate sheet.

Key words

Researchers are often asked to identify up to five 'key words'. These words are 'identifiers' – words that capture the essence of what the report is all about. The key words are needed for cross-referencing during library searches.

List of contents

Depending on the context, this can range from being just a list of chapter headings and their starting page through to being an extensive list, including details of the contents within the major section of the report; for instance, based on headings and sub-headings.

List of tables and figures

This should list the titles of the various tables and figures and their locations.

Preface

This provides the opportunity for the researcher to give a personal statement about the origins of the research and the significance of the research for the researcher as a person. In view of the importance of the 'self' in the research process, the Preface offers a valuable place in the research report to explore, albeit briefly, how the research reflects the personal experiences and biography of the researcher.

Acknowledgements

Under this heading, credit can be given to those who have helped with the research. This can range from people who acted as 'gatekeepers' in relation to fieldwork, through to academic supervisors, through to those who have commented on early drafts of the research report.

List of abbreviations

If the nature of the report demands that many abbreviations are used in the text, these should be listed, usually alphabetically, under this heading, alongside the full version of what they stand for.

The main text

The main text is generally divided into sections, whether this be chapters as in the case of a larger piece of work, or headings as in the case of shorter reports. These generally follow the logical sequence below.

Introduction

For the purposes of writing up research there needs to be an introduction. This may, or may not, coincide with a section or chapter titled as an 'Introduction', depending on how much discretion is open to the researcher and how far this is taken. The important thing is to recognize that, at the beginning, the reader needs to be provided with information about:

▶ the *background* to the work (in relation to significant issues, problems, ideas);

▶ the *aims* of the research;

▶ key *definitions* and concepts to be used;

▶ optionally, in longer pieces, an *overview* of the report (mapping out its contents).

Literature review

This may be presented as an integral part of the 'Introduction' or it may appear as a separate chapter or section. It is, though, essential that in the early stages of the report there is a review of the material that already exists on the topic in question. The current research should build on existing knowledge, not 'reinvent the wheel'. The literature review should demonstrate how the research being reported relates to previous research and, if possible, how it gives rise to particular issues, problems and ideas that the current research addresses.

Methods of investigation

At this point, having analysed the existing state of knowledge on a topic, it is reasonable to describe the methods of investigation. See the section below on 'The research methods chapter or section' for guidance on how this should be done.

Findings

This is where the reader gets introduced to the data. Aspects of the findings are singled out and described. The first step is to say, 'This is what was found with respect to this issue . . . This is what was found with respect to another issue . . .'

The aim for the researcher is to be able to present relevant findings before going ahead to analyse those findings and see what implications they might have for the issues, problems or ideas that prompted the research. First things first: let's see what we have found. Then, and only then, as a subsequent stage, will we move on to considering what significance the data might have in the context of the overall aims of the research.

Discussion and analysis

Here, the findings that have been outlined are subjected to scrutiny in terms of what they might mean. They are literally discussed and analysed with reference to the theories and ideas, issues and problems that were noted earlier in the report as providing the context in which the research was conceived. The researcher 'makes sense' of the findings by considering their implications beyond the confines of the current research.

Conclusions and recommendations

Finally, in the main text, the researcher needs to draw together the threads of the research to arrive at some general conclusion and, perhaps, to suggest some way forward. Rather than let the report fizzle out as it reaches the end, this part of the report should be constructive and positive. It can contain some of the following things:

▶ a retrospective evaluation of the research and its contribution;

▶ recommendations for improving the situation, guidelines or codes of practice;

▶ identification of new directions for further research.

The end matter

Appendices

This is the place for material which is too bulky for the main body of the text, or for material which, though directly relevant to the discussion, might entail too much of a sidetrack if placed in the text. Typical things that can be lodged in an appendix are:

▶ extensive tables of data;

▶ questionnaires used in a survey;

▶ extracts from an interview transcript;

▶ memos or minutes of meetings;

▶ technical specifications.

Notes

These will mainly occur when the researcher is using a numerical referencing system. They also offer the opportunity for scholarly details to be added which would interrupt the flow of the reading were they to be put directly into the text.

References

See the section on the Harvard system of referencing above.

Index

Provision of an index is usually restricted to large reports and books. It is unlikely that the kind of report produced by a project researcher would require an index.

When a *word count* becomes crucial, such as is often the case with academic dissertations, it is worth noting that the total normally includes only those sections from the introduction to the conclusions/recommendations. References, appendices and indexes are not normally included, nor is the initial material before the introductions, such as the contents page, preface etc.

It is always worth checking, however, that this convention applies in each specific instance when submitting a research report.

8 Writing up qualitative research

For the qualitative researcher, the presentation of research in sections under the headings of 'abstract', 'introduction', 'findings', 'methods', 'discussion' and 'conclusions' might seem inappropriate and not in keeping with the way the research actually evolved. Headings like these might seem to accord with a design and execution of research more in line with experiments and surveys than ethnography or grounded theory, and therefore pose a difficulty for the qualitative researcher when it comes to meeting the conventions associated with writing up research. They would seem to be artificial and inappropriate.

Rather than ditch such headings, however, qualitative researchers might well consider using them as a template for constructing their accounts of the research – a template which gives some structure to the accounts and which is comfortably recognized by those coming from different traditions within the social sciences. While acknowledging that writing up qualitative research involves much more of a retrospective reconstruction of what actually happened than would be the case with more positivist approaches, it still needs to be recognized as just that – a retrospective *account* rather than a literal depiction of the rationale and the events. By latching on to the traditional conventions, the interpretive social researcher is provided with a template for reporting the research. The template, in this case, does not provide a means for faithfully reporting in some structured sequential manner what actually happened in the process of research. It does, however, provide a means for reconstructing and presenting the research in a way that:

▶ addresses and highlights the key issues;

▶ is clearly comprehendable to the reader;

▶ is logically ordered.

9 The research methods chapter or section

In all accounts of research there needs to be some description and justification of the methods used to collect the data. In larger works, this appears in a separate chapter. In shorter reports and articles, it tends to be curtailed to a section under a 'research methods' heading or to a clearly identifiable paragraph or two. Within the confines of the available space, the researcher needs to explain how the research was conceived, designed and executed. This is vital in order for the reader to make some informed evaluation of the study. Basically, if the reader is not told how and why the data were collected, he or she cannot make any judgement about how good the research is and whether any credibility should be given to its findings or conclusions.

Within the confines of the space available, the methods section should do three things.

Describe how the research was conducted

Precise details need to be given, using specific and accurate numbers and dates.

▶ *What* method(s) were used (the technical name)?

▶ *When* did the research take place (month and year, duration of research)?

▶ *Where* did the research take place (location, situation)?

▶ How was *access* to the data or subjects obtained?

▶ *Who* was involved in the research (the population, sample, cases, examples)?

▶ *How many* were involved in the research (precise numbers)?

▶ *How* were they selected (sampling technique)?

Justify these procedures

An argument needs to be put forward supporting the choice of method(s) as:

▶ feasible in terms of the resources and time available;

▶ appropriate under the circumstances for collecting the necessary type of data;

▶ suitable for addressing the issues, problems or questions that underpin the research;

▶ having rigour, coherence and consistency – a professional standard;

▶ producing data that are representative, valid and reliable;

▶ conforming with ethical standards.

Acknowledge any limitations to the methods employed

Good research evaluates the weaknesses as well as the strengths of its methodology.

▶ What unexpected factors arose during the research, and what effect did they have?

▶ In what ways, if any, did resource constraints influence the quality of the findings?

▶ Are there any reservations about the authenticity, accuracy or honesty of answers?

▶ In retrospect, could the methods have been improved?

Checklist for writing up research

When writing up your research you should feel confident about answering 'yes' to the following questions:

1 Is there a suitable *structure* and logical development to the report? ☐

2 Is the text written in a clear *style*, free of spelling and grammatical errors? ☐

3 Does the writing style meet the expectations of the main *audience* for the research? ☐

4 Have the necessary *conventions* been followed in the writing up of the research? ☐

5 Are the *references* complete and do they follow a recognized style (e.g. Harvard)? ☐

6 Are the *tables*, *figures*, *illustrations* and *diagrams* properly labelled? ☐

Do they enhance the visual attractiveness of the report, as well as supplying *necessary* information in a succinct manner? ☐

7 Has a detailed and precise *description* of the research process been provided? ☐

8 Has the choice of method(s) been *justified* in relation to the type of data required and the practical circumstances surrounding the research? ☐

9 Have the *limitations* of the research methodology been acknowledged? ☐

© M. Denscombe, *The Good Research Guide*. Open University Press.

FREQUENTLY ASKED QUESTIONS

What is analysis?

Analysis means the separation of something into its component parts. To do this, of course, the researcher first needs to identify what those parts might be, and this links with a further meaning of analysis, which is to trace things back to their underlying sources. Analysis, then, involves probing beneath the surface appearance of something to discover the component elements which have come together to produce it. By tracing things back in this fashion, the researcher aims to expose some *general* principles that can be used to explain the nature of the thing being studied and can be applied elsewhere to other situations.

What is a concept?

A concept is a basic idea. It is an idea that is generally abstract and universal rather than concrete and specific. And it is basic in the sense that it cannot be easily explained in terms of other ideas or equated to other ideas. In terms of ideas, then, a concept is a basic building block that captures the *essence* of a thing (e.g. 'love', 'relevance').

What is positivism?

Positivism is an approach to social research which seeks to apply the natural science model of research to investigations of the social world. It is based on the assumption that there are patterns and regularities, causes and consequences in the social world, just as there are in the natural world. These patterns and regularities in the social world are seen as having their own existence – they are real. For positivists, the aim of social research is to discover the patterns and regularities of the social world by using the kind of scientific methods used to such good effect in the natural sciences.

What is reflexivity?

Reflexivity concerns the relationship between the researcher and the social world. Contrary to positivism, reflexivity suggests that there is no prospect of the social researcher achieving an entirely objective position from which to study the social world. This is because the concepts the researcher uses to make sense of the world are also a part of that social world. Reflexivity is an awkward thing for social research. It means that what we know about the social world can never be entirely objective. A researcher can never stand outside the social world he or she is studying in order to gain some vantage point from which to view things from a perspective which is not contaminated by contact with that social world. Inevitably, the sense we make of the social world and the meaning we give to events and situations are shaped by our experience as social beings and the legacy of the values, norms and concepts we have assimilated during our lifetime. And these will differ from person to person, culture to culture.

What is reliability?

Researchers need to feel confident that their measurements are not affected by a research instrument that gives one reading on the first occasion it is used and a different reading on the next occasion when there has been no real change in the item being measured. This is why they are concerned with the 'reliability' of a research instrument. A good level of reliability means that the research instrument produces the same data time after time on each occasion that it is used, and that any variation in the results obtained through using the instrument is due entirely to variations in the thing being measured. None of the variation is due to fluctuations caused by the volatile nature of the research instrument itself. So a research instrument such as a particular experiment or questionnaire is said to be 'reliable' if it is *consistent*, and this is generally deemed to be a good thing as far as research is concerned.

What is a theory?

A theory is a proposition about the relationship between things. In principle, a theory is universal, applying at all times and to all instances of the thing(s) in question. In the social sciences, the notion of 'theory' needs to be treated more cautiously than in the natural sciences, because of the *complexity* of social phenomena and because people react to knowledge about themselves in a way that chemicals and forces do not.

What is validity?

In a broad sense, validity means that the data and the methods are 'right'. In terms of research data, the notion of validity hinges around whether or not the data reflect the truth, reflect reality and cover the crucial matters. In terms of the methods used to obtain data, validity addresses the question, 'Are we measuring suitable indicators of the concept and are we getting accurate results?' *The idea of validity hinges around the extent to which research data and the methods for obtaining the data are deemed accurate, honest and on target.*

▶ ▷ ▷

REFERENCES

Ball, S. (1990) Self-doubt and soft data: social and technical trajectories in ethnographic fieldwork, *International Journal of Qualitative Studies in Education*, 3: 157–71.

Becker, H. and Geer, B. (1957) Participant observation and interviewing: a comparison, *Human Organization*, 16(3) : 28–35.

Boutilier, M., Mason, R. and Rootman, U. (1997) Community action and reflective practice in health promotion research, *Health Promotion International*, 12(1): 69–78.

Bryman, A. (1989) *Research Methods and Organization Studies*. London: Routledge.

Burgess, R.G. (1984) *In the Field: an Introduction to Field Research*. London: Allen and Unwin.

Croll, P. (1986) *Systematic Classroom Observation*. London: Falmer.

Delamont, S. (1992) *Fieldwork in Educational Settings*. London: Falmer.

Denscombe, M. (1983) Interviews, accounts and ethnographic research on teachers. In M. Hammersley (ed.) *The Ethnography of Schooling: Methodological Issues*. Driffield: Nafferton Books.

Edwards, A. and Talbot, R. (1994) *The Hard-pressed Researcher: a Research Handbook for the Caring Professions*. London: Longman.

Elliott, J. (1991) *Action Research for Educational Change*. Buckingham: Open University Press.

Festinger, L., Reicken, H. and Schachter, S. (1956) *When Prophecy Fails*. Minneapolis: University of Minnesota Press (republished 1964, London: Harper & Row).

Fielding, N. (1993) *Analysing Qualitative Data by Computer*, Social Research Update No. 1. Guildford: University of Surrey.

Fielding, N. and Lee, R. (eds) (1993) *Using Computers in Qualitative Research*, 2nd edn. London: Sage.

Flanders, N.A. (1970) *Analysing Teacher Behavior*. Reading, MA: Addison-Wesley.

Galton, M., Simon, B. and Croll, P. (1980) *Inside the Primary Classroom*. London: RKP.

Geertz, C. (1973) Thick description: toward an interpretive theory of culture. In C. Geertz (ed.) *The Interpretation of Cultures*. New York: Basic Books.

Gerbner, G., Holsti, O., Krippendorf, K., Paisley, W. and Stone, P. (eds) (1969) *The Analysis of Communication Content*. New York: Wiley.

Glaser, B. and Strauss, A. (1967) *The Discovery of Grounded Theory*. Chicago: Aldine.

Griffin, J. (1962) *Black Like Me*. London: Collins.

Grundy, S. and Kemmis, S. (1988) *Educational research in Australia: the state of the art (an overview)*. In S. Kemmis and R. McTaggart (eds) *The Action Research Reader*, 3rd edn. Geelong, Victoria: Deakin University Press.

Hammersley, M. (1983) *The Ethnography of Schooling: Methodological Issues*. Driffield: Nafferton Books.

Hammersley, M. (1990) What's wrong with ethnography? The myth of theoretical description, *Sociology*, 24: 597–615.

Hammersley, M. (1992) *What's Wrong with Ethnography?* London: Routledge.

Hammersley, M. and Atkinson, P. (1983) *Ethnography: Principles in Practice*. London: Tavistock.

Hoinville, G., Jowell, R. and associates (1978) *Survey Research Practice*. London: Heinemann.

Howell, N. (1990) *Surviving Fieldwork: a Report of the Advisory Panel on Health and Safety in Fieldwork*. Washington, DC: American Anthropological Association.

Humphreys, L. (1970) *Tearoom Trade*. Chicago: Aldine.

Irvine, J., Miles, I. and Evans, J. (1979) *Demystifying Social Statistics*. London: Pluto Press.

Kirk, J. and Miller, M. (1986) *Reliability and Validity in Qualitative Research*. Beverly Hills, CA: Sage.

Layder, D. (1993) *New Strategies in Social Research*. Cambridge: Polity Press.

Lee, R. (1995) *Dangerous Fieldwork*. Thousand Oaks, CA: Sage.

Lewin, K. (1946) Action research and minority problems, *Journal of Social Issues*, 2: 34–46.

Lewis, A. (1992) Group child interviews as a research tool, *British Educational Research Journal*, 18: 413–32.

Lincoln, Y. and Guba, E. (1985) *Naturalistic Enquiry*. Newbury Park, CA: Sage.

Malinowski, B. (1922) *Argonauts of the Western Pacific*. London: Routledge and Kegan Paul.

Maykut, P. and Morehouse, R. (1994) *Beginning Qualitative Research: a Philosophical and Practical Guide*. London: Falmer.

Mead, M. (1943) *Coming of Age in Samoa: a Study of Adolescence and Sex in Primitive Societies*. Harmondsworth: Penguin.

Mead, M. (1963) *Growing Up in New Guinea*. Harmondsworth: Penguin (first published in 1930).

Miles, M. and Huberman, A. (1994) *Qualitative Data Analysis*. Thousand Oaks, CA: Sage.

Milgram, S. (1974) *Obedience to Authority*. New York: Harper and Row.

Oakley, A. (1981) Interviewing women: a contradiction in terms. In H. Roberts (ed.) *Doing Feminist Research*. London: Routledge and Kegan Paul.

O'Connell Davidson, J. (1995) The anatomy of 'free choice' prostitution, *Gender, Work and Organization*, 2: 1–10.

Platt, J. (1981) Evidence and proof in documentary research, *The Sociological Review*, 21(1): 31–66.

Polsky, N. (1967) *Hustlers, Beats and Others*. Harmondsworth: Penguin.

Porter, S. (1993) Critical realist ethnography: the case of racism and professionalism in a medical setting, *Sociology*, 27: 591–601.

Ragin, C. (1994) *Constructing Social Research*. Thousand Oaks, CA: Pine Forge Press.

Ragin, C. and Becker, H. (1992) *What Is a Case? Exploring the Foundations of Social Enquiry*. New York: Cambridge University Press.

Reimer, J. (1979) *Hard Hats: the Work World of Construction Workers*. Beverly Hills, CA: Sage.

Richards, L. and Richards, T. (1993) The transformation of qualitative method: computational paradigms and research processes. In N. Fielding and R. Lee (eds) *Using Computers in Qualitative Research*, 2nd edn. London: Sage.

Schön, D. (1983) *The Reflective Practitioner: How Professionals Think in Action*. New York: Basic Books.

Scott, J. (1990) *A Matter of Record*. Cambridge: Polity Press.

Seidel, J. (1993) Method and madness in the application of computer technology to qualitative data analysis. In N. Fielding and R. Lee (eds) *Using Computers in Qualitative Research*, 2nd edn. London: Sage.

Silverman, D. (1985) *Qualitative Methodology and Sociology*. Aldershot: Gower.

Silverman, D. (1993) *Interpreting Qualitative Data: Methods for Analyzing Talk, Text and Interaction*. Thousand Oaks, CA: Sage.

Simon, A. and Boyer, G. (1970) *Mirrors of Behavior: an Anthology of Classroom Observation Instruments*. Philadelphia: Research for Better Schools.

Somekh, B. (1995) The contribution of action research to development in social endeavours: a position paper on action research methodology, *British Educational Research Journal*, 21(3): 339–55.

Spector, P. (1981) *Research Designs*. Beverly Hills, CA: Sage.

Stake, R. (1995) *The Art of Case Study Research*. Thousand Oaks, CA: Sage.

Strauss, A. (1987) *Qualitative Analysis for Social Scientists*. Cambridge: Cambridge University Press.

Strauss, A. and Corbin, J. (1990) *Basics of Qualitative Research: Grounded Theory Procedures and Techniques*. London: Sage.

Susman, G. and Evered, R. (1978) An assessment of the scientific merits of action research, *Administrative Science Quarterly*, 23(4): 582–603.

Tesch, R. (1990) *Qualitative Research: Analysis Types and Software Tools*. Basingstoke: Falmer Press.

Tesch, R. (1993) Software for qualitative researchers: analysis needs and program capabilities. In N. Fielding and R. Lee (eds) *Using Computers in Qualitative Research*, 2nd edn. London: Sage.

Thomas, R. and Purdon, S. (1995) *Telephone Methods for Social Surveys*, Social Research Update 8. Guildford: University of Surrey.

Whyte, W.F. (1981) *Street Corner Society: the Social Structure of an Italian Slum*, 3rd edn. Chicago: University of Chicago Press (first published 1943).

Winter, R. (1996) Some principles and procedures for the conduct of action research. In O. Zuber-Skerritt (ed.) *New Directions in Action Research*. London: Falmer Press.

Woods, P. (1979) *The Divided School*. London: RKP.

Woods, P. (1996) *Researching the Art of Teaching: Ethnography for Educational Use*. London: Routledge.

Worthington, H. and Holloway, P. (1997) Making sense of statistics, *International Journal of Health Education*, 35(3): 76–80.

Yin, R. (1994) *Case Study Research: Design and Methods*, 2nd edn. Newbury Park, CA: Sage.

Zuber-Skerritt, O. (ed.) (1996) *New Directions in Action Research*. London: Falmer Press.

INDEX

access to research settings, 76, 111, 152, 156
  authorization, 40, 52, 119
  gatekeepers, 77, 78
action research, 57–67, 224
  and change, 58
  cyclical process, 58, 60, 65
  emancipatory approach, 61, 62, 64
  generalizability, 64
  practical action, 57, 58, 62
  professional self-development, 59, 65
analysis, 173–6, 215, 219, 239
arrays of raw data, 181
Atkinson, P., 78

Ball, S., 74
bar charts, 185, 186
basic statistics, 192
Becker, H., 36, 38, 147
Boutilier, M., 61
Boyer, G., 139
Bryman, A., 52, 59
Burgess, R.G., 77

case studies, 30–42
  boundaries, 37–9
  generalize from a case study, 35–7
  selection of cases, 33, 34, 35
chi-squared test, 185, 200, 204
concept, 239
content analysis, 134, 167–9
contingency tables, 185, 200
continuous data, 179, 188
Corbin, J., 211

correlations, 203, 204
Croll, P., 139

Delamont, S., 154
Denscombe, M., 109
descriptive statistics, 193–8
discrete data, 179, 185
documentary research, 10, 158–71
  authenticity, 162, 167, 170

Edwards, A., 59
Elliott, J., 61
empirical research, 6, 27
ethics, 5, 104, 237
  in action research, 63
  and deception, 54, 156
  in ethnographic research, 77, 80
  informed consent, 109, 151
ethnography, 68–81, 235
  covert research, 76, 77
  fieldwork, 68, 150
  idiographic approach, 71
  naturalism, 71
  nomothetic approach, 72
  reflexivity, 73
  self, 74–6
Evered, R., 58, 66
experimental approach, 43–56
  cause and effect, 43, 46, 47
  control groups, 43–6
  controls, 43, 44
  laboratory experiments, 48
  observation and measurement, 48
  standardized tests, 50–2

factor analysis, 203
feasibility, 5, 104, 105
Festinger, L., 153
field experiments, 52, 62, 70
field notes, 120, 122, 151
Fielding, N., 218, 220
Flanders, N.A., 139
frequency distributions, 182, 204

Galton, M., 144
Geer, B., 147
Geertz, C., 175
Gerbner, G., 168
Glaser, B., 25, 78, 176, 214, 215, 217
Griffin, J., 153
grounded theory, 214–18, 235
    theoretical sampling, 216
    theoretical saturation, 216
Grundy, S., 61
Guba, E., 25, 176, 213

Hammersley, M., 32, 36, 71, 72, 74, 78
histogram, 187, 188
Hoinville, G., 23
Holloway, P., 204
horizontal axis, 184
horizontal bar charts, 186
Howell, N., 154
Huberman, A., 26, 211, 212, 219, 221
Humphreys, L., 149, 153

independent variable, 46, 230
interval data, 179, 194, 195, 204
interviewer effect, 116, 137
interviews, 109–38, 234
    computer assisted, 113
    equipment, 123
    focus groups, 115
    group interviews, 114
    interview skills, 124–8
    one-to-one, 8, 9, 114
    planning and preparation, 118–20
    recording, 120–4
    semi-structured interviews, 113
    structured interviews, 112
    telephone, 9, 120, 122, 123
    transcribing, 128–32
    unstructured, 113

Kemmis, S., 61
Kirk, J., 212

Layder, D., 33, 217
Lee, R., 154, 155, 218, 220

Lewin, K., 58
Lewis, A., 114
library-based research, 159
Likert scale, 103, 178
Lincoln, Y., 25, 176, 213
line graph, 189
literature review, 158, 233

Malinowski, B., 68, 69, 73
Maykut, P., 176, 221
Mead, M., 53, 68, 70
mean, 193, 194, 197, 204
median, 193, 194, 196, 204
Miles, M., 26, 211, 212, 219, 221
Milgram, S., 48–50
Miller, M., 212
mode, 195, 204
Morehouse, R., 176, 221
multiple methods, 83–6
    and case studies, 31, 39

nominal data, 102, 178, 185, 195, 204
null hypothesis, 199

O'Connell Davidson, J., 149, 153
Oakley, A., 117
objectivity, 212
observer effect, 41, 47, 48
ordinal data, 102, 178, 194, 195, 204

participant observation, 147–57
    dangers, 154, 155
    going native, 154
pictograms, 185
pie chart, 189, 190
Platt, J., 167
Polsky, N., 77
Porter, S., 72
positivism, 239
probability, 199
Purden, S., 9

qualitative research, 173–6
    audit trail, 211, 213
    coding the data, 210, 218
    computer-aided analysis of data,
        218
    decontextualizing the meaning, 219,
        222
quantitative research, 173–6, 177–207
    coding the data, 180
    grouping the data, 181, 182, 201
    presentation of the data, 182–92
quartiles, 196

questionnaires, 87–108, 234
  constructing the questions, 97–100
  costs, 90
  length and appearance, 95
  open and closed questions, 101
  order of questions, 100
  postal questionnaires, 7, 88, 105,
    106
  routine essentials, 91
  types of questions, 100, 101

Ragin, C., 35, 36, 38
range, 196, 204
ratio data, 179, 194, 195
raw data, 181, 210
referencing, 226, 227, 230
  Harvard referencing system, 228–30,
    235
reflexivity, 212, 239
  in action research, 63
regression analysis, 204
Reimer, J., 70
reliability, 136, 146, 156, 213, 237,
    239
research design, 177
research reports, 224–38
  audiences, 224, 226
  structure of reports, 231–5
  style, 225, 227, 229
  with qualitative research, 235
response rates, 19, 23, 104, 136
  bias from non-responses, 20
Richards, L., 218
Richards, T., 218

sampling, 11–27
  cluster sampling, 14
  convenience sampling, 16
  multi-stage sampling, 14
  non-probability sampling, 12, 15,
    25
  probability sampling, 11, 12
  purposive sampling, 15
  quota sampling, 13
  random sampling, 12
  sampling frame, 17–19
  size of the sample, 21–3, 27, 216
  in small-scale research, 24
  snowball sampling, 16
  stratified sampling, 12
  systematic sampling, 12
  theoretical sampling, 16, 26, 216
  with qualitative research, 25–7

scatter plot, 188, 203
Schön, D., 60
Scott, J., 167
Seidel, J., 220
self, 152–5, 208, 209, 212, 221
  insider knowledge, 63, 80
  participation in research, 58, 61,
    62
  personal beliefs, 116
  personal expertise, 153
  personal interests, 66
  presentation, 117
  researcher involvement, 117, 176
semantic differential, 104
Silverman, D., 109, 212
Simon, A., 139
social surveys, 6–11
Somekh, B., 58, 65
Spector, P., 44
stacked bar chart, 187
Stake, R., 34
standard deviation, 197, 204
strategic choices, 3, 4, 32, 173–6
statistical tests of significance, 198–200
Strauss, A., 25, 78, 173, 176, 211, 214,
    215, 216, 217
surveys
  documents, 10–11
  face-to-face interviews, 8–9
  observations, 11
  postal survey, 7–8
  qualitative research, 25–7
  response rates, 19–21
  sample size, 21–5, 27
  sampling, 11–27
  telephone surveys, 9–10
Susman, G., 58, 66
systematic observation, 11, 139–47
  observation schedules, 141–5

tables and charts, 183, 184, 230
Talbot, R., 59
tallies of frequencies, 181
Tesch, R., 207, 218, 219
theory, 33, 208, 214, 216, 217, 219,
    239
thick description, 72, 220
Thomas, R., 9
triangulation, 83–6, 214, 215
  and case studies, 40
t-test, 201–4

validity, 85, 132, 136, 213, 237, 239

web-site/internet, 8, 160, 161
Whyte, W.F., 68, 77, 78, 153
Winter, R., 63
Woods, P., 70–2, 75, 76
Worthington, H., 204

x axis, 184, 188, 190, 230

y axis, 184, 190
Yin, R., 33, 36

Zuber-Skerritt, O., 61, 62